ASPEN PUBLISHERS

Property

Fourth Edition

Neil C. Blond

Yoram Chen

John Marafino

D1531347

Wolters Kluwer

Law & Business

AUSTIN   BOSTON   CHICAGO   NEW YORK   THE NETHERLANDS

About Wolters Kluwer Law & Business

Wolters Kluwer Law & Business is a leading provider of research information and workflow solutions in key specialty areas. The strengths of the individual brands of Aspen Publishers, CCH, Kluwer Law International and Loislaw are aligned within Wolters Kluwer Law & Business to provide comprehensive, in-depth solutions and expert-authored content for the legal, professional and education markets.

CCH was founded in 1913 and has served more than four generations of business professionals and their clients. The CCH products in the Wolters Kluwer Law & Business group are highly regarded electronic and print resources for legal, securities, antitrust and trade regulation, government contracting, banking, pension, payroll, employment and labor, and healthcare reimbursement and compliance professionals.

Aspen Publishers is a leading information provider for attorneys, business professionals and law students. Written by preeminent authorities, Aspen products offer analytical and practical information in a range of specialty practice areas from securities law and intellectual property to mergers and acquisitions and pension/benefits. Aspen's trusted legal education resources provide professors and students with high-quality, up-to-date and effective resources for successful instruction and study in all areas of the law.

Kluwer Law International supplies the global business community with comprehensive English-language international legal information. Legal practitioners, corporate counsel and business executives around the world rely on the Kluwer Law International journals, loose-leafs, books and electronic products for authoritative information in many areas of international legal practice.

Loislaw is a premier provider of digitized legal content to small law firm practitioners of various specializations. Loislaw provides attorneys with the ability to quickly and efficiently find the necessary legal information they need, when and where they need it, by facilitating access to primary law as well as state-specific law, records, forms and treatises.

Wolters Kluwer Law & Business, a unit of Wolters Kluwer, is headquartered in New York and Riverwoods, Illinois. Wolters Kluwer is a leading multinational publisher and information services company.

CHECK OUT THESE OTHER GREAT TITLES:

BLOND'S LAW GUIDES
Comprehensive, Yet Concise . . . JUST RIGHT!

Each Blond's Law Guide book contains: Black Letter Law Outline • EasyFlow™ Charts • Case Clips • Mnemonics • Free Digital Version

Available titles in this series include:

Blond's Civil Procedure

Blond's Constitutional Law

Blond's Contracts

Blond's Criminal Law

Blond's Criminal Procedure

Blond's Evidence

Blond's Property

Blond's Torts

ASK FOR THEM AT YOUR LOCAL BOOKSTORE
IF UNAVAILABLE, PURCHASE ONLINE AT
HTTP://LAWSCHOOL.ASPENPUBLISHERS.COM

How To Use This Book

Law school is very different from your previous educational experiences. In the past, course material was presented in a straightforward manner both in lectures and texts. You did well by memorizing and regurgitating. In law school, your fat casebooks are stuffed with material, most of which will be useless when finals arrive. Your professors ask a lot of questions but don't seem to be teaching you either the law or how to think. Sifting through voluminous material seeking out the important concepts is a hard, time-consuming chore. We've done that job for you. This book will help you study effectively. We hope to teach you the law and how to think.

Preparing for Class

Most students start their first year by reading and briefing all their cases. They spend too much time copying unimportant details. After finals they realize they wasted time on facts that were useless on the exam.

Case Clips

Case Clips help you focus on what your professor wants you to get out of your cases. Facts, Issues, and Rules are carefully and succinctly stated. Left out are details irrelevant to what you need to learn from the case. In general, we skip procedural matters in lower courts. We don't care which party is the appellant or petitioner because the trivia is not relevant to the law. Case Clips should be read before you read the actual case. You will have a good idea what to look for in the case, and appreciate the significance of what you are reading. Inevitably you will not have time to read all your cases before class. Case Clips allow you to prepare for class in about five minutes. You will be able to follow the discussion and listen without fear of being called upon.

"Should I read all the cases even if they aren't from my casebook?"

Yes, if you feel you have the time. Most major cases from other texts will be covered at least as a note case in your book. The principles of these cases are universal and the fact patterns should help your understanding. The Case Clips are written in a way that should provide a tremendous amount of understanding in a relatively short period of time.

EasyFlow™ Charts

A very common complaint among law students is that they "can't put it all together." When you are reading 400 pages a week it is difficult to remember how the last case relates to the first and how November's readings relate to September's. It's hard to understand the relationship between different torts topics when you have read cases for three or four other classes in between. Our EasyFlow™ Charts will help you put the whole course together. They are designed to help you memorize fundamentals. They reinforce your learning by showing you the material from another perspective.

Outlines

More than one hundred lawyers and law students were interviewed as part of the development of this series. Most complained that their casebooks did not teach them the law and were far too voluminous to be useful before an exam. They also told us that the commercial outlines they purchased were excellent when used as hornbooks to explain the law, but were too wordy and redundant to be effective during the weeks before finals. Few students can read four 500-page outlines during the last month of classes. It is virtually impossible to memorize that much material and even harder to decide what is important. Almost every student interviewed said he or she studied from homemade outlines. We've written the outline you should use to study.

"But writing my own outline will be a learning experience."

True, but unfortunately many students spend so much time outlining they don't leave time to learn and memorize. Many students told us they spent six weeks outlining, and only one day studying before each final!

Mnemonics

Most law students spend too much time reading, and not enough time memorizing. Mnemonics are included to help you organize your essays and spot issues. They highlight what is important and which areas deserve your time.

TABLE OF CONTENTS

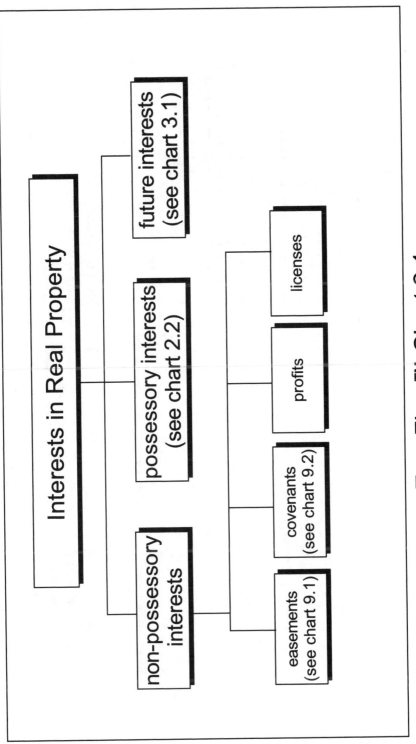

EasyFlow™ Chart 2.1

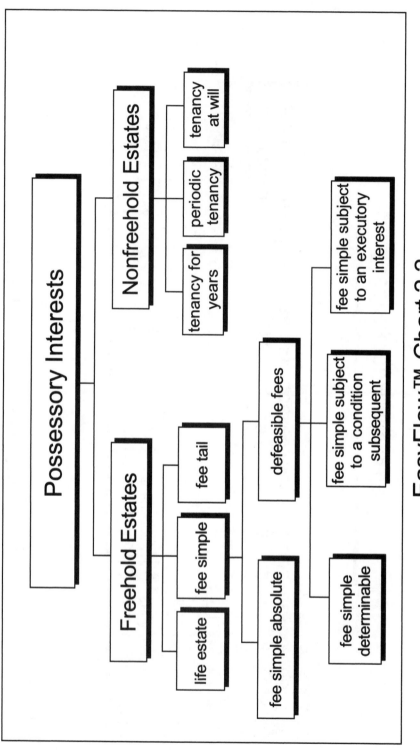

EasyFlow™ Chart 2.2

Freehold Estates

"to A," "to A and his heirs"	"so long as," "until," "while"	"but if used for"	"so long as," "until," "while"	"to A and the heirs of A's body"	"to A for life"
indefinite	until condition is broken	until condition is broken and grantor re-enters	until specified event occurs	indefinite, passed to heirs	until death of the measuring life
created without specific language	wording must be explicit	wording must be explicit	wording must be explicit	abolished	effective
freely alienable	freely alienable subject to the condition	freely alienable subject to the condition	freely alienable subject to the condition	none	grantee may transfer his rights, but property reverts to grantor at grantee's death
✕	grantor	grantor	third party	✕	grantor or third party

EasyFlow™ Chart 2.3

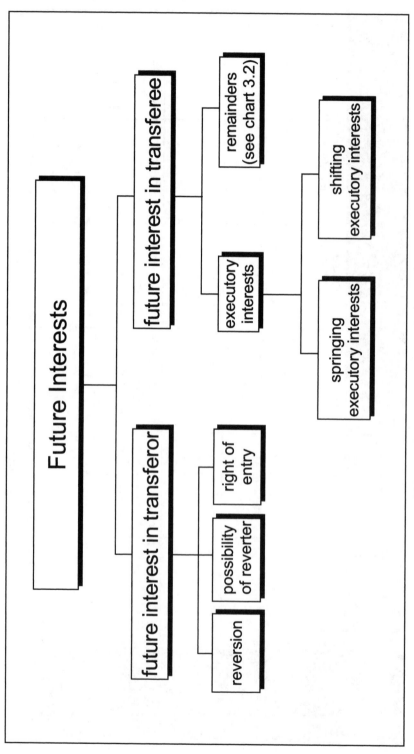

EasyFlow™ Chart 3.1

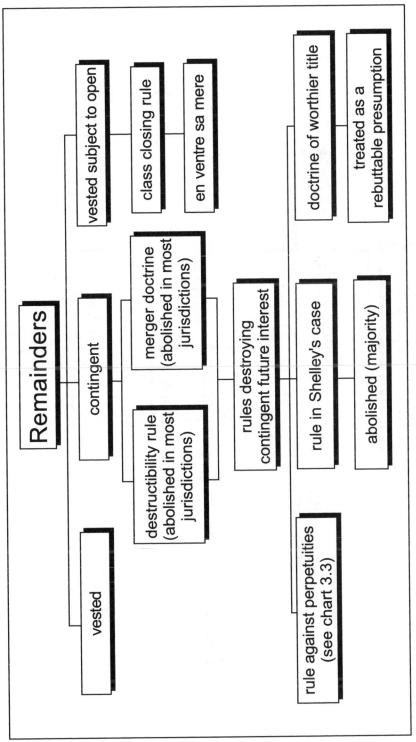

EasyFlow™ Chart 3.2

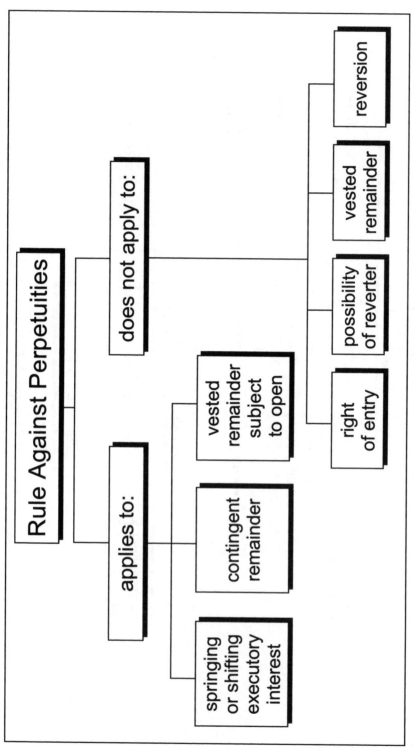

Rule Against Perpetuities

applies to:
- springing or shifting executory interest
- contingent remainder
- vested remainder subject to open

does not apply to:
- right of entry
- possibility of reverter
- vested remainder
- reversion

EasyFlow™ Chart 3.3

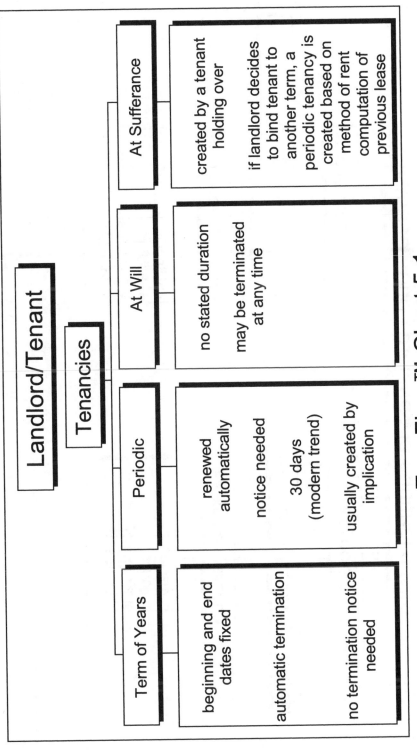

Landlord/Tenant

Tenancies

Term of Years
- beginning and end dates fixed
- automatic termination
- no termination notice needed

Periodic
- renewed automatically
- notice needed
- 30 days (modern trend)
- usually created by implication

At Will
- no stated duration
- may be terminated at any time

At Sufferance
- created by a tenant holding over
- if landlord decides to bind tenant to another term, a periodic tenancy is created based on method of rent computation of previous lease

EasyFlow™ Chart 5.1

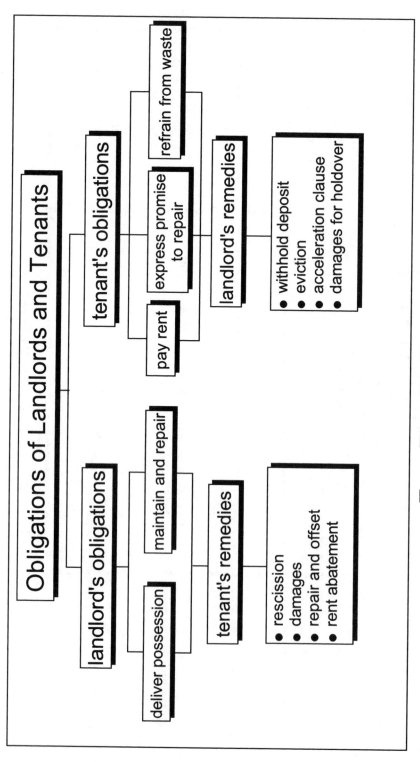

Obligations of Landlords and Tenants

- landlord's obligations
  - deliver possession
  - maintain and repair
- tenant's remedies
  - rescission
  - damages
  - repair and offset
  - rent abatement

- tenant's obligations
  - pay rent
  - express promise to repair
  - refrain from waste
- landlord's remedies
  - withhold deposit
  - eviction
  - acceleration clause
  - damages for holdover

EasyFlow™ Chart 5.2

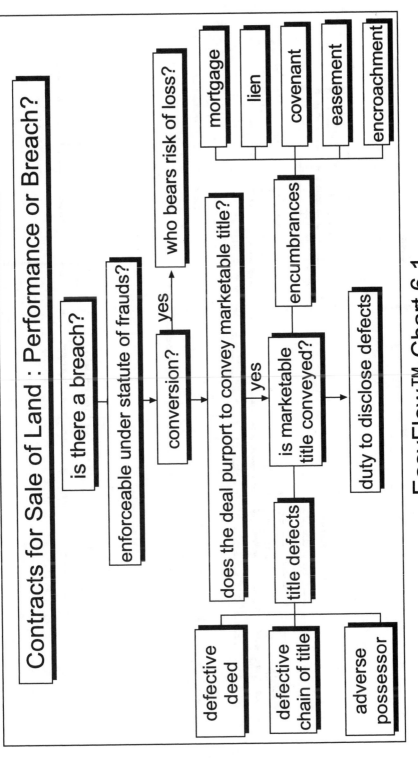

Contracts for Sale of Land : Performance or Breach?

is there a breach?

enforceable under statute of frauds?

conversion?

yes → who bears risk of loss?

does the deal purport to convey marketable title?

yes → is marketable title conveyed?

encumbrances
- mortgage
- lien
- covenant
- easement
- encroachment

title defects
- defective deed
- defective chain of title
- adverse possessor

duty to disclose defects

EasyFlow™ Chart 6.1

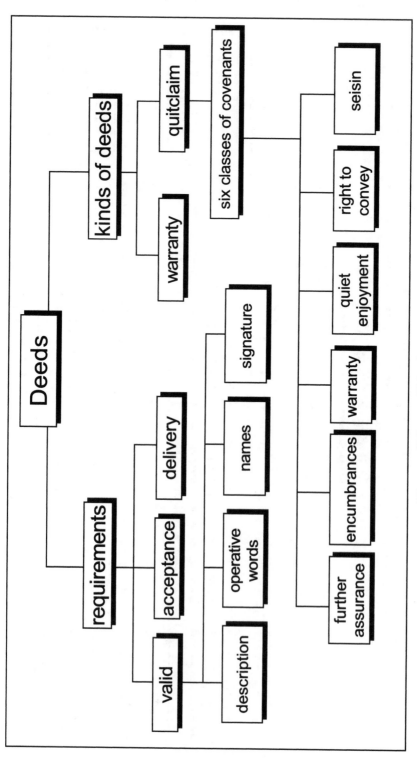

EasyFlow™ Chart 7.1

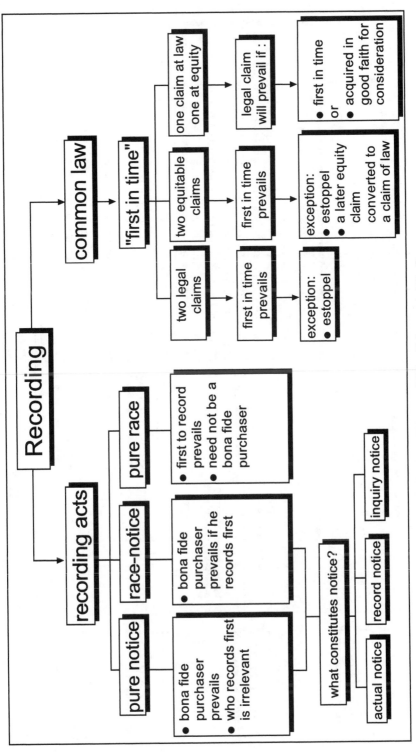

EasyFlow™ Chart 7.2

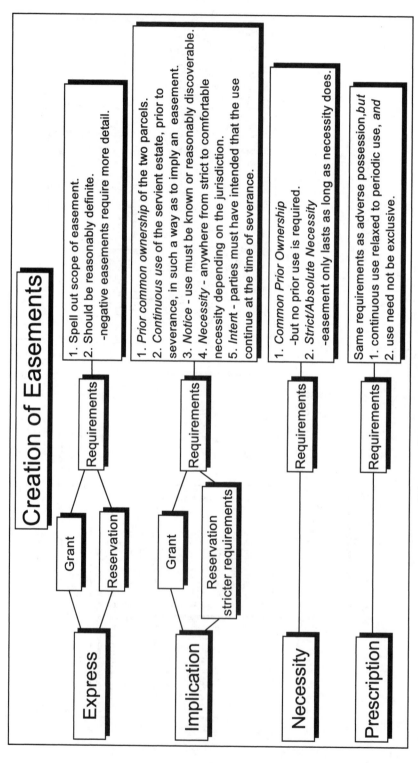

Creation of Easements

Express

Requirements

1. Spell out scope of easement.
2. Should be reasonably definite.
   - negative easements require more detail.

Branches: **Grant**, **Reservation**

Implication

Requirements

1. *Prior common ownership* of the two parcels.
2. *Continuous use* of the servient estate, prior to severance, in such a way as to imply an easement.
3. *Notice* - use must be known or reasonably discoverable.
4. *Necessity* - anywhere from strict to comfortable necessity depending on the jurisdiction.
5. *Intent* - parties must have intended that the use continue at the time of severance.

Branches: **Grant**, **Reservation stricter requirements**

Necessity

Requirements

1. *Common Prior Ownership*
   - but no prior use is required.
2. *Strict/Absolute Necessity*
   - easement only lasts as long as necessity does.

Prescription

Requirements

Same requirements as adverse possession, *but*
1. continuous use relaxed to periodic use, *and*
2. use need not be exclusive.

EasyFlow™ Chart 9.1

Real Covenants

Requirements for covenant to run with the land at law:

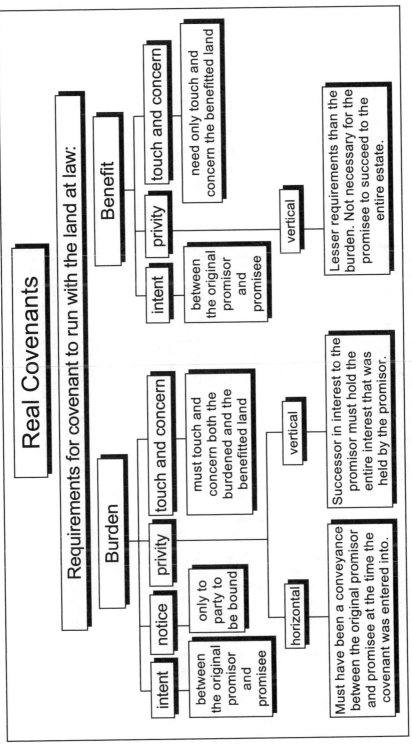

Burden

- **intent**
  - between the original promisor and promisee
- **notice**
  - only to party to be bound
- **privity**
  - horizontal
    - Must have been a conveyance between the original promisor and promisee at the time the covenant was entered into.
  - vertical
    - Successor in interest to the promisor must hold the entire interest that was held by the promisor.
- **touch and concern**
  - must touch and concern both the burdened and the benefitted land

Benefit

- **intent**
  - between the original promisor and promisee
- **privity**
  - vertical
    - Lesser requirements than the burden. Not necessary for the promisee to succeed to the entire estate.
- **touch and concern**
  - need only touch and concern the benefitted land

EasyFlow™ Chart 9.2

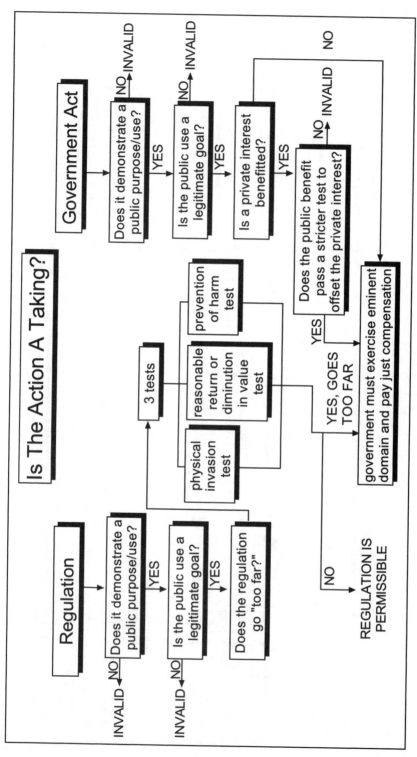

EasyFlow™ Chart 10.1

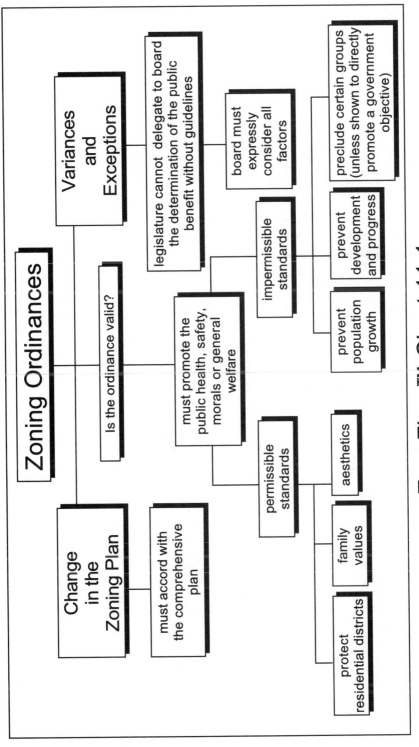

EasyFlow™ Chart 11.1

CHAPTER 1 MISCELLANEOUS TOPICS

I. CAPTURE OF WILD ANIMALS
(ferae naturae)

A. The exercise of dominion and control over a wild animal constitutes possession of the animal and ownership is vested in the possessor.

    1. Mortally wounding or trapping an animal or fish constitutes constructive possession, provided the hunter pursues the wounded animal and, in the case of trapping, capture is virtually complete.

    2. Mere pursuit of a wild animal does not create a property right.

B. A trespasser's title to a killed or captured animal is inferior to that of the land's owner.

C. The owner of a captured animal loses title if the animal escapes and resumes its natural state.

D. If a captured wild animal escapes, the captor retains title only if the escaped animal has been tamed and forms a habit of periodically returning to the captor, or the animal is not indigenous to the area, so that a potential captor is put on notice that it belongs to someone else.

II. LOST, MISLAID, AND ABANDONED CHATTELS

A. When an owner of a chattel accidentally and involuntarily parts with it and does not know where to find it, the chattel is considered *lost*.

B. When an owner of a chattel intentionally puts the chattel in a certain place but forgets to retrieve it, it is considered *mislaid*.

C. When the owner of a chattel intentionally and voluntarily relinquishes both title and possession it is considered *abandoned*.

D. Title to a lost or mislaid chattel remains with the rightful owner. One who reduces a lost chattel to possession is its finder and only acquires a possessory right to the chattel.

E.   A finder's rights to a lost chattel are generally superior to all except the rightful owner.

F.   A finder's possessory right to a lost chattel found when the finder was on another's property with consent (express or implied) is generally superior to that of the property's owner.

    1. If one finds a chattel on private premises open to the public (e.g. the public area of a shop), the finder's possessory rights are superior to all except the rightful owner.

    2. If a chattel is found in a private portion of a landowner's premises, the landowner (not the finder) acquires a possessory right to the chattel.

G.   Mislaid Chattel
The owner of the property where a mislaid chattel is found acquires a possessory right to the chattel that is superior to all but the rightful owner.

H.   One who finds a chattel by virtue of a trespass generally does not acquire a possessory right superior to that of the owner of the property upon which the finder has trespassed.

    1. One who wrongfully (i.e., by trespass) obtains possession of a lost chattel may sue to recover possession from a third party (i.e., persons other than the rightful owner or the owner of the property) interfering with his possession.

    2. One who finds but then loses a chattel may sue to recover the chattel from a third person who subsequently finds the same.

I.   A landowner, not a finder, acquires a possessory right, based on constructive possession, to objects (e.g., meteorites) embedded in soil located on his property.

J.   Unclaimed gold, silver, currency, etc. intentionally concealed or buried by an unknown owner (i.e., a treasure trove) belongs either to the finder or to the landowner, depending on the jurisdiction.

K.   Due Care

As a quasi-bailee, a possessor must exercise due care toward a lost or mislaid chattel in his custody.

1. If a possessor knows, or can reasonably ascertain, a rightful owner's identity, he has a duty to do so. A breach of this duty is grounds for a charge of larceny and an action for conversion.

2. A possessor's obligations persist until either sufficient time has passed to constitute abandonment, or the statute of limitations has run.

L.   Gaining Title

1. A possessor gains title to lost or mislaid property when either the statute of limitations has run or the chattel is held to be abandoned.

2. Most jurisdictions have enacted estray statutes under which a lost or mislaid chattel is placed with proper authorities who register it. If the chattel is unclaimed after a certain amount of time, the possessor becomes the owner.

M.   Statute of Limitations
Every jurisdiction has a statute of limitations prescribing the period during which the rightful owner must bring suit to recover possession of a lost or mislaid chattel. (See Adverse Possession of Real Property, below.) Modern courts tend to depart from the rule applying adverse possession to chattels and apply the *discovery rule,* which dictates that a rightful owner's cause of action accrues "when he first knew, or reasonably should have known through the exercise of due diligence, of the cause of action, including the identity of the possessor. . . ."

III.   ACCESSION

A.   Definition
Improving the value of another's chattel (usually with labor or added materials).

B.   Ownership of the improved chattel is at issue when the added value cannot be separated from the original chattel or the original chattel has so changed as to constitute a different species (e.g., wheat is ground into flour).

1. The "different species test" (traditional rule).
   When the original chattel is completely changed, the party who made the change, not the owner, will be awarded title to the new product.

2. The "disproportionate value test" (modern rule).
   The party who made the change will be awarded title when the value added is wholly disproportionate to the original chattel's value.

3. The original owner may recover damages for conversion.

C.   One who improves another's chattel must act in good faith. A willful trespasser will never be awarded title by accession. An original owner may elect to sue a willful trespasser for damages (conversion) or return of possession (replevin).

D.   An improver who was denied title does not generally have a right to compensation.

1. Damages at law are usually denied even in good faith situations.

2. Equitable relief may be obtained.

IV.   CONFUSION

A.   Definition
Confusion is the mingling of separately owned fungible goods so that they cannot be distinguished.

B.   Regardless of the facts surrounding the event, the parties become tenants in common with an interest in the whole proportional to their respective share, if the contribution of each party is known.

C.   When the contribution of each party is unknown, the parties share equally as tenants in common.
Exception: When the confusion is wrongfully occasioned and the wrongdoer fails to prove his share, the innocent party takes the whole.

V. BAILMENTS

A. Definition
A bailment is a temporary transfer of the right to possess property from the owner (bailor) to the bailee.

1. A contract is not essential to creating a bailment.

2. To constitute a bailment, the bailee must:

   a. have physical control of the property;

   b. intend to assume custody of the property; and

   c. consent to the bailment.

3. Even if the bailee lacks an intent to assume custody of property, a constructive or involuntary bailment may arise.
Example: Someone finding an umbrella left behind at a restaurant is a bailee.

B. Bailee's Rights and Duties

1. A bailee has a right to possession superior to all, except the owner. The bailee can maintain a suit against third parties interfering with his possession.

2. Absent a contrary agreement, a bailee has no right to use the bailed goods. Any intentional unauthorized use resulting in loss makes the bailee absolutely liable. Incidental use essential to the performance of the bailee's duty is permitted.

3. The bailee must redeliver the property to the bailor at the termination of the bailment. A bailee is strictly liable for misdelivery of the bailed property. Constructive bailees are liable only for negligent misdelivery. If the bailee either refuses to return the property or departs without authorization from the terms of the bailment, strict liability attaches.

4. If a bailee's use of the bailed property harms a third party, the bailee (not the bailor) is liable due to his possession and control of the property.

5. Though not an insurer, the bailee owes a duty of care regarding the treatment of the bailed property. The standard of care turns on who is benefited by the bailment.

    a. If the bailment solely benefits the bailor, the bailee is liable only if he is grossly negligent.

    b. If the bailment is mutually beneficial, the bailee must exercise ordinary due care.

    c. If the bailment solely benefits the bailee, the bailee must exercise extraordinary care.

VI.   ADVERSE POSSESSION OF REAL PROPERTY

A.   Generally
The doctrine of adverse possession obligates the title holder of land to eject, within a statutorily prescribed period, a wrongful possessor of the land. Provided certain other elements are satisfied, a title holder who fails this obligation will lose title to the land in question to the adverse possessor.

B.   Elements of Adverse Possession
Possession must be open and notorious, continuous, hostile, and under a claim of right, for the statutory period.

1. Open and Notorious
Possession is "open and notorious" when the adverse possessor actually uses a reasonable percentage of the claimed land in a manner similar to that of typical owners of similar land, and this use is sufficient to put the true owner or the community on notice of his possession.

2. Continuous
The adverse possessor must "continuously" occupy the land throughout the statutory period, in a manner consistent with the normal uses of similar land. Although intermittent occupancy is insufficient, an adverse possessor need not occupy the land every day of every year during the statutory period, (e.g., if the land is normally used only in the summer, seasonal possession suffices to satisfy this requirement).

3. Hostile
Possession is "hostile" when the adverse possessor occupies land without the title holder's consent and in a manner inconsistent with his rights.

4. Claim of Right
Possession is under a "claim of right" when the adverse possessor indicates, by words or conduct, that he holds the land as against all others.

   a. The majority view is that the "hostile" and "claim of right" elements are synonymous.

   b. The minority view, however, is that the adverse possessor must have a bona fide belief that he has title to the land.

5. Statutory Period
An adverse possessor must remain in possession for a statutorily prescribed period, usually twenty years.

C. Constructive Possession Doctrine
One actually possessing under "color of title" (i.e., the possessor holds a defective conveyance document) a portion of a large, unitary tract of land may gain title by adverse possession to the whole tract as described in the defective document, even if never actually possessing or using the entire tract. The portion actually possessed must be in reasonable proportion to the whole, such that it is sufficient to put the true owner or community on notice.

D. Concurrently Held Land
To gain title by adverse possession to concurrently owned land, the adverse possessor must oust his cotenant.

E. Tacking
When possession is continuous, and the parties are in privity (i.e., a blood relation, oral or written transfer, will or intestacy), the time in possession of successive adverse possessors may be added together to fulfill the statutory period.

F. Tolling the Statute of Limitations

1. Disabilities

If at the time of an adverse possessor's entry onto the land the title owner is disabled, the statute of limitations is tolled for the duration of the disability.

   a.   Most jurisdictions recognize insanity, infancy, and imprisonment as disabilities.

   b.   Disabilities may not be tacked.

2. Future Interests

   a.   If at the time of the adverse possessor's entry onto the land another holds a future interest in the land, the statute of limitations is tolled until the future interest becomes possessory.

   b.   However, if the future interest is created after the adverse possessor enters the land, the statute of limitations runs against the future interest holder prior to such interest becoming possessory.

G.   The adverse possession doctrine does not apply to government owned land and to land registered under the Torrens System.

H.   Rights of an Adverse Possessor

   1. An adverse possessor may convey his possessory right to property.

   2. In conflicts between adverse possessors of the same land, a first possessor's right to the land is generally superior to the rights of subsequent possessors.

   3. An adverse possessor may bring trespass and ejectment actions against third parties.

CASE CLIPS

State v. Shack (1971)

Facts: Pursuant to federal statutes mandating legal and other aid for migrant workers, the defendants, Tejeras and Shack, entered a farmer's land to see certain workers. The farmer executed a complaint alleging violation of the state trespass statute.

Issue: Do landowners have an absolute right to exclude others from their property?

Rule: Real property rights are not absolute. Hence, private or public necessity may justify entry upon the lands of another.

Sierra Club v. Morton (S.Ct. 1972)

Facts: Sierra Club brought suit against various federal officials, alleging that a proposed development of a National Game Refuge would destroy its flora and fauna as well as future generations' enjoyment of the refuge. However, Sierra Club failed to plead that it, or any of its members, use the Refuge and would thereby be injured in fact.

Issue: Under the Administrative Procedure Act, may one seek judicial review of a Federal Agency's actions when injury in fact is not alleged?

Rule: (Stewart, J.) A mere interest in a federal action is not sufficient by itself to render a person or organization "adversely affected" or "aggrieved" under the APA, but rather, an injury in fact is requisite for standing to seek judicial review of an agency's actions.

Dissent: (Blackmun, J) The court should solve the problem by adopting one of two alternatives. It should either allow Sierra Club to amend its complaint accordingly, or it should expand the definition of standing to encompass the interests of organizations with a provable, sincere, dedicated, and established status.

Dissent: (Brennan, J) The court should recognize organizations like the Sierra Club as having standing to bring suit.

Dissent: (Douglas, J) Standing to sue should be conferred upon the environmental object itself and representative counsel should be appointed to argue for the preservation of its existence.

Jones v. Alfred H. Mayer Co. (1968)

Facts: Jones alleged that the defendant's refusal to sell him a home was based solely on racial discrimination, and thus in contravention of 42 U.S.C.A. § 1982.

Issue: Does § 1982 prohibit all private and public racial discrimination in the sale or rental of property?

Rule: (Stewart, J) § 1982 bars all racial discrimination, private as well as public, in the sale or rental of property.

Edwards v. Sims (1929)

Facts: Edwards filed a writ of prohibition against Judge Sims, following an earlier proceeding in which judgment was entered against him. The writ was sought in order to prevent the enforcement of an order of the lower court directing surveyors to enter upon Edwards' land for the purpose of surveying a cave.

Issue: To determine the property rights of surface landowners, may a court order a survey of a privately owned cave?

Rule: A court of equity has the power to compel a cave owner to permit a survey of it at the institution of a suit of a party who can show reasonable ground for suspicion that the cave owner is trespassing under his property.

Johnson v. McIntosh (S.Ct. 1823)

Facts: The plaintiff, who purchased land from a Native American tribe, brought an ejectment action against the defendant who acquired the same land by a grant from the United States.

Issue: Is a title to real property conveyed by Native American tribes recognized by courts of the United States?

Rule: (Marshall, CJ.) A title conveyed by a Native American tribe cannot be valid unless it was granted to the tribe by the United States Government.

Shelley v. Kraemer (S.Ct. 1948)

Facts: Shelley's property was impressed with a restrictive covenant prohibiting occupancy or ownership of his house by blacks.

Issue: Does the Equal Protection clause of the Fourteenth Amendment prohibit judicial enforcement by state courts of restrictive covenants based on race or color?

Rule: (Vinson CJ.) The granting of equitable judicial enforcement of restrictive covenants that deny property rights available to other members of the community is prohibited by the Equal Protection Clause of the Fourteenth Amendment.

Goddard v. Winchell (1892)

Facts: Goddard claimed ownership of a meteorite that was found by a third party on Goddard's property and subsequently sold to the defendant without Goddard's knowledge.

Issue: Are natural deposits embedded in the soil considered lost or abandoned and thus the property of the finder?

Rule: Natural deposits on property become a part of the realty and are not lost or abandoned. Hence, they belong to the realty's owner.

Eads v. Brazelton (1861)

Facts: Planning to salvage its cargo, Brazelton discovered and marked the location of a sunken ship abandoned by its owners. Due to his delays, the defendant located the ship and raised some of its cargo. Brazelton brought suit to enjoin the defendant from removing any more cargo from the ship and to recover the previously removed cargo.

Issue: Will mere discovery of a lost or abandoned chattel give the finder a property right in the found chattel?

Rule: The occupation or possession of a chattel lost, abandoned or otherwise without an owner depends on an actual taking of the property, as is reasonable under the circumstances, coupled with an intent to reduce it to possession.

Armory v. Delamirie (1722)

Facts: The plaintiff found a jewel and brought it to a jeweler for appraisal. The jeweler's apprentice removed the stones from the jewel and the plaintiff brought an action for money damages.

Issue: What is the nature of the title held by the finder of a chattel?

Rule: The finder of a lost chattel has superior title in the chattel as against everyone but the rightful owner.

Bridges v. Hawkesworth (1851)

Facts: Bridges found bank notes lying on the floor of the defendant's shop which he requested the defendant hold until the rightful owner claimed them. Three years later, the defendant refused to return the still unclaimed notes to Bridges.

Issue: When a chattel is found in the public area of a shop, does the shop owner or the finder acquire a property right in it?

Rule: Since not intentionally left behind, a chattel lost in a public shop is not within the shop owner's custody. Consequently, the finder of an article lost in a public shop is entitled to possession of it as against all parties except the true owner.

South Staffordshire Water Co. v. Sharman (1896)

Facts: The defendant found two rings upon the property of the plaintiff while in the process of cleaning out the plaintiff's pool. The plaintiff brought suit to regain possession of the rings.

Issue: Does the finder of lost property or the owner of the land upon which it is found acquire a right to possess the property?

Rule: The owner of the land upon which the lost property is found acquires a superior possessory interest to that of the finder if the owner exercises actual control over the locus in quo (the land) and the things upon it.

Hannah v. Peel (1945)

Facts: The plaintiff found a brooch in a house owned by the defendant but never occupied by him.

Issue: Does the finder of a lost chattel have a superior claim to possess the chattel than the owner of the freehold on which it was found?

Rule: Where the owner of the freehold was never physically in possession of the premises the finder of a chattel lost on the freehold has a superior claim to the chattel?

McAvoy v. Medina (1866)

Facts: The plaintiff, a customer in the defendant's barbershop, found a pocketbook accidentally left behind by one of the defendant's prior patrons.

Issue: Does the lost-mislaid distinction play a part in determining ownership of a chattel found by one person on premises owned by another?

Rule: In a case where the court finds that the chattel has been mislaid (inadvertently forgotten) the owner of the premises is awarded possession. However, property that is lost goes to the finder.

Schley v. Couch (1955)

Facts: The plaintiff found money buried in a glass jar on Schley's property.

Issue: In jurisdictions not recognizing the treasure trove doctrine, does the finder of buried money or the owner of the property upon which it is found acquire a possessory right in the money?

Rule: Money found embedded in soil under circumstances repelling the idea that it was involuntarily parted with through inadvertence constitutes a mislaid chattel to which the owner of the property acquires a possessory interest, good against all but the true owner. However, when it appears that the true owner involuntarily parted with it through inadvertence, it is lost property and may be retained by the finder as against all but the true owner.

Parking Management, Inc. v. Gilder (1975)

Facts: Gilder's car was vandalized while parked in the defendant's garage.

Issue: Does a commercial parking lot operator have an implied duty of reasonable care to protect a patron's car?

Rule: Where a patron reasonably expects that reasonable care will be exercised to prevent tampering with his car, an implied duty of reasonable care by the lot operator to protect the auto from theft or malicious mischief is created.

Shamrock Hilton Hotel v. Caranas (1972)

Facts: The Caranases, guests at the defendant hotel, lost a purse containing thirteen thousand dollars in jewelry in the hotel dining room. A hotel employee found it and gave it to a superior, who mistakenly gave it to a stranger. The Caranases filed suit for negligent misdelivery of the purse.

Issue: To establish a bailment, must the bailor knowingly intend to entrust the property to the bailee?

Rule: A constructive bailment arises if it is apparent that the loser of the property was aware of the circumstances and would have expected the person finding the property to have kept it safely for its subsequent return to him.

Porter v. Wertz (1979)

Facts: Porter, the plaintiff, entrusted a Maurice Utrillo painting to Harold Von Maker (a con artist), hoping that the latter would buy the painting. Acting in concert with one Peter Wertz, a delicatessen employee, Von Maker sold the painting to an art dealer, Feigen, who subsequently sold it to Brenner. Ultimately the painting wound up in Venezuela, and Porter brought suit against all of the above named actors.

Issue 1: May a rightful owner be statutorily estopped from recovering his stolen property from a subsequent purchaser for value based on UCC § 2-403?

Rule 1: An owner will not be statutorily estopped from asserting his title against a person who is not "a buyer in the ordinary course of business," defined in UCC § 1-201 as "a person who in good faith and without knowledge that the sale to him is in violation of the ownership rights or security interest of a third party in the goods buys in ordinary course from a person in the business of selling goods of that kind."

Issue 2: May an owner be equitably estopped from asserting his title against a bona fide purchaser for value?

Rule 2: If an owner invests another with the usual evidence of title or an apparent authority to dispose of his property, he will not be allowed to make a claim against an innocent purchaser dealing on the faith of such apparent ownership.

Sheridan Suzuki, Inc. v. Caruso Auto Sales (1981)

Facts: The plaintiff, Sheridan Suzuki, Inc., sold a motorcycle to Bouton who, except for obtaining a statutorily required Certificate of Title, had all indicia of ownership. The next day, Bouton sold it to the defendant. Subsequently, Bouton's check to Sheridan bounced.

Issue: Can a bona fide purchaser for value obtain good title from someone who holds a voidable unperfected title to a motor vehicle?

Rule: Although a bona fide purchaser for value is able to obtain good title when buying from one with voidable title under the U.C.C., he does not obtain good title when he buys from one who has not perfected title pursuant to the State Uniform Vehicle Certificate of Title Act.

Anderson v. Gouldberg (1892)

Facts: The plaintiffs wrongly removed timber from land that did not belong to them, and brought it to a mill. The owner of the mill promptly appropriated the timber for himself.

Issue: Is bare possession of property, though obtained through improper means, a sufficient interest to enable the wrongdoer to maintain an action of replevin against another wrongdoer who subsequently takes the property from him?

Rule: One who has acquired possession of property, whether by finding, bailment, or even by tort, has a right to retain possession as against a wrongdoer who is a stranger to the property.

Russell v. Hill (1900)

Facts: Russell bought timber from one who mistakenly believed that she had title to the land from which the timber came. Subsequently, the defendant wrongfully took the logs from Russell and disposed of them. Russell sued in trover to recover damages for the conversion.

Issue: May one maintain an action in trover when he cannot show that he has both title and possession, or a present right of possession?

Rule: An action in trover is not maintainable unless a satisfaction of the judgment will have the effect of vesting a good title in the defendant, except where the property is restored, and the conversion was temporary.

Therefore, in order to maintain an action in trover, a plaintiff must show title and possession, or a present right of possession.

Chapin v. Freeland (1886)

Facts: The plaintiff purchased a chattel from a vendor who became the owner of it by adverse possession. Freeland, the original owner of the chattel, used self help and simply took the chattel from the plaintiff.

Issue: Does the running of the statute of limitations for bringing suit to recover personalty bar the owner from using self help to recover the personalty from a subsequent purchaser?

Rule: A purchaser from one against whom the remedy is already barred by the running of the statute of limitations is entitled to stand in as good a position as his vendor. Thus, the original owner may not use self help to recover the chattel from the vendee.

O'Keeffe v. Snyder (1980)

Facts: In 1946 three of Georgia O'Keeffe's paintings were stolen from a gallery, but she took no formal action to recover them. In 1976, she instituted suit against the defendant, the owner of an art gallery who was then in possession of the paintings.

Issue: When does the statute of limitations begin to run on an action for replevin of chattels?

Rule: Under the discovery rule the statute of limitations on an action for replevin begins to run when the owner knows or reasonably should know of her cause of action and the identity of the possessor of the chattel.

Wetherbee v. Green (1871)

Facts: Wetherbee cut the plaintiff's timber without his consent and made hoops from it. The plaintiff brought an action in replevin to regain possession of his improved property.

Issue: Does one who has taken the property of another and significantly increased its value, gain title to the property if it was taken in good faith and in reliance upon a supposed right, without intention to commit wrong?

Rule: When one takes another's property in good faith and adds value to it which is wholly disproportionate to the original material's value, he gains title to the property. The remedy of the owner of the original materials is to recover damages for unintentional trespass.

Isle Royale Mining Co. v. Hertin (1877)

Facts: Isle Royale Mining Co. took possession of cord wood that the plaintiff mistakenly cut on its land. The plaintiff brought an action for the value of the labor expended on the operation.

Issue: Will one receive compensation for his labor when he mistakenly, but in good faith, takes and improves another's property, but does not thereby greatly increase the property's value?

Rule: When there is no great disparity between the value of raw materials and the value added by the labor of one who had mistakenly and in good faith taken and improved them, the laborer has no right to be compensated for his work when the raw material's true owner reclaims his property.

Hardy v. Burroughs (1930)

Facts: The plaintiff mistakenly built a house on Burroughs' land and brought suit to recover the value of the improvements.

Issue: May one who mistakenly improves another's land recover the value of the improvements?

Rule: One who improves another's land in good faith and is evicted by the true owner, may sue in equity for the value of the improvements.

In Re Cohn (1919)

Facts: Leopold Cohn made a gift to his wife of certain stock certificates which he did not have in his physical possession. The gift was evidenced by an unambiguous writing, which was also witnessed by several individuals. Several days later he died without having the opportunity to make actual delivery of the stock certificates to his wife.

Issue: Is an inter vivos gift valid without actual delivery of the thing given?

Rule: When a gift is evidenced by an instrument of gift executed and delivered to the donee, and the circumstances surrounding the making of the gift afford a reasonable and satisfactory excuse for not making actual delivery of the object constituting the gift, a constructive or symbolical delivery is sufficient to establish the legal validity of the gift.

Gruen v. Gruen (1986)

Facts: Victor Gruen (decedent) made an inter vivos gift of a painting but reserved a life estate. His son, the recipient of the gift, brought suit against his stepmother for possession of the painting.

Issue: Is an inter vivos gift valid when the donor has reserved a life estate in the chattel and the donee never had physical possession before the donor's death?

Rule: As long as the evidence establishes an intent to make a present and irrevocable transfer of title or the right of ownership, there is a present transfer of some interest and the gift is effective immediately.

Foster v. Reiss (1955)

Facts: Just prior to her death, Ethel Reiss wrote a note to her husband expressing her desire that he receive some of her personalty upon her death. She did not actually deliver the personalty to him. The plaintiffs in the case were the representatives of the deceased's estate.

Issue: To be a valid gift causa mortis, must the thing given be actually delivered?

Rule: To be a valid gift causa mortis, the delivery of the thing must be such as is actual, unequivocal, and complete during the lifetime of the donor, wholly divesting the donor of the possession, dominion, and control thereof.

Note: This case represents a minority position.

Scherer v. Hyland (1977)

Facts: Prior to committing suicide, Ms. Wagner (the plaintiff's cohabitor) endorsed a blank check, wrote a note expressing her desire to leave it to the plaintiff, and left it where the plaintiff would be sure to find it. The defendant, Hyland, was the administrator of her estate.

Issue: Absent actual delivery, when is constructive delivery sufficient to support a gift causa mortis?

Rule: Where there is unequivocal evidence of the donor's intent to presently transfer the subject matter of the gift to the donee, and the donor did all that she could or thought necessary to do to effect such a transfer, constructive delivery is sufficient to support a gift causa mortis.

In Re Estate of Michaels (1965)

Facts: Helen Michaels established a joint bank account registered in the name of "Helen Michaels or Harry Michaels." However, Harry Michaels, her son, had no knowledge of this account during his mother's lifetime and she retained complete control over the funds. Upon her death proceedings were instituted to determine whether the bank account should be treated as owned individually by her, or in joint tenancy with Harry Michaels.

Issue: Under what circumstances will the survivor (donee/payee) of a joint bank account be required to hold title in trust for another, upon the death of the (donor/depositor)?

Rule: Legal title to a joint bank account is in the survivor (donee/ payee) upon the death of the (donor/depositor), unless clear and satisfactory evidence indicates that the donor/depositor did not intend the right of survivorship. In the event of such a showing the survivor will be required to hold the title in trust until such time when the proper beneficiary is ascertained.

Ferrell v. Stinson (1953)

Facts: Mary Kamberling (decedent) deeded land to the defendants but did not deliver the deed. Bedridden from tuberculosis, Kamberling instructed a friend to mail the deed to the defendants after her death.

Issue: Is manual delivery essential to complete a conveyance when the grantor intended to relinquish dominion and control over a deed and have it take effect as a present conveyance of title?

Rule: Because a grantor's intent is the paramount factor, effective delivery may be made by placing the deed in the hands of a third person without reserving the right to recall it and with instructions to deliver it to the grantee after the grantor's death.

Pierson v. Post (1805)

Facts: The plaintiff, Lodowick Post, brought an action against Pierson for killing a fox that Post himself was pursuing and about to capture.

Issue: What acts are required in order to acquire ownership of a wild animal?

Rule: Mere pursuit of a wild animal confers no property right to the animal. The pursuer must deprive the animal of its natural liberty by wounding, ensnaring, or otherwise subjecting it to his control.

Ganter v. Kapiloff (1986)

Facts: The Kapiloff brothers owned valuable stamps and did not realize that they had lost them until they saw the stamps being advertised in a publication. The stamps were found by Ganter, with whom they had no relation. The Kapiloffs brought an action for replevin to obtain the return of the stamps.

Issue: Does the finder of lost property acquire absolute ownership of it?

Rule: The finder of lost property has a superior right to the property as against everyone *but* the true owner.

Favorite v. Miller (1978)

Facts: Miller found a piece of a 200-year-old statue of King George III buried on the plaintiff's property. He unearthed and removed the artifact without the plaintiff's permission and contracted to sell it to the Museum of the City of New York. Upon learning of the discovery, the plaintiff brought suit to regain possession of the valuable find.

Issue: May the finder of lost property retain possession of it, even if it was found by trespassing upon another's land?

Rule: The finder of lost property upon the land of another does not acquire a possessory interest in the property if it was buried in the ground or discovered by trespass. In these two instances, the owner of the land is entitled to possession of the property.

Monroe v. Rawlings (1951)

Facts: Monroe brought an ejectment action against Rawlings who entered upon the land, paid taxes on it, built and used a hunting lodge, and otherwise exercised dominion over it for the statutory period.

Issue: To establish title by adverse possession, must one live on the land or improve it, fence it off or otherwise attempt to exclude others?

Rule: To establish title by adverse possession, it is sufficient if the acts of ownership are of such a character as to openly and publicly indicate an assumed control or use that is consistent with the character of the premises in question.

Peters v. Juneau-Douglas Girl Scout Council (1974)

Facts: The defendants held title to a piece of beachfront property, but Peters used the property continuously and openly for over 40 years. During this period, people other than Peters occasionally made use of the land. Peters brought suit to establish his title to the property.

Issues: Will a claim of title by adverse possession be defeated because parties other than the adverse possessor also made use of the property?

Rule: To satisfy the "exclusivity" element of the adverse possession doctrine the possessor must only hold the land for himself, as his own, and not for another.

Mannillo v. Gorski (1969)

Facts: Mannillo's and Gorski's lots shared a boundary. Unknowingly, when making improvements on his house, Gorski encroached on Mannillo's lot by 15 inches. Mannillo filed a trespass action. In defense, Gorski claimed title by adverse possession.

Issue: To establish title by adverse possession, must the possession be accompanied by an intention to invade the property rights of another?

Rule: Any entry and possession for the required time which is exclusive, continuous, uninterrupted, visible, and notorious, even though under mistaken claim of title, is sufficient to support a claim of title by adverse possession.

Porter v. Posey (1979)

Facts: The Porters purchased land, part of which was acquired by adverse possession by the grantor, but their deed did not describe the adversely acquired portion of the property. However, the same land was in the deed by which the Poseys acquired their adjacent property. The dispute led the Porters to bring suit to establish their right to the parcel in question.

Issue: May title to property acquired by adverse possession be transferred by a deed that did not contain a description of that property?

Rule: Title to property acquired by adverse possession may be transferred without a written conveyance where the title owner intends to transfer the property and the transferee takes possession of that property.

Taffinder v. Thomas (1977)

Facts: The Taffinders claimed ownership by adverse possession of land that they used for eight years, but their period of usage fell two years short of the statutorily prescribed period for acquiring title by adverse possession. However, the Taffinders proposed to tack their period of possession onto that of a tenant of their grantor, who had been occupying his leased premises for more than the statutory period.

Issue: May title be acquired through adverse possession by tacking a tenant's occupation onto that of the grantees in order to comply with the statute of limitations?

Rule: Where the area in question is either expressly or impliedly within the terms of a lease, prescriptive rights can be established through a tenant.

Peet v. Roth Hotel Co. (1934)

Facts: The Roth Hotel Co. lost a ring left with it by the plaintiff for delivery to a third party. The plaintiff sued to recover the value of the ring.

Issue 1: For there to be a valid bailment, must the bailor divulge the value of the property left with the bailee?

Rule 1: Even if he erroneously underestimates its value, a bailee is liable for the value of the property entrusted to his care when the identity of the property and all its attributes, except its value, are known to him.

Issue 2: Must a bailee exercise a degree of care commensurate to the hazard?

Rule 2: A bailee must exercise that degree of care which an ordinarily prudent person would have exercised in the same or similar circumstances.

Allen v. Hyatt Regency-Nashville Hotel (1984)

Facts: Allen parked his car in the defendant's garage, which had only one exit and was guarded by an attendant. He was not required to surrender his keys. The car was stolen, and Allen brought suit against the owners of the garage.

Issue: Is a commercial parking garage liable to a customer for the theft of a vehicle if it has only one exit and has attendants monitoring the exit?

Rule: A bailment is created when an owner leaves his vehicle in the custody of a parking garage with limited access, and where the patron must present a ticket to an attendant upon leaving the premises. On proof of nondelivery, the patron is entitled to plead a presumption of negligence.

Borough of Westville v. Whitney Home Builders, Inc. (1956)

Facts: Whitney Home Builders, Inc. discharged treated sewage into a stream that flowed through the plaintiff's land and emptied into the plaintiff's pond.

Issue: May a riparian owner discharge treated sewage into a stream?

Rule: The discharge of treated sewage effluent into a stream is not a per se unreasonable riparian use. Courts must weigh the reasonableness, under all the circumstances, of the use being made by the defendant and of the materiality of the harm, if any, visited by such use on the reasonable uses of the water by the complaining owner.

Pendergrast v. Aiken (1977)

Facts: After Aiken altered the drainage on his land, the plaintiff's land, which was located upstream from Aiken's, flooded whenever heavy rains fell.

Issue: Is a landowner liable whenever he interferes with the natural flow of surface water to the detriment of another in the use and enjoyment of his land?

Rule: Each possessor is legally privileged to make a reasonable use of his land, even though the flow of surface water is altered thereby and causes some harm to others, but liability is incurred when his harmful interference with the flow of surface waters is unreasonable and causes substantial damage.

Finley v. Teeter Stone, Inc. (1968)

Facts: Due to the quarrying on and pumping water from the defendants' land the Finleys suffered damage to their land due to substantial subsidence.

Issue: Is a landowner liable for damage to an adjacent landowner's property caused by his use of the percolating water under his land?

Rule: A landowner incurs no liability by using the percolating water under his land if it is used for any reasonable purpose connected with the legitimate use of his land.

Puckett v. Sullivan (1961)

Facts: The defendant excavated dirt on his own property, thereby causing landslides and damaging noncontiguous property owned by the Pucketts.

Issue: Is an excavator liable when his removal of land's lateral support causes damage to a noncontiguous tract?

Rule: Because the right to lateral support is not confined to adjoining lands, if land is negligently excavated, the excavator is liable for damage caused to noncontiguous tracts.

Keeble v. Hickeringill (1707)

Facts: The plaintiff owned a pond to which he attracted ducks with decoys so as to kill and bring them to market. By discharging guns nearby the defendant purposefully scared the fowl away.

Issue: Does an action for damages lie against one who purposely scares away wild animals that another has induced to come to his property so as to capture for market?

Rule: An action lies in all cases where a violent or malicious act is done to a person's occupation, profession, or way of getting a livelihood.

Note: This rule is inconsistent with the rule announced in Pierson v. Post (above) and no longer represents valid law.

Young v. Hichens (1844)

Facts: Young had placed a net almost completely around a shoal of fish when Hichens interfered with the operation and captured the fish for himself. Young brought a suit for trespass.

Issue: Can one acquire a property interest in a wild animal without reducing it to possession?

Rule: Until a party takes actual possession of a wild animal, he has no property interest in it.

Ghen v. Rich (1881)

Facts: The plaintiff (libelant) brought suit to recover the market value of a whale that his ship had harpooned. The defendant (respondent) had purchased the whale from a third party who had found it washed up on the beach. According to the local custom of the Massachusetts coastal whaling trade, one who harpooned a whale acquired an ownership interest in it, vis-à-vis any finder of the dead whale. Unique markings were used on the harpoons of each whaling vessel for identification purposes.

Issue: Is it possible to acquire a property right in a wild animal without actually reducing it to possession and control?

Rule: Where one undertakes the only act of appropriation that is possible in the nature of the case, and otherwise does all that is possible to make the animal his own, he acquires a property right in the wild animal.

Glave v. Michigan Terminix Co. (1987)

Facts: Peggy Glave alleged that the defendants' act of chasing away pigeons from certain city buildings caused the birds to flock to her property and thereby caused her to contract an infection.

Issue: Under what circumstances can a defendant be held responsible for the actions of ferae naturae (wild animals)?

Rule: Individuals can only be held liable for the actions of wild animals if they have asserted dominion over them in the form of taming or confinement, and have not later relinquished this control.

The Queen v. Ashwell (1885)

Facts: The defendant asked Keogh to lend him a shilling (12 pence). Keogh mistakenly gave the defendant a sovereign (240 pence), which the defendant appropriated after discovering the error.

Issue: When a borrower of money is mistakenly lent more than he had requested, is he guilty of larceny if he fails to return the excess?

Rule: One commits larceny when he finds a lost chattel and, not believing it to be abandoned, carries it away with a felonious intent. Consequently, a borrower of money commits larceny if he intends to, and does, appropriate the excess at the moment he realizes he received more than both he and the lender intended.

Cowen v. Pressprich (1922)

Facts: The plaintiffs delivered the wrong bond to the defendants. In an attempt to return it, the defendants handed it to a messenger who they mistakenly believed was employed by the plaintiffs. Consequently, the negotiable bond was lost and never recovered. The plaintiffs brought suit to obtain the return of the bond.

Issue: Is a constructive bailee absolutely liable for the goods in his possession?

Rule: When a constructive bailee exercises any dominion over the bailed goods, his duty to deliver the bailed goods to the proper person is absolute. Hence, he is absolutely liable for the value of misdelivered goods.

Dissent: An implied contract of bailment with its consequent obligations arises only where a person in possession of the property of another does some act which is inconsistent with the view that he does not accept the possession which has been thrust upon him.

Note: On appeal, this case was reversed and the dissent's position adopted.

Gillespie v. Dew (1827)

Facts: Duncan Dew removed timber from land to which the plaintiff had title, though he was never in possession of it. The plaintiff brought an action for trespass.

Issue: To maintain a trespass action, must the title holder be in actual possession of his land?

Rule: Where there is no adverse possession, the titleholder of realty has constructive possession and may maintain a trespass action.

State v. Schingen (1865)

Facts: Buhler entrusted his employee, the defendant, with horses and a wagon to deliver goods. The defendant attempted to sell the horses and wagon and actually sold the harness.

Issue: Will an employer be able to maintain an action for trespass and larceny where an employee takes his property if the employer is not in actual possession of the property?

Rule: An employer who entrusts property to an employee is considered to be in constructive possession of the property. Therefore, actions for trespass and larceny lie against an employee who, having temporary custody of the property, converts it to his own use.

Ewing v. Burnet (S.Ct. 1837)

Facts: Through a common grantor, both the plaintiff and the defendant had title to the same unimproved lot, though the plaintiff's grant was earlier in time. The defendant, however, publicly exercised dominion and control over it for the statutory period. The plaintiff brought an action of ejectment.

Issue: Must an adverse claimant actually possess, cultivate, fence, or otherwise improve land to sustain a claim of adverse possession?

Rule: (Baldwin, J.) When property is so situated as not to admit of any permanent useful improvement, a claim of adverse possession is sustainable upon evidence of public acts of ownership such as would be exercised by an owner over property being claimed as his own.

Brumagim v. Bradshaw (1870)

Facts: The plaintiff's predecessor in interest repaired a wall on the neck of a 1,000 acre peninsula and used it for pasturage. Bradshaw entered upon the land and the plaintiff sought ejectment.

Issue: To sustain a claim of adverse possession, must the claimant use a reasonable percentage of the claimed land?

Rule: Where the inclosure consists wholly or partially of natural barriers, the acts of dominion and ownership which establish actual possession must reasonably correspond to the size of the tract and its condition and appropriate use, and the acts must be such as usually accompany the ownership of land similarly situated.

Mendonca v. Cities Service Oil Co. (1968)

Facts: The Cities Service Oil Co. built a fence on its property twenty-four feet from the common boundary of its own and the plaintiff's lots. Except for a three week period, during which a contractor working for the Oil Co. stored material on the disputed strip and tore down and replaced the fence, the plaintiff used the strip for the statutory period without the objection of the City Services Oil Co. The plaintiff brought suit to enjoin the defendant from entering upon the strip and to recover damages for trespass.

Issue: Will a brief re-entry by the owner defeat the "continuity of possession" element needed to establish adverse possession?

Rule: An adverse claimant must prove all the elements of adverse possession and a brief re-entry by the owner, even if not for the purpose of regaining possession, interrupts, and thereby defeats, the continuous possession element.

United States v. Stubbs (1985)

Facts: The United States sued Stubbs in order to quiet title to a tract of land which it claimed to have acquired either through a valid conveyance or by adverse possession.

Issue: Does the doctrine of adverse possession apply to the United States Government?

Rule: The United States can acquire title by adverse possession in the same way as a private individual. However, a person can not acquire land by adverse possession against the government.

The Winkfield (1901)

Facts: The British Postmaster General sued the owners of the *Winkfield* which collided with and sank another ship that was laden with mail and parcels. In his capacity as the bailee of the mailed materials the Postmaster General was not liable to the multiple bailors under British law.

Issue: May a wrongdoer defend against a claim brought by a bailee on the ground that the bailee himself is not liable to the bailors, and therefore the bailors themselves are the only ones with standing to bring the suit?

Rule: As between a bailee and a third party, possession gives the bailee title. Consequently, the stranger cannot defend against the bailee's claim for damage to the bailed property by showing that title was in the bailor.

Zimmerman v. Shreeve (1882)

Facts: When Zimmerman unlawfully cut and removed timber from a lot, the life tenant sued for damages in trespass.

Issue: May a life tenant recover in trespass for the full amount of damage done to the property?

Rule: A life tenant may recover damages in trespass only to the extent that his interest is injured.

Rogers v. Atlantic, Gulf & Pacific Co. (1915)

Facts: The plaintiff, a life tenant, sued to recover for all of the damage, both to the life estate and the future interest, caused by a fire set by the defendant, which was negligently allowed to spread.

Issues: May a life tenant recover for all the damages to an estate wholly caused by a third party, or should the recovery be limited to the damage to the life estate?

Rule: Since a wrongdoer should not escape liability by asserting rights of a third party under whom he does not claim, a life tenant may recover for all the damage to the estate, and such recovery bars an action by the remaindermen against the wrongdoer.

Tapscott v. Cobbs (1854)

Facts: Having been in prior possession, Cobbs, who did not have legal title, brought an ejectment action against Tapscott who, without title, took possession of the land.

Issue: May an action for ejectment be maintained upon the force of mere prior possession?

Rule: A peaceable prior possessor may maintain ejectment as against all the world except the rightful titleholder.

Winchester v. City of Stevens Point (1883)

Facts: The plaintiff sued for permanent damages due to the depreciation in value sustained by her property as a result of the actions of the defendant City of Stevens Point. Although in possession of the property the plaintiff could not prove a complete chain of title.

Issue: Can a party in actual possession of land, but without a perfect chain of title, recover both present and future damages for an injury to the freehold against a wrongdoer who neither has nor claims any title to or possession of the premises?

Rule: To recover for permanent damage to realty, a claimant in possession must prove valid title.

Lasalle County Carbon Coal Co. v. Sanitary District (1913)

Facts: Lasalle County Carbon Coal Co. took possession of land to which it did not have title. The land was later damaged by floods caused by the defendant. Five years later, Lasalle's adverse possession ripened into title, and it brought suit to recover for permanent damage to the land.

Issue: Can one recover damages for permanent injury to his land if the cause of action accrued before he gained title through adverse possession?

Rule: An owner may not rely on title by adverse possession to recover damages for injury to realty unless his possession had ripened into title before the cause of action accrued.

Illinois & St. Louis Railroad & Coal Co. v. Cobb (1879)

Facts: Cobb adversely possessed certain land which, prior to the ripening of this possession into title, the defendant entered and damaged. Cobb brought a trespass action seeking damages.

Issue: May a trespasser escape liability for damage to a freehold by showing that the party in possession of the property has no title to it?

Rule: A trespasser who is not claiming title to the property may not escape liability for damage to the freehold because the possessor of the estate does not have a valid title. Therefore, a recovery against a wrongdoer is not limited to the possessory interest of the party in possession, but is determined by the full amount of the damage done to the freehold.

Hammonds v. Central Kentucky Natural Gas Co. (1934)

Facts: After legally extracting gas from a natural underground field the defendant refilled it with gas brought in from other fields. A small portion of the field was located under the plaintiff's land and she brought an action for trespass, charging that the gas was placed there without her knowledge or permission.

Issue: How does the migratory nature of oil and gas affect the property rights associated with their extraction?

Rule: Generally oil and gas do not belong to anyone until captured and reduced to possession, and only the owner of the property directly under which these resources lie has the right to extract them. However, by analogy to wild animals, if the oil or gas is captured and then escapes or is released all ownership interest is destroyed.

Cheney Brothers v. Doris Silk Corp. (1929)

Facts: Doris Silk copied one of Cheney Brothers' popular designs and then undercut plaintiff's price.

Issue: May a party duplicate another party's property?

Rule: In the absence of a right or statute stating otherwise, an individual's property is limited to the chattels which embody his invention. Others may imitate these at their pleasure.

International News Service v. Associated Press (S.Ct. 1918)

Facts: Associated Press sought to enjoin the International News Service from selling news taken from its publications.

Issue: May a news organization be restrained from appropriating news published by a competing organization for the purpose of selling it to its own clients?

Rule: (Pitney, J.) Generally, published news materials are not regarded as property and may be used for any purpose whatsoever by the general public. However, between competing professional organizations published news materials are quasi-property. Therefore, a competitor must postpone distributing or reproducing news it gathers from another news organization's publications, but only to the extent necessary to prevent that competitor from reaping the benefit of the other news organization's efforts and expenditures.

Smith v. Chanel, Inc. (1968)

Facts: A perfume company claimed in an advertisement that its product was the equivalent of the more expensive Chanel No. 5.

Issue: May a party advertise its product as comparable to another when the original party put great effort and expense into its product's creation.

Rule: If a product is unpatented, a party has the right to copy it. The public interest in a competitive market is maintained in part through the ability of a marketer to identify the copied article by its tradename.

Moore v. The Regents of the University of California (1990)

Facts: Dr. Golde removed plaintiff's spleen and other bodily tissues after learning that the cells were unusually useful to his genetic research. A cell wall was then developed by Golde and his colleagues that was licensed for commercial development.

Issue: Does an individual have a sufficient legal interest in his own bodily tissues following their removal from his body?

Rule: An individual does not retain an ownership interest in his cells when they are removed for medical research. Such an individual is without an action for conversion, which is a tort that protects against interference with possession and ownership interests in personal property. However, a physician who is seeking a patient's consent for a medical procedure must disclose all facts relevant to that consent, including, personal interests unrelated to the patient's health that may affect his medical judgment.

Van Valkenburgh v. Lutz (1952)

Facts: The defendant, Lutz, claimed title by adverse possession to a lot that was purchased by the plaintiffs. He built a *dwelling* on the lot, cultivated a large portion of it, and used the property as his own for over twenty five years.

Issue: What facts need to be established to satisfy the "actual" and "hostile and under claim of right" requirements of acquiring title by adverse possession?

Rule: The requirement of "actual" possession is satisfied when the adverse possessor improves, cultivates, or encloses the premises to such an extent that he generally appears to be the rightful owner. The "hostile and under claim of right" requirement is met if the adverse possessor knows that he is not the rightful owner of the property but claims it as his own anyway.

Note: The remaining requirements for acquiring title by adverse possession involve proof that the occupancy is "exclusive," "open and notorious," and "continuous" for the period of time required under the applicable statute of limitations.

CHAPTER 2 POSSESSORY ESTATES

I. HISTORY—FEUDALISM AND TENURE
    During the Middle Ages, land was transferred through a system of tenures. The central feature of feudalism was the relationship of lord and vassal. All land was owned in the first instance by the sovereign, who then "tenured" it to his chief lords. They were obligated to render services in return. The chief lords then granted parts of their estates to their vassals, in return for services. Through this process of subinfeudation, a pyramid was formed, with the king at the top and the peasants at the bottom. In between were successive layers of chiefs and mesne lords, who were vassals to those above them and lords to those below.

A. Tenure
    The holding of the land by the vassal in exchange for the rendering of services to his lord was said to be "in tenure." Every time a vassal granted part of the land he possessed to another party (e.g., the vassal's vassal), a new tenure was created.

B. Feudal Tenures and Services

    1. Free Tenures
       These tenures involved services that were defined and fixed as to quantity and manner of performance. The tenant who held in free tenure could sue anyone who disturbed his possession in the King's court. There were four principal types of free tenures, differentiated by the nature of services the vassal had to render in return for possession of the land.

       a. Military Tenure
           Also called tenure by knight service. This was the most common type of tenure. The vassal was required to provide his lord with a previously agreed upon quota of knights for the king's host. As the art of war progressed, a monetary contribution (scutage) was given so that a professionally trained mercenary army could be hired.

       b. Serjeanty Tenure
           The serjeanty tenant had to perform a personal service which was definite as to time and often localized to a specific place.

Types of services that were performed included working in the King's or lord's household (e.g., cook, chamberlain, butler, etc.), or supplying the lord with specific goods and military service by the tenant/vassal himself. As the practice of hiring servants became widespread, serjeanty tenants paid rent instead of performing services.

c. Religious Tenure (Frankalmoign)
    These tenures were granted to churches or other religious bodies or officials in return for the performance of religious services.

d. Economic Tenure (Socage)
    Tenants in socage tenure were required to perform specified agricultural work on the lord's land or to supply a fixed amount of agricultural produce. Sometimes the tenant had to pay a fixed monetary sum, either nominal or substantial, instead of giving crops.

2. Unfree Tenures: Villenage
Each lord kept possession of some of his land, apart from the land he "tenured out." The lord used villeins (serfs) who lived on manorial property in exchange for working it. The serf, unlike a slave, had the rights of a free man against all persons except his lord. A serf was held in unfree tenure. His home and plot of land could be arbitrarily taken by his lord. The amount of services that the serf had to render was not fixed and would vary according to his lord's wishes. The serf could only enforce his rights in his lord's court. The arbitrary nature of unfree tenures gradually disappeared as serfs were granted a greater degree of freedom. Eventually, the obligations of villein tenants were fixed by custom, and were no longer decided by whim.

C. Feudal Incidents
    A lord was also entitled to the incidents of tenure. These obligations were created by the feudal relationship, (i.e., lord-vassal) and existed regardless of the specific terms of the tenure agreement. There were five principal incidents:

1. Homage and Fealty

Homage was a feudal ceremony in which an unarmed tenant knelt before his lord and pledged loyalty. Fealty was the oath which the tenant swore.

2. Aids

A tenant was obligated to financially assist his lord in some situations.

3. Liabilities at Death of Tenant

    a.   Relief and Primer Seisin

        At the death of a tenant, his heir had to pay a relief for the right to take over the land. If the tenant was by socage tenure, relief was equal to one year's rent. At the death of a tenant in chief (i.e., one who was a direct tenant to the King), the King was entitled to primer seisin (i.e., first possession) of all of the tenant's lands and the accompanying reliefs.

    b.   Wardship and Marriage

        If a military or grand serjeanty tenant died leaving a male heir under 21 or a female under 14, the lord was entitled to the rents and profits from the land until the male heir reached majority or the female heir either married or reached 16. The lord was entitled to arrange a marriage for the male heir and pocket the profit. Socage tenure was not subject to these incidents.

4. Escheat

If a tenant died without heirs the land returned to the lord.

D.   Statute Quia Emptores (1290)

Two ways in which land was transferred during the Middle Ages were subinfeudation and substitution. Subinfeudation was the process by which a tenant transferred lands in his possession to others, who became his tenants. He was entitled to both services and incidents from his tenants. He could also modify the incidents (i.e., lower them). Substitution involved the transfer of all of a tenant's interests in the land to another party who took the place of the original tenant. Thus, the original tenant was removed from the chain of ownership and received neither services nor incidents. The new tenant was directly responsible to the former tenant's lord. The

Statute Quia Emptores was enacted to permit free alienation of land by substitution only. It forbade subinfeudation and relieved tenants from a previously existing fine that was levied every time they transferred land. Thus, it permitted greater alienability of land and preserved valuable incidents for the lords.

II.   THE SYSTEM OF ESTATES

Although tenure is of little practical value, common law estates have survived to this day. An estate in land is an interest which: (a) is possessory or may become possessory (unlike easements, covenants, rents, and other land interests); and (b) is ownership measured in terms of duration of possession. (Rest. § 9). A key factor in classifying the various types of estates is the length of time during which the grantee (i.e., one receiving possession) is entitled to possess the land. Duration can vary from a few years (i.e., a term for years), to infinity (i.e., fee simple absolute).

Estates also differ with regard to the time at which they become possessory. The holder of a presently possessory estate is entitled to immediate possession of the land. Future interests, discussed in the following chapter, become possessory only at the expiration of a prior estate or upon the happening of a required event.

A.   Words of Purchase and Limitation

Because an estate has two components (i.e., possession and duration), every conveyance of an estate must indicate who is to receive possession and the length of time that possession will last. Thus, the words of every grant are divided into two groups.

1. Words *of purchase* designate the grantee.

2. Words of *limitation* designate the quantum of interest transferred.

Example: In the grant "To B for life," "To B" are words of purchase, indicating that B is the grantee. "For life" are words of limitation, defining the duration of B's possession.

B.   Freehold Estates (present interests)

Another distinction between estates, though mainly historical, involved the concept of seisin, the highest level of ownership at common law. To be "seized" of land meant to occupy it under claim of having a freehold estate in it (non-freehold estates are discussed under Landlord-Tenant). The following are the various types of freehold estates.

1. Fee Simple Absolute

a. Creation
A grant "To A," "To A and his heirs," or "To A in fee simple." Today, there is a presumption in favor of fee simple conveyances. Thus, a vague or uncertain grant is construed as a fee simple absolute if possible.

b. Duration
A fee simple absolute can potentially last forever. It is the largest possible estate in terms of duration.

c. Alienability
A fee simple absolute is freely alienable. If no conveyance was made during the grantee's life, the estate passes to his devisees, then to his lineal heirs and even to collateral heirs if there is no one else to claim it. In the absence of other claimants the estate escheats (i.e., goes to the state).

d. Common Law
At common law a fee simple absolute could only be created by use of the specific words, "To A and his heirs." This is no longer the case today.

2. Fee Simple Determinable (defeasible fee)

a. Creation
A grant "To A and his heirs, so long as they use the land for specified purposes only" creates this estate. Critical words are "so long as," "until," and "while."

b. Duration
A fee simple determinable is also of potentially infinite duration, as long as the condition is not violated. If the condition is broken, the estate automatically terminates and possession reverts to the grantor. The grantor's future interest is called "possibility of reverter."

c. Alienability

A fee simple determinable is freely alienable. The new owner also holds subject to the condition, and possession may revert to the original grantor. Upon the death of the grantee the estate goes to his devisees, then to his heirs if no inter vivos transfer was made. There is a possibility of escheat.

d. Public Policy

Courts are hostile to the fee simple determinable because it often results in forfeitures. If the wording of the grant is not explicit or is open to other interpretations, courts will be reluctant to construe a clause as creating a fee simple determinable.

3. Fee Simple Subject to a Condition Subsequent (defeasible fee)

a. Creation

A grant "To A and his heirs, but if the land is used for other than specified purposes, G or his heirs shall have the right to enter and declare the estate forfeited" will create a fee simple subject to a condition subsequent.

b. Duration

The grantee keeps possession until the grantor enters and terminates the estate. Unlike a fee simple determinable, violation of the condition does not lead to automatic forfeiture of the property. The grantor must enter and terminate. If the condition is not broken, or if the grantor decides not to terminate, the estate can last forever. By keeping the right to enter and the power to terminate the estate, the grantor has not conveyed all of his interests in the land.

c. Alienability

The estate is freely alienable, but always subject to the condition. If no inter vivos transfer was made, then heirs are entitled to possession. Escheat is also possible.

d. Public policy

Courts are generally hostile to this type of estate and will construe the condition as a restrictive covenant, if possible, in order to avoid a forfeiture. The grantor must specifically and expressly retain his right of entry and power of termination (see future interests) because they will not be assumed absent clear language.

4. Fee Simple Subject To An Executory Interest (defeasible fee)
   This type of fee simple is like an ordinary fee simple determinable or one subject to a condition subsequent, except that if the condition is broken the estate goes to a third party and not the grantor.

   Example: G grants to "A and his heirs, but if the land is used to sell alcohol then to B and his heirs," or ". . . B and her heirs shall have the right to enter and declare the estate forfeited," or ". . ., but if A has no sons then to B and his heirs."

5. Life Estate

   a. Creation
      A grant "To A for life" creates this estate.

      Note: At common law, any grant that was intended to create a fee simple absolute but failed to use the specific words "To A and his heirs" was deemed to create a life estate.

   b. Duration

      i. Grantee's Lifetime
         A life estate lasts until the death of the grantee, whereupon possession of the land reverts to the grantor or his heirs. Thus, the grantor has only transferred possession of his land for the grantee's life. The estate can terminate prior to the grantee's death if he *renounces* it.

      ii. Per Autre Vie
          Life estate whose duration is measured by the life of a third party. Sometimes a grant will state "To B, for A's life." A life estate "per autre vie" is created because the

life that is used to measure the duration of possession is not that of the party actually in possession. Possession only terminates at the death of the measuring life. If the party in possession (i.e., B) dies first, the estate goes to his heirs, devisees, purchasers, or even by escheat, until the death of the measuring life.

c. Alienability
The grantee is free to make inter vivos transfers, but possession of the land by the third party terminates at the death of the original grantee. Obviously this type of estate is not inheritable by the grantee's heirs.

d. Defeasible Life Estate
As with a fee simple, a life estate can be conditioned upon a certain event, the occurrence of which will entitle the grantor either to automatic reversion or to enter and reclaim possession.

e. Duties and Powers of a Life Tenant
A life tenant has certain obligations to his remaindermen (i.e., those who will take possession after the tenant's death). These obligations include the following:

Mnemonic: If you only own a life estate, you better not **WRITE** on the walls.

i. no <u>w</u>aste (i.e., unreasonable impairment of the future value of the property);

ii. reasonable <u>r</u>epairs (does not include rebuilding structures destroyed by natural causes);

iii. <u>i</u>nterest charges on the mortgage (does not have to repay principal). Obligation is limited to value of income received from the land; and

iv. property <u>t</u>axes on <u>e</u>state.
The life tenant is entitled to all rents and profits from the estate.

6. Fee Tail

a. Creation
A grant "To A and the heirs of A's body" created this estate at common law. The purpose of this type of grant was to keep ownership of land within a family.

Note: This grant is different from "To A and his heirs."

b. Duration
At common law, the grantee received an estate for his life which passed to his first heir at his death. The heir also held for life and then it passed to his heir, and so on.

c. Alienability
At common law, the grantee could not transfer an interest in the estate that exceeded his lifetime. At the grantee's death, the only persons who could take the estate were his lineal heirs. If he had no lineal heirs, the estate would revert to the grantor and his heirs.

d. Modern View
Most states have abolished the fee tail or greatly modified its effect. Some courts treat such a grant as creating an ordinary fee simple absolute. Others construe it as a fee simple conditional, so that a grantee has a fee simple conditioned upon having *issue* (i.e., children). Once the grantee has a child, he acquires a freely alienable fee simple. Still another approach has been to allow the fee tail to exist for one generation only.

CASE CLIPS

In Re O'Connor's Estate (1934)

Facts: The estate of John O'Connor escheated to the state of Nebraska for want of heirs.

Issue: When real estate escheats, is the state liable for the payment of an inheritance tax?

Rule: Since escheated real estate reverts to the state, and the inheritance tax is applicable to property acquired by a right of succession only, no inheritance tax is due on escheated realty.

Cole v. Steinlauf (1957)

Facts: Steinlauf contracted with Cole to sell land and convey a "marketable title." Subsequently, Cole refused to close the transaction and sued for return of his deposit because, he said, the title was not clear.

Issue: Is a title marketable when there is doubt as to the validity of a prior grantor's deed?

Rule: When there is enough doubt in the chain of title to make the plaintiff believe that he risks a future title contest, the title is not marketable.

Lewis v. Searles (1970)

Facts: The plaintiff received all of the decedent's property subject to a condition that if she were to marry the property would be divided evenly between her and two other relatives of the decedent.

Issue: Is a will provision which reduces a devise in the event of the beneficiary's marriage always contrary to public policy?

Rule: If the provision is incorporated in the will for legitimate purposes, and is not intended to restrict marriage unreasonably or maliciously, it will not be voided on public policy grounds.

Moore v. Phillips (1981)

Facts: The remaindermen of the life tenant's estate sued for damages resulting from the life tenant's neglect of the property.

Issue: Will a mere delay in instituting suit for waste result in dismissal of the claim?

Rule: The affirmative defense of laches will not succeed because of delay unless the delay resulted in a disadvantage to another party.

Oldfield v. Stoeco Homes, Inc. (1958)

Facts: The plaintiffs deeded land to Stoeco Homes, Inc. with the condition that the land be filled and graded within one year.

Issue: Does a durational requirement create a fee simple determinable or a fee simple subject to condition subsequent?

Rule: Absent an intent that time is of the essence, courts will construe durational requirements as creating a fee simple subject to condition subsequent.

Roberts v. Rhodes (1982)

Facts: Without reversion or other language of limitation, grantor deeded land conditioned on its being used for school purposes. When no longer so used, Roberts, the successor in interest to the original grantor, claimed title to the land by reversion.

Issue: Does a statement of purpose, without more, limit a grant?

Rule: When the grantee accepts and uses for a reasonable time land on which a use condition is imposed, and the deed does not contain language limiting the grant, a fee simple, not a determinable fee, is conveyed.

Martin v. City of Seattle (1986)

Facts: When the city of Seattle bought a parcel of land from the plaintiff's predecessor in title, the deed contained a condition requiring the city to acquire the land necessary for the grantor to build a boathouse. A breach of the condition allowed the grantor or the successors to reenter and forfeit the grant. The original grantor did not hold the city to its promise, but the grantor's successor asked the defendant to acquire the land for the boathouse nearly 80 years later. The defendant refused.

Issue: Will the passage of time, without more, extinguish the grantor's right to exercise a condition subsequent in a deed, and if so, does the state's failure to perform amount to an unconstitutional taking?

Rule: The passage of time does not prevent a landowner from exercising the right to a condition subsequent, and the state's failure to perform is a restriction of the use of the land amounting to an unconstitutional taking.

Johnson v. City of Wheat Ridge (1975)

Facts: Paul Johnson, the plaintiff, claimed title when grantee failed to satisfy a condition of the conveyance.

Issue: May a right of reentry be time-barred?

Rule: A condition subsequent is subject to the statute of limitations which begins to run when the stated event occurs.

Leeco Gas & Oil Co. v. County of Nueces (1957)

Facts: The defendant gave fifty acres of land to Nueces County, so long as the land would be used as a public park. Subsequently, the county began condemnation proceedings against the defendant's reversionary interest.

Issue: May the state condemn a possibility of reverter on land given to the state and pay mere nominal damages to the owner of the reversionary interest?

Rule: When a governmental entity is the grantee in a gift deed in which the grantor retains a reversionary interest, if the same governmental entity condemns the reversionary interest, it must pay as compensation the amount by which the value of the unrestricted fee exceeds the value of the restricted fee: not merely nominal damages.

Caccamo v. Banning (1950)

Facts: The decedent willed property to the plaintiff. The will stated that she forfeit the land if she should die without issue. The plaintiff contracted to sell the land to Banning. Banning breached, arguing that the title was not marketable due to the restriction.

Issue: Do the words "should die without leaving lawful issue of her body" give rise to a definite or indefinite failure of issue construction?

Rule: Absent a contrary expression of a decedent's intent, an indefinite failure of issue construction obtains, and a fee tail estate will be created.

Note: This case represents a minority view.

Wood v. Board of County Commissioners of Fremont County (1988)

Facts: The Woods conveyed land to the defendant "for the purpose of constructing and maintaining" a memorial hospital. The land was used for a hospital for thirty-five years before the hospital's location changed. The Woods filed suit to regain possession of the land.

Issue: Does a conveyance "for the purpose of constructing and maintaining a hospital" create either a fee simple determinable or a fee simple subject to a condition subsequent?

Rule: Unless the deed clearly states either that the property will automatically revert if the purpose is not fulfilled or that grantor intended to create discretionary power to terminate the estate, neither a fee simple determinable nor a fee simple subject to condition subsequent is created.

Baker v. Weedon (1972)

Facts: A life tenant's income from the decedent's property provided insufficient support. She petitioned the court for judicial sale of the property and investment of the proceeds.

Issue: May a court of equity order property sold when future interests are affected?

Rule: Necessity must be demonstrated for a court of equity to order a sale of property in which there are future interests. The court will consider whether a sale is necessary for the best interest of all the parties.

White v. Brown (1977)

Facts: The decedent devised her house to Evelyn White "to live in and not to be sold." White filed an action to obtain a construction of the will to determine whether the house was conveyed in fee simple or as a life estate.

Issue: When interpreting an ambiguous will, is a construction that conveys the whole estate preferred over a partial conveyance?

Rule: Where a will is ambiguous, a construction that conveys the entire estate is preferred if it is reasonable and consistent with the general scope and provisions of the will.

Mahrenholz v. County Board of School Trustees (1981)

Facts: The grantor conveyed land which was "to be used for school purposes only; otherwise to revert to grantor". The land was not used as directed.

Issue: Does the granting clause create a fee simple determinable or a fee simple subject to a condition subsequent?

Rule: The difference between a fee simple determinable and a fee simple subject to a condition subsequent is solely a matter of judicial interpretation of the words of a grant. Generally a grant of exclusive use, followed by an express provision for reverter when that use ceases, will be interpreted as creating a fee simple determinable.

Mountain Brow Lodge No. 82, Independent Order Of Odd Fellows v. Toscano (1968)

Facts: The Toscanos deeded land to the plaintiff, a non-profit corporation, on condition that if any or all of the land was sold or transferred, or if the plaintiff failed to use the land, it would revert to the grantor. The plaintiff brought an action to quiet title.

Issue: May a grantor restrict the use of land?

Rule: A restriction on the "use" of land does not constitute a restraint on alienation and is not void as against public policy.

CHAPTER 3 FUTURE INTERESTS

I. INTRODUCTION
    Chapter two discussed estates that are possessory (immediate possession). The distinguishing feature of a future interest is that, though the interest presently exists, possession will only be transferred in the future.

II. FUTURE INTERESTS IN THE TRANSFEROR
    A transferor who conveys (or wills) his property to another can retain part of his interest. Remember that ownership is measured by the duration of possession. Thus, if a person holding a fee simple absolute (i.e., infinite duration) transfers an estate of shorter duration (e.g., fee simple determinable, life estate, etc.), possession reverts to the transferor at the expiration of that estate. There are three types of future interests that a transferor can have.

A. Reversion
    A reversion in the transferor is automatically created if he transfers an estate of a shorter duration than the one he holds. At the expiration of the shorter estate, this future interest becomes possessory and the property reverts to the transferor.

    Example: If B, who has a fee simple absolute, transfers a life estate to C, at C's death the life estate terminates and possession of the land reverts to B. A transferor does not have to expressly reserve this future interest.

    1. Divestment
       A reversion can be divested (i.e., extinguished). This occurs if the condition necessary for reversion cannot be met. For example, O grants "To B for life, then to C, if she outlives B" (B has a life estate). Two things can happen at B's death. If C is dead, then possession reverts to O, because there are no other takers; but if C is alive, she takes possession in fee simple absolute and the reversion is extinguished.

    2. Alienability
       A reversion is freely alienable (inter vivos), devisable or inheritable (there is also a possibility of escheat). However, the new holder of the reversion also runs the risk of divestment.

B.   Possibility (Right) of Reverter
     A possibility of reverter is the name of the residual future interest held by a transferor of a fee simple determinable only. Thus, a grant "To A for so long as no alcohol is sold on the property" creates a possibility of reverter in the grantor.

   1. Duration
      The possibility of reverter runs with the fee simple determinable that was conveyed. It is a future interest that only becomes possessory, if at all, when the condition is broken. It entitles the grantor to automatic repossession of the property.

      Note: A grantee who stays in possession after the condition is broken is considered to be in adverse possession.

   2. Alienability
      This future interest is freely alienable and inheritable (majority rule).

   3. Public Policy
      Courts are generally hostile to possibilities of reverter because they cause forfeiture and encumber the free use and transfer of land. Unless the language is completely unambiguous, courts will construe the restrictions as only a suggestion or a covenant.

C.   Right of Entry
     A right of entry is the residual future interest in the transferor of a fee simple upon a condition subsequent, where the transferor expressly reserves the right to reenter the land and reclaim possession.

     Example: "To A, but if the land is used to sell alcohol, G or his heirs shall have the right to enter and declare the estate forfeit."

   1. Duration
      The right of entry runs with the land and can be asserted against any subsequent grantee of the original transferee. It only becomes possessory if the condition is broken. However, to take possession of the land, the transferor must actually enter it and declare the prior possessor's claim void. A grantor who fails to enter within a reasonable time is later barred by laches.

2. Alienability
This future interest is devisable and inheritable but cannot be transferred inter vivos (majority rule).

3. Public Policy
Rights of entry are not favored by courts, and unless expressly reserved will not be allowed. If at all possible, courts will try to construe the grant otherwise (i.e., restrictive covenant).

D. Legislation
Rights of entry and possibilities of reverter are presently limited by statute. States have taken the following approaches.

1. Some limit the permissible duration of these interests.

2. Some require the holders of these interests to rerecord them periodically.

3. Some only allow equitable remedies such as injunction, but do not permit forfeiture.

4. Some adopt the approach taken in (3) above, but hold that the restrictive covenant is unenforceable if neighborhood conditions sufficiently change.

III. FUTURE INTERESTS IN THE TRANSFEREE
A transferee can also receive a future interest. This occurs if the transfer is made to several sequential transferees or if the transferor places some condition to delay possession (e.g., "To A when he graduates"). There are two types of future interests that a transferee can have.

A. Remainders
A remainder is a future interest in one transferee which becomes possessory upon the natural expiration of a prior life estate held by another transferee.

Example: "To A for life, remainder to B," A has a life estate and B has a vested remainder in fee simple, which becomes possessory when A dies. Remember that a remainder always follows a life estate.

1. Vested vs. Contingent

There are two types of remainders.

a. Vested

A vested remainder is one that becomes possessory at the termination of the prior life estate and is subject to no other condition precedent.

Example: "To A for life, remainder to B." B has a vested remainder in fee simple, which becomes possessory at A's death. Once the transferee's interest has vested, he is entitled to possession when the prior estate ends. There is no requirement that B must outlive A. If B is dead, possession goes to his grantees, devisees, heirs, or even by escheat. A vested remainder can be lost only if it is subject to a condition subsequent (see executory interests).

b. Contingent

A contingent remainder is one that becomes possessory only at the termination of the prior life estate and the fulfillment of some other condition precedent.

i. **Example:** "To A for life, then to B's children" and B has no children, or "then to B if she outlives A." In both these cases it is not enough for A to die, (i.e., B must either have children or outlive A) for the estate to become possessory. A reversion in the grantor is automatically created by the conveyance of a contingent remainder because of the possibility that the contingency will not be met (e.g., B predeceases A). If the condition is not met, the remainder is extinguished. If the condition is met, the remainder vests and the grantor's reversion is extinguished.

ii. **Example:** More than one contingency.
"To A for life, then to the lineal heirs of B," and B has no children yet. (Lineal heirs are children, grandchildren, etc.) The children must be born, but they also must survive B to become his heirs. (Note that this

contingent remainder vests and becomes possessory simultaneously, if at all).

c. Vested or Contingent?
Whether a remainder is vested or contingent is often a difficult question, and frequently depends on technical distinctions. A few rules do exist to facilitate this determination.

   i. Grammatical construction.
   If the condition is contained in the clause which creates the interest, then the interest will be interpreted as a contingent remainder. If the condition is stated in a clause separate from that which creates the interest, then it will be construed as a vested remainder subject to a condition subsequent.

   ii. Reversion.
   A contingent remainder creates a reversion in the grantor. A vested remainder creates an executory interest in a third party.

   Example: "To A for life, remainder to B, but if B dies before A then to C." B has a vested remainder in fee simple subject to total divestment by a condition subsequent. "To A for life, remainder to B if B survives A." B has a contingent remainder. B's interest is subject to a condition precedent. The remainder is vested in the grantor until the condition is satisfied.

2. The Destructibility Rule
This rule only applies to contingent remainders. At common law, a contingent remainder was automatically extinguished at the time the prior estate expired if it was not vested by then.

Example: "To A for life, then to B's children," where B has no children. If at A's death (i.e., expiration of prior estate), B was still childless (i.e., remainder still contingent), the remainder was destroyed under the destructibility rule and possession reverted to the grantor.

a. Merger Doctrine

Another common law method of destroying contingent remainders was the merger doctrine. The doctrine provides that when successive vested estates are held by the same person the smaller of the two is absorbed by the larger.

Example: "To A for life, remainder to A and his heirs." (i.e., A has a life estate and a remainder in fee simple absolute). A's life estate is merged into his remainder and A has one estate in fee simple absolute. If another estate intervenes between the two estates, merger does not occur if the intervening estate is vested. But, if it is contingent, merger occurs and the intervening estate is destroyed. Contingent remainders were not viewed as an estate by common law standards. **Example:** C grants "To B for life, then to A if he marries." C then conveys his reversion to B before A gets married. B has a life estate and a reversion in fee simple; A has a contingent remainder in fee simple. B's interests merge into a fee simple, destroying A's contingent remainder.

b. Modern View

Most jurisdictions today have abolished the destructibility rule. Remainders which are still contingent are not destroyed at the expiration of the prior life estate. Instead, the original grantor is allowed to retake possession (i.e., reversion) subject to the remainder. Thus, the grantor can take the property back until B has children, at which time the remainder vests and becomes possessory and the grantor's reversion ends. If B dies without having children, the remainder is extinguished due to impossibility of vesting. The merger doctrine has also been abolished in most states.

3. Open

A remainder that is granted to a group of persons.

Example: "To A for life, then to the children of B" may be completely contingent, (e.g., B has no children yet), or it may be vested subject to open (e.g., some members of the class of grantees are living, but the class is still open to further additions if B has more children). The significance of "open" is that the living class members hold a vested remainder that is subject to partial divestment if members are added to the class.

a.   Class Closing Rule
Existing members can move to close their class when their interest becomes presently possessory.

Example: "To A for life, then to B's children." B has two children. B later has another child, then A dies. At A's death, his life estate is terminated and the vested remainder of B's children becomes possessory. B's three children can move to close the class, so that if B has more children at a future date, they will not receive a share of the estate. But, if no class members are alive at the time the estate becomes possessory, the class must stay open and includes all children born after that time.

b.   En Ventre Sa Mere
This is an exception to the class closing rule. Children "conceived before but born after" the estate becomes possessory are deemed to be alive at the time of possession. Generally, any child born within nine months of the time that an estate becomes possessory is considered to be a life in being at the time possession was taken.

4. Alternative Contingent Remainders
These are future interests created where occurrence or non-occurrence of the same condition lead to mirror image results.

Example: O grants "To A for life, remainder to B if B survives; if not to C" B has a contingent remainder in fee simple subject to the condition that he outlives A. C has an alternative contingent remainder in fee simple subject to the condition that B dies before A. (i.e., both remainders are contingent until either A or B dies).

5. Secondary Life Estate
A secondary life estate is a life estate granted in a remainder.

Example: "To A for life, then to B for life." A has a presently possessory life estate and B has a secondary life estate, also called a remainder in life estate. A secondary life estate is treated as vested despite the implied condition of surviving the previous owner. A secondary life estate can be contingent (e.g., "To A for life, then to B's children for life") where B has no children.

6. Alienability
Vested remainders are freely transferable by deed, will, inheritance, etc. Contingent remainders are also freely transferable in most states, although at common law, they could not be conveyed inter vivos.

B.   Executory Interests
An executory interest is the second type of future interest that a transferee can hold. Unlike a remainder, an executory interest always follows and shortens a fee simple.

Example: "To A and his heirs, but if A has no issue, to B and his heirs." A has a present possessory fee simple subject to divestment by B's shifting executory interest. There are two types of executory interests, springing and shifting.

1. Springing Executory Interest
A springing executory interest is one that limits a fee simple in the grantor.

Example: G grants "to A and his heirs, when A is 25," A is 22. Or "To B for life, and one day later to C." In the first case, G has given a fee simple to A that will begin in the future. A has a springing executory interest in fee simple subject to a condition precedent (i.e., that he reaches 25). G has a present possessory fee simple subject to total divestment by A's springing executory interest. In the second example, B has a present possessory life estate. However, C does not take possession when it terminates (he must wait a day). The estate reverts to G for the one day gap, and then C takes possession, cutting short G's "fee simple subject to a springing executory interest in C."

2. Shifting Executory Interest

A shifting executory interest is one that limits a fee simple held by a previous grantee.

Example: G grants "To A and his heirs, but if A has no issue, then to B and his heirs," A has a present possessory fee simple subject to total divestment by B's shifting executory interest. Notice that this time B's interest cuts short that of another grantee.

3. Duration

Executory interests last as long as they are applicable. If the condition precedent to their becoming possessory cannot be met, they are extinguished. In the example above, if A has children, B's shifting executory interest is extinguished. (Note that A's children receive nothing since "and his heirs" are only words of limitation; once A has a child, A acquires a fee simple absolute.) **Note:** Executory interests are *not* subject to destructibility or merger.

4. Alienability

Executory interests are freely transferable, devisable and inheritable. There is also a possibility of escheat.

5. Common Law

All executory interests were prohibited at common law, but this is not the case today.

IV. RULES FURTHERING MARKETABILITY BY DESTROYING CONTINGENT FUTURE INTERESTS

A. The Rule in Shelley's Case

If a conveyance creates a life estate in a grantee and a remainder in fee simple in the heirs of the grantee, the words "heirs of . . ." are treated as words of limitation and the grantee is given a fee simple absolute.

1. **Example:** "To A for life, remainder to the heirs of A," or "to the children of A." In both cases the Rule in Shelley's Case will treat A as having a present possessory fee simple absolute and his children/heirs will not have any interest.

2. Modern View

This rule is abolished in most jurisdictions. In the example above, A gets a life estate and his heirs have a contingent remainder in fee simple absolute.

B.   The Doctrine of Worthier Title

If a grantor creates a life estate in the grantee and then grants the remainder in fee simple to the grantor's heirs, the remainder is construed as a reversion in fee simple absolute in the grantor.

1. **Example:** G grants "to A for life, remainder to G's heirs." A has a presently possessory life estate and G has a reversion in fee simple absolute, G's heirs do not have any interest. This rule is only applied to inter vivos transfers.

2. Modern view

Most states treat "Worthier Title" as a presumption only, which is rebuttable by evidence of the grantor's actual intent. Some states have abolished the doctrine.

C.   The Rule Against Perpetuities

The rule states that "no interest other than one in the grantor is good unless it must vest, or fails to vest if it is a remainder, or become possessory or fails to become possessory, if at all, no later than 21 years plus a gestation period after the death of all lives in being." The basic thrust of the rule is that the effect of every contingent or executory interest must be known with certainty no later than 21 years after the death of all "lives in being." The rule does not mean that a remainder has to vest or that an executory interest has to become possessory within the measuring period (21 years). They must either fail or succeed within that time, so that their effect will be known with certainty.

1. Interests subject to the rule:

   a. springing and shifting executory interests;

   b. contingent remainders;

   c. vested remainders subject to open—as long as the class of grantees is still open, the rule applies.

2. Interests that are NOT subject to the rule:

   a.   reversions;

   b.   rights of entry;

   c.   possibilities of reverter; and

   d.   vested remainders.

3. Effect
   The rule goes into effect at the time the interest is created. For a will, that means at the death of the grantor; for a deed it is the time of transfer. The rule operates as follows: If it is possible to create a scenario, no matter how improbable, under which one of the future interests subject to the rule will neither succeed nor fail within the measuring period, then that interest is invalid and eliminated from the grant. The analysis is done at the time of the grant.

   Infectious invalidity—If cutting out a piece of the grant will defeat the purpose of the entire grant, the court will strike down the entire grant, not just the specific part.

4. Life in Being
   A "life in being" is any party, living at the time the transfer was made, who has a causal effect on when and whether the future interests will vest or become possessory. Lives in being are usually named expressly in the grant, although they don't have to be. There is no requirement that they must receive an interest.

   a.   **Example:** O grants "To A for life, remainder to A's children for life, remainder to A's grandchildren living at death of A's last child." Lives in being are A, any of his children who are alive at the time of transfer, and any of his grandchildren who are alive at that time.

   Rationale: A has a causal effect because he can have more children, which affects the vesting of the secondary life estate. His children have a causal effect because their very existence affects vesting and they affect the class of grandchildren. Finally, the very existence of the grandchildren affects the vesting of their future interest.

b. **Example:** O grants "To my children for life, remainder to their grandchildren." Lives in being are O, any of his children living at the time the grant was made, and any of O's grandchildren and his children's grandchildren living at the time of transfer.

   Rationale: O has a causal effect because he can have more children. O's children have an effect both on the vesting of their life estate and on having more children of their own. Their children (O's grandchildren) have a direct effect on the size of the class of grandchildren. (Note that O's grandchildren are neither named nor have any interest). Finally, the children's grandchildren have an effect on the vesting of their future interest.

5. Time
The perpetuities period runs for 21 years after the death of the last life in being. Gestation periods (i.e., 9 months) are added.

6. Procedure
To determine whether a future interest violates the rule, go through the following steps:

a. Identify all interests created in the grant, will, etc.

b. Identify all "lives in being."

c. Add 9 months to guard against gestation period.

d. Add a "nonlife in being" who is a potential taker or the source of a taker.

e. Kill off all "lives in being."

f. Will the future interests definitely vest or fail to vest within 21 years?

g. If there is uncertainty, the void provision is struck and possession reverts to the preceding estate or to the grantor.

h. **Example:**
O grants "To A for life, remainder to A's children for life, remainder to his grandchildren at the death of A's last child," where A has two sons and a grandchild at the time of transfer.

Step 1
A has a present possessory life estate (not subject to the rule); A's sons have a vested remainder in a life estate, which is subject to open (and to the rule); A's grandchildren have a vested remainder subject to open (and to the rule).

Step 2
A, A's sons and grandchildren living at the time of transfer are all "lives in being."

Step 3
If A has another child within nine months, that child will also be a life in being.

Step 4
A could have a son two years after the grant is made. Although the child affects the vesting of his life estate with his brothers and has a causal effect on the class of grandchildren, he was not alive at the time of transfer.

Step 5
A, his two sons, and his grandchild could all die in a plane crash a year later, so that only the third son remains alive. The perpetuities period starts.

Step 6
The surviving son's life estate becomes possessory upon the death of A, and the class is also closed by that event, so that his estate does not violate the rule. However, he could live for longer than 21 years, or he could die sooner. Thus there is no guarantee that the grandchildren's remainder in fee simple will close (remember that it is vested already) or not within 21 years. The remainder violates the rule and is struck

out. Possession reverts to O, or his heirs, after the surviving son dies.

7. Charity to Charity Exception
Transfers from one charity to another are not subject to the rule, even if they violate it.

8. Statutory Remedies
The harsh effects of the Rule Against Perpetuities have led most jurisdictions to modify it in one of three ways:

   a. "Wait and see" statutes
   Instead of making an immediate decision as to whether or not a future interest violates the rule, "wait and see" if it ends up violating the rule. Thus, the court will only strike out an interest if, 21 years after the death of the last life in being, the interest actually did not succeed or fail.

   b. Cy-pres (comme possible) statutes
   Instead of striking out the invalid provision, courts try to reform the grant to achieve the grantor's intent as nearly as possible without violating the rule. The process, however, is done at the time the grant is made.

   c. Cy-pres and "wait and see" statutes
   Some jurisdictions have combined both, so that courts will "wait and see" until a problem actually arises and will then reform the grant if possible.

V. RULE AGAINST RESTRAINTS ON ALIENATION
Courts will invalidate some restrictions placed on the alienation of land in the grant as a matter of public policy.

A. Three Types of Restrictions

1. Disability
A grant states that any transfers made by the grantee are of no force or effect.

2. Forfeiture
A grant states that the grantee forfeits the land if he makes a transfer.

3. Promissory

A grant has a covenant forbidding alienation. Remedy is either injunction or damages for breach of contract.

B. Effect of Rule

The type of estate that was conveyed influences the effect of the rule.

1. Fee Simple

If a fee simple was conveyed, all restrictions are meaningless and unenforceable.

2. Life Estate

Disabling restraints will not be enforced, but others may be enforced.

3. Leaseholds

Forfeiture and promissory restraints are enforceable. Disabling restraints are also likely to be enforced by most courts.

CASE CLIPS

Kost v. Foster (1950)

Facts: A deed drawn by his parents gave Kost a life tenancy with the remainder in his children. One child was bankrupt. Local law allowed the trustee in bankruptcy to sell vested but not contingent remainders. The trustee sold the bankrupt son's remainder. The parties disputed whether the remainder was vested or contingent.

Issue: How should a court determine whether a remainder is vested or contingent?

Rule: Whether a remainder is vested or contingent depends upon the grammatical structure employed. If the condition is contained in the clause which creates the interest, then the interest will be interpreted as a contingent remainder. If the condition is stated in a clause separate from that which creates the interest, then it will be construed as a vested remainder subject to a condition subsequent.

Abo Petroleum Corp. v. Amstutz (1979)

Facts: The Amstutzes conveyed a life estate to their children, with contingent remainders in their grandchildren, the defendants. The parents retained a reversionary interest. Later, the parents purported to convey the same property in fee simple absolute to their children. The children subsequently attempted to convey fee simple interests to the predecessors of the Abo Petroleum Corporation (plaintiff). The defendants argued that the first deed gave their parents only life estates.

Issue: Under the doctrine of destructibility of contingent remainders, when a grantor conveys land and creates a contingent remainder in a third party, but reserves a reversionary interest in himself, will that remainder be destroyed by a subsequent conveyance in fee simple by the same grantor to the same grantee?

Rule: The doctrine of destructibility of contingent remainders is obsolete. Therefore, a conveyance of property in fee simple will not destroy contingent remainders which have been created previously.

Sybert v. Sybert (1953)

Facts: The testator, J.H. Sybert, bequeathed a life estate to his son, Fred Sybert (the defendant's husband), "to vest in fee simple in the heirs of his body." The son died intestate without issue. The life tenant's brothers (plaintiffs) contended that they should inherit the testator's reversion. The defendant contended that the Rule in Shelley's Case converted the heir's contingent remainder into a fee simple in her husband.

Issue: Is the Rule in Shelley's Case applicable to Testator's devise?

Rule: Unless language qualifying the words "heirs of his body" establishes that a testator did not intend the words to be used in their technical sense, the Rule in Shelly's case will apply.

Braswell v. Braswell (1954)

Facts: James Braswell conveyed land to his son, Nathaniel Braswell, "during his natural life . . . and if said (son) should die leaving no lawful heir . . . then the land herein conveyed shall revert back to the grantor or to his lawful heirs." Nathaniel died without issue, devising all his real property to Charles Braswell. Charles was not a lawful heir of James Braswell Charles brought suit against the lawful heirs of James Braswell for partition.

Issue: Will a remainder left to a grantor's heirs become a reversion in the grantor under the Doctrine of Worthier Title?

Rule: The Doctrine of Worthier Title, a rule of construction, creates a presumption in favor of reversions which may be rebutted by indication of the grantor's contrary intent gathered from the instrument as a whole.

Stoller v. Doyle (1913)

Facts: Lawrence Doyle first conveyed a fee to Frank Doyle with a contingent interest in the wife and children of the grantee and a reversion in the grantor. Later, Lawrence executed a new deed purporting to remove all restrictions of the first grant. Frank Doyle subsequently conveyed the land to Stoller. Stoller sued to quiet title.

Issue: Did the first grant create a contingent remainder subject to destruction or an executory interest not subject to destruction?

Rule: An interest following a fee held by one other than the grantee or grantor is an executory interest not subject to destruction.

Capitol Federal Savings & Loan Ass'n v. Smith (1957)

Facts: The owners of certain lots agreed to forbid the sale of those lots to blacks. Failure to abide by the agreement resulted in automatic divestment of ownership rights.

Issue: Are future interests subject to equal protection analysis?

Rule: A future interest arising from a racially restrictive covenant violates the Fourteenth Amendment.

The City of Klamath Falls v. Bell (1971)

Facts: A corporation granted land to the City to be used as a library. The deed provided that if not so used, title should pass to the descendants of the corporation's shareholders. Subsequently, the City ceased using the land as a library. The City filed an action against the shareholders' descendants for declaratory judgment.

Issue: Does a grantor who alienates his possibility of reverter destroy it?

Rule: An attempt by a grantor to transfer his possibility of reverter does not destroy his interest.

Brokaw v. Fairchild (1929)

Facts: Brokaw, a life tenant, sought to demolish a mansion and erect an apartment building in its place.

Issue: May a life tenant exercise rights of ownership over an estate?

Rule: Although a life tenant may make reasonable use of an estate and improve its value, he cannot so change the inheritance as to preclude its transfer to the remaindermen or reversioners.

Baker v. Weedon (1972)

Facts: A life tenant's income from the decedent's property provided insufficient support. She petitioned the court for judicial sale of the property and investment of the proceeds.

Issue: May a court of equity order property sold when future interests are affected?

Rule: Necessity must be demonstrated for a court of equity to order a sale of property in which there are future interests. The court will consider whether a sale is necessary for the best interest of all the parties.

Harrison v. Marcus (1985)

Facts: Irving K. Taylor conveyed in trust two parcels of land for the exclusive use of a Boy Scout Troop. The terms of the conveyance specifically stated that if the parcels were no longer used for this purpose the trustees were to convey the land back to the grantor or his heirs or their assigns. The Boy Scout Troop disbanded and its successor in interest, as well as the trustees, brought suit to quiet title to the parcels.

Issue: Do the words "so long as" used in the conveyance necessarily indicate that the trustees held title in fee simple determinable or is there a possibility that they held title in fee simple absolute despite the phrasing of the document?

Rule: Generally the words "so long as" are interpreted as creating a fee simple determinable but the particular terms of a conveyance cannot stand on their own and must be interpreted in light of the general purposes of the instrument as a whole.

City Bank & Trust Co. v. Morrissey (1983)

Facts: A testamentary trust gave the trustee discretion to distribute it in kind or after a cash conversion to the beneficiary's heirs at law following the beneficiary's death. The defendant contended that the trustee's power to convert the assets resulted in creating two estates of unequal kind, realty and personalty, and that therefore, the Rule in Shelley's Case is inapplicable.

Issue 1: Does the discretionary power of a trustee to distribute assets in kind or in cash effect an equitable conversion triggering the Rule in Shelley's Case?

Rule 1: To effect an equitable conversion, the trustee must be mandated to convert the assets.

Issue 2: To trigger the Rule in Shelley's Case, must estates be of equal quality?

Rule 2: There are three requisites for the application of the Rule in Shelly's Case: (1) a freehold estate must be granted to the ancestor; (2) a remainder must be limited to his heirs, general or special; and (3) the two estates, freehold and remainder, must both be of the same quality, either legal or equitable.

Estate of Annie I. Kern (1979)

Facts: The testator devised all her property to her only son, Ralph, who predeceased her. Pursuant to Iowa's antilapse statute, the collateral heirs of the testator's deceased husband claim the property should have been divided among Ralph's heirs. The testator's collateral heirs contend that the Doctrine of Worthier Title compelled the division of her property entirely among them alone.

Issue: Is the testamentary branch of the Worthier Title Doctrine operative in an antilapse statute context?

Rule: The Worthier Title Doctrine is prospectively abrogated in antilapse situations.

Jee v. Audley (1787)

Facts: Audley willed that in default of issue by Mary Hall, the estate should pass to the daughters of John and Elizabeth Jee.

Issue 1: When does a failure of issue of an individual occur?

Rule 1: A failure of issue occurs when an individual is dead and all of the individual's descendants are dead.

Issue 2: At what age does the law recognize that a person can no longer have children?

Rule 2: Every individual is presumed to be capable of having offspring at any time before the individual's death.

Issue 3: Can a will contain a limitation that upon failure of issue of a certain living individual, an estate passes to the offspring of a third party?

Rule 3: Limitations on personal estates are void unless they necessarily vest within 21 years of a life in being when the interest was created. Any person alive at the testator's death may be employed as a measure of "lives in being."

Broadway Nat'l Bank v. Adams (1882)

Facts: The creditor sued an income beneficiary in an attempt to attach the trust income. The grantor had expressly provided that the income shall remain "free from the interference or control of his creditors."

Issue: May the founder of a trust attach to the trust a condition that the income from it cannot be alienated?

Rule: A person may create a trust in favor of a beneficiary, and provide that it shall not be alienated by him, nor be seized by his creditors in advance of its payments to him.

Brown v. Independent Baptist Church of Woburn (1950)

Facts: The defendant held a determinable fee that might last indefinitely.

Issue: Can the Rule Against Perpetuities prevent a possibility of reverter from passing through a will's residuary clause?

Rule: The Rule Against Perpetuities does not apply to reversionary interests such as possibility of reverter.

Central Delaware County Auth. v. Greyhound Corp. (1991)

Facts: Two parcels of land had been conveyed to Central Delaware. Both deeds contained a fee simple interest subject to a restrictive covenant, giving the grantor or its successor the right to repurchase the land if the Authority ceased to use it for public purposes.

Issue: Does a deed restriction which states that a grantor or its successor may repurchase a property after the tract has ceased to be used for its deeded purpose, fall under the Rule Against Perpetuities?

Rule: Where a clause maintains that upon abandonment, payment of a certain sum of money will follow, the interest can be seen as either a repurchase option or a fee simple subject to a condition subsequent. The distinction is important because a repurchase option is subject to the Rule Against Perpetuities, while a fee simple subject to a condition subsequent, being a vested interest, is not.

Note: The court held that this restriction was a repurchase option rendered void by the rule against perpetiuties.

CHAPTER 4 CONCURRENT OWNERSHIP

I.   CONCURRENT OWNERSHIP
     Situations arise where two or more persons have simultaneous rights of present or future possession. There are three main types: the joint tenancy, the tenancy in common, and the tenancy by the entirety.

A.   Joint Tenancy
     Each joint tenant has an equal interest in the whole property.

     1. Right of Survivorship is the outstanding characteristic of the joint tenancy. When one joint tenant dies, the decedent's interest is extinguished and the survivors continue to hold an undivided right in the property. The decedent's will has no impact on the property.
     Note: A deceased joint tenant's creditor cannot reach the surviving joint tenant's interest.

     2. Four Unities were essential to a joint tenancy at common law and in many states today.
     Mnemonic: **T**he **P**ig **I**s **T**enant

        a.   **T**ime
             The interests of each joint tenant must be acquired at the same time.

        b.   **P**ossession
             Each joint tenant must have an equal right to possess the whole property.

        c.   **I**nterest
             All the joint tenants must have identical interests in the property, both as to duration and fractional share.

        d.   **T**itle
             All joint tenants must acquire title by the same instrument.

     3. Creation of Joint Tenancies
     At common law, there was a presumption that a cotenancy was a joint tenancy.

a. Modern statutes now presume that a cotenancy is a tenancy in common (see below) in the absence of language which clearly indicates an intention to create a joint tenancy.

b. Explicit language is required to create a joint tenancy (e.g., "to A and B as joint tenants with right of survivorship, and not as tenants in common").

c. A wants to convert his fee simple into a joint tenancy with B.

   i. Common Law View
   This could not be accomplished by conveying "from A to A and B" because the requirements of unity of time and unity of title would not be satisfied. Strawman transfers were the solution to this problem at common law. A transfers to X who then transfers to A and B jointly so that the unities of time and title are not broken.

   ii. Modern statutes allow a property owner to create a joint tenancy in himself and another party without the use of a strawman.

4. Severance of a joint tenancy by destroying one of the unities leaves the parties as tenants in common. There are many ways to sever a joint tenancy.

   a. Inter vivos conveyance by one of the joint tenants to a third party destroys unity of title and time because the third party received the interest by a different instrument and at a different time than the remaining original joint tenant. The joint tenancy is severed and the third party is a tenant in common with the remaining original joint tenant.

      i. More Than Two Original Joint Tenants.
      A conveyance by one of the joint tenants to an outsider will result in a tenancy in common between the outsider and the remaining joint tenants, but the joint tenancy will stay intact as between the remaining original joint tenants.

   ii. **Example:** A, B, and C are joint tenants. C transfers his interest to X. X now holds an undivided one-third interest in the property as a tenant in common with A and B, A and B hold the remaining two-thirds as joint tenants with the right of survivorship. If A dies, his interest is shifted to B. If X dies, his devisees or heirs receive his interest.

b. Lease

Although unities of interest and possession are destroyed once a lease is granted to an outside party, some courts hold that a joint tenancy is not severed by a joint tenant's execution of a lease. There is disagreement over this issue.

c. Mortgage

There is disagreement over whether the granting of a mortgage by a joint tenant destroys the joint tenancy. It depends on the theory of mortgages to which the jurisdiction adheres.

   i. Lien Theory (Majority Rule)

This principle views a mortgage as a lien to secure payment and, therefore, does not consider the execution of a mortgage as a transfer of title to the mortgagee. According to this majority rule, a mortgage does not sever a joint tenancy.

   ii. Title Theory

This principle views the execution of a mortgage as a transfer of title from the mortgagor to the mortgagee. According to this minority rule, a mortgage does sever a joint tenancy.

d. Mutual Agreement

A joint tenancy may be terminated by mutual agreement of the owners, express or implied.

e. Judicial Sale

A creditor of a joint tenant can levy execution during the lifetime of the debtor and terminate the joint tenancy. If the debtor joint tenant dies before the creditor is able to secure a judicial sale, the surviving joint tenant is entitled to the property free from the claims of the creditor.

B. Tenancy in Common
Tenants in common have separate but undivided interests in the property.

1. No right of survivorship exists in a tenancy in common. A deceased tenant's interest will pass to his heirs or devisees.

2. Requires Only One Unity
A tenancy in common must only have unity of possession (i.e., each tenant is entitled to possess the whole property). Unities of interest, title, and time are not needed. Therefore, tenants in common can obtain unequal interests by different deeds at different times.

3. A statutory or common law presumption favoring tenancies in common over joint tenancies exists in most states.

4. Heirs taking an estate are classified as tenants in common.

C. Tenancy by the Entirety
A concurrent ownership which can only he created in a husband and wife who are legally married. This tenancy is recognized in less than half of the states.

1. The four unities (time, title, interest, and possession) are required just as they are for joint tenancies.

2. Presumption
In most states that recognize this tenancy, there is a presumption that a property grant to a husband and wife is intended to establish a tenancy by the entirety.

Note: A man or a woman cannot transfer a partial interest to his/her spouse and create a tenancy by the entirety because unities of time and interest are absent.

3. Right of Survivorship
The surviving spouse has a right of survivorship (just as the surviving joint tenant).

4. Not Subject to Severance

Neither spouse can terminate the tenancy and thereby defeat the other's right of survivorship by unilateral action (e.g., by inter vivos transfer or judicial partition).

Termination results when:

a. there is a mutual agreement to terminate.

b. one spouse dies.

c. judgment is executed against husband and wife by a joint creditor of both.

d. there is a divorce (which leaves the parties as tenants in common).

5. Management

At common law, the husband had exclusive right to manage marital property (see marital interest section below). Married Women's Acts gave the woman equal rights with her husband to manage the property.

a. Most states hold that neither husband nor wife may sell or burden the property without the consent of the other spouse.

b. Creditors in most states cannot encumber a debtor spouse's property while the other spouse is still living. If the debtor spouse dies first, the surviving spouse's interest supersedes the creditor's interest. Only if the debtor survives his spouse may the creditor's claim be satisfied.

6. Personal Property

The majority rule is that a tenancy by the entirety may exist with respect to personal property.

II.   RIGHTS AND RESPONSIBILITIES OF COTENANTS
(Applicable To The Three Main Types Of Cotenancies)

A.   Right of Possession

Each cotenant has the right to possess the entire property (i.e., unity of possession). No cotenant has the right to exclusive possession of the premises.

B.   Possession by One Cotenant

Because there is unity of possession, the cotenant in sole possession does not ordinarily have a duty to account (i.e., to pay the other cotenant one-half the rental value of the property).

1. Duty to Account If an Ouster Occurs

If the cotenant in sole possession wrongfully excludes his cotenants from the property, an ouster occurs. The tenant in possession must pay the ousted cotenant his share of the rental value of the property.

2. Duty to Account If the Tenant in Sole Possession Depletes the Land

If the cotenant lessens the value of the land by taking away and selling resources such as coal, timber, etc., he will have to account to his cotenant for the fair share of the revenues he received.

3. Duty to Account for Lease to a Third Party

If one cotenant makes use of the property for his own benefit, he is not required to account for the reasonable rental value. However, if the cotenant rents the property to a third party, he must pay his cotenants their fair share of the rents collected.

C.   Contribution

A cotenant may wish to receive contributions from the other cotenants for certain payments he has made to benefit the property. If the cotenant has a duty to account, he may deduct the contribution owed him before paying the other cotenants their fair share of the property's proceeds.

1. Real Estate Taxes and Mortgage Payments

Paid to benefit the entire property for both cotenants. Contribution will be enforced for such outlays.

2. Improvements

The cotenant who pays for improvements will almost never be compensated. However, the cotenant can receive the portion of land containing the improvements in a partition in kind or the value of the improvement in a partition by sale (see below).

3. Repairs
If one cotenant makes repairs without the consent of the other, most courts will not enforce contribution. However, there is a trend to allow contribution if the repairs were necessary, especially if possession is shared by the cotenants. Adjustments for uncompensated repairs may be made before a property is partitioned (see below).

D. Partition
Any cotenant, except a tenant by the entirety, may bring an action for the partition of property.

1. Partition in Kind is when the property is physically divided to reflect each cotenant's proportional interest.

2. Partition by Sale is executed when partition in kind is inequitable (e.g., when a family home is involved). The property is sold and the proceeds are divided to reflect the proportional interests of the cotenants.

3. The partition will be adjusted to account for uncompensated repairs, improvements, tax payments, and rents (see section C above).

III. MARITAL INTERESTS
How are a man and woman's property interests affected after they enter into a marriage? At common law, a married woman occupied a lowly legal position. This was reflected in the treatment of marital estates. Significant changes in a married woman's status did not take place until the nineteenth century.

A. Husband's Interest in Wife's Property

1. Jure Uxoris (i.e., estate by marital right) was a legal life estate whereby the husband was entitled to the use of *all* the lands his wife possessed before, or acquired during, the marriage.

    a.   The husband had a right to occupy and alienate his wife's land and to collect all its rents and profits.

    b.   Termination of jure uxoris occurred upon the death of the husband or wife or upon divorce.

2. Curtesy Initiate
Upon the birth of a live child (survival of the child was not necessary), jure uxoris was transformed into curtesy initiate. The effect of this was that the husband no longer lost his rights to his wife's property if she predeceased him (as he did in jure uxoris).

3. Curtesy Consummate
Upon his wife's death, the husband's curtesy was transformed into a curtesy consummate. There is little practical difference between the two types of curtesy.

4. Modern View

    a.   Jure Uxoris was effectively destroyed in the nineteenth century when the Married Women's Property Acts were passed, which allowed a woman to dispose of her property during the marriage.

    b.   Curtesy has been abolished by statute in most, but not all, states. Modern statutes give the husband an outright interest in a percentage of his wife's property (usually a one-third or one-half interest). In the jurisdictions which still have curtesy, the husband can choose between curtesy and the statutory share.

B.   Rights of the Wife in Husband's Property

1. Dower
Originally, a wife was not her husband's heir and received nothing upon his death. To ensure that a widow was provided for, dower was developed which gave the woman a one-third *life estate* in her husband's property at his death.

    a.   Requirements.

i. The property must have been owned and possessed by the husband at some point during the marriage, not only at death.

ii. The property would have to be inheritable by issue of the marriage, if there were issue.
Note: there is no requirement that there actually be a child.

2. Dower Inchoate means that a wife will receive a one-third interest in her husband's property if he predeceases her.

a. Not Destructible
A wife's expectancy in the property which her husband owned at *some point* during the marriage cannot be destroyed even if the husband sold the property or has creditors who claim the property to settle debts he owes.

b. Termination of dower rights occurs upon divorce or the death of the wife.

3. Dower Consummate is the term used to describe the dower once the husband predeceases his wife. The widow then has the right to her one-third life estate in her husband's property.

4. Modern View of Dower

a. Abolished in Most States
In these states, if a husband dies intestate, his wife is considered an heir and receives a share of his property that is prescribed by statute. If there is a will, the wife may elect between the will's provisions and a statutory share (normally the intestate share).

b. Retained in a Few States
In these states, the wife may elect between dower and the statutory share. The principal benefit of choosing dower is that it passes free from the claims of the decedent's creditors.

IV. THE COMMUNITY PROPERTY SYSTEM
Eight states (Arizona, California, Idaho, Louisiana, Nevada, New Mexico, Texas, and Washington) have a system of community

property. The system's basic assumption is that the husband and wife contribute equally to the economic achievements of the marriage.

A. Effect
    All property acquired during the marriage by either spouse is community property owned jointly by husband and wife. This has its greatest effect when a marriage is dissolved or when property is sold.

B. Strong Presumption That Property Acquired or Possessed During Marriage Is Community Property.

    1. Community Property Includes:

        a. Income from Community Property (even if the property is only listed in one spouse's name).

        b. Earnings by both spouses during the marriage.

    2. The presumption can be rebutted by a preponderance of the evidence proving that the property is separately owned.

C. Separate Property includes:

    1. Property obtained by either spouse before marriage.

    2. Property obtained by either spouse by gift, devise, or descent.

    3. Five out of eight community property states also include income from all separate property in this category.

D. Separate Property Can Be Transformed Into Community Property by the Act of the Spouse Who Owns the Property. Neither spouse can change community property into separate property without the consent of the other.

E. Management

    1. Prior to 1960
       The husband had exclusive control over community property as a fiduciary. However, he could not convey real property without his wife's consent in most cases.

2. Present
Community property states give each spouse equal control over the property.

F.   Comparison With the Common Law

1. None of the eight states uses the concepts of dower, curtesy, or tenancy by the entirety.

2. Tenancies in common and joint tenancies are recognized as separate property, but cannot be simultaneously held as community property.

G.   Death
Community property is considered to be owned by each spouse in equal halves. As a result, each spouse has the power to devise half the property. If there is no will, some states grant the property to the surviving spouses; others pass the property onto the decedent's heirs.

H.   Divorce
Some states evenly divide the property upon divorce. Others require the courts to make an equitable distribution.

I.   Conflict of Laws Rule
Property acquires its character at the time of procurement.

1. Personal Property is classified in accordance with the law of the couple's domicile at the time of acquisition.

2. Real Estate is always classified in accordance with the laws of the state where it is situated.

CASE CLIPS

In Re Estate of Michael (1966)

Facts: A deed's language failed to explicitly create a joint tenancy, though it did state that the grantees had a "right of survivorship."

Issue: Does a devise to two or more persons (not husband and wife or trustees) with a right of survivorship create, without more, a joint tenancy?

Rule: Within the four corners of the instrument, a grantor's intent to create a joint tenancy must be clearly expressed, otherwise no right of survivorship exists, and a tenancy in common, not a joint tenancy, is created.

Laura v. Christian (1975)

Facts: Laura, the plaintiff, and Christian were cotenants of property threatened with foreclosure. The plaintiff averted foreclosure by paying a lien without contribution from the defendant. The plaintiff sued to quiet title in himself. After the property's value increased, the defendant asserted that he could redeem his interest.

Issue: Does a derelict cotenant have an option to reimburse his fellow cotenants who, in order to avert foreclosure on commonly held property, paid a lien on the property without contribution?

Rule: When a cotenant pays an obligation, on common property subject to contribution, the fellow cotenants can exercise their option, within a reasonable time, to redeem or prevent loss of their interest by proportionately reimbursing the paying cotenant cotenant.

Goergen v. Maar (1956)

Facts: Goergen (defendant) was one of four cotenants, but exclusively occupied the common property, collected and retained the rent, and paid the taxes and maintenance expenses. The other cotenants sought a partition and accounting.

Issue: May cotenants not in possession of the commonly held property impose on the possessing cotenant's interest an equitable charge when the possessing cotenant retained more than his proportionate share of the rents?

Rule: Any item of rent received by a cotenant in excess of his share of the income of the property is an equitable charge against his interest, and any expenditure made by a cotenant in excess of his share of the obligation is a charge against the interests of his cotenants.

White v. Smyth (1948)

Facts: The plaintiff and defendant were tenants in common. White (plaintiff) mined the land and kept for himself all proceeds of the mining operation. The defendant sought partition by sale and division of the profits already realized in proportion to each party's interest in the property.

Issue: Must a cotenant who kept all the profits realized from the common property account to his co-owners for the profits realized from the common property?

Rule: When a co-owner of mineral property works the property and disposes of the minerals produced, he must account to his cotenants for all profits made.

Michalski v. Michalski (1958)

Facts: A husband and wife held property as tenants in common. They agreed in writing that neither would convey or mortgage their interest without the others' consent and that neither party "shall do or permit anything in respect thereto to defeat the common tenancy of said properties by said parties," A year later, they divorced. The husband (plaintiff) sought to partition some of the property by sale.

Issue: May tenants in common agree to prohibit partition of property?

Rule: Although the right of partition between cotenants is absolute, cotenants can, if they explicitly state or clearly manifest their intent, bar partition for a reasonable time. If, however, the agreement is no longer fair and equitable due to changed circumstances, a court can decline to enforce it.

Miller v. Riegler (1967)

Facts: An aunt reregistered stock in which she had sole title. The reregistered stock listed the aunt and her niece, Mary Jane Riegler, as joint tenants. Upon the aunt's death, Marjorie Miller, also a niece, argued that a joint tenancy was not created.

Issue: Is the common law requirement of unity of time essential to the creation of a joint tenancy?

Rule: Where it is grantor's intent to create a joint tenancy, the absence of unity of time is not fatal. A grantor can convey her own property to herself and another as joint tenants.

Jackson v. O'Connell (1961)

Facts: Three sisters held property as joint tenants. One sister conveyed her interest to another sister, who devised her property by will to her heirs. The heirs (plaintiffs) sued the third sister, O'Connell, to partition the real estate.

Issue: Does a conveyance by one joint tenant of real estate to another of the joint tenants destroy the joint tenancy in its entirety or merely sever the joint tenancy with respect to the undivided interest so conveyed, leaving the joint tenancy in force and effect as to the remaining interest?

Rule: Where one joint tenant conveys her interest to one of her cotenants, the cotenant grantee holds the share conveyed as a tenant in common and her original share is held with the remaining cotenants as a joint tenancy.

Palmer v. Flint (1900)

Facts: A bank (defendant) conveyed property to a married couple as "joint tenants, and not as tenants in common, to them and their assigns and to the survivors, and the heirs and assigns of the survivor forever." After a divorce, Alice Flint, the wife conveyed the premises to her ex-husband. His sister, Roxa Palmer (plaintiff) subsequently acquired the property. The defendants claimed the bank's conveyance to Flint and her ex-husband created a joint life estate with a contingent remainder in the survivor.

Issue: Does the use of the word "heirs" in the phrase "and the heirs of the survivor forever," and in no other part of the granting or habendum clauses of a deed, preclude a severance of the property and thus create a life estate in the grantees with a contingent fee in the survivor?

Rule: If the intention of the parties to create a joint tenancy clearly expressed in a deed is in conflict with technical rules of common law in the construction of deeds, the intent takes precedence and overrides the technical rules of the common law.

Jones v. Green (1983)

Facts: Dorothy Jones (plaintiff) and James Green (defendant) purchased property together as joint tenants, each with full rights of ownership. They were unmarried. The plaintiff sued to partition the property.

Issue: May property conveyed to unmarried individuals as joint tenants and not as tenants in common be partitioned?

Rule: Real estate owned by joint tenants may not be partitioned.

People v. Nogarr (1958)

Facts: Elaine Wilson and her husband, Calvert, owned real estate as joint tenants. Before his death, Calvert executed and delivered to the State of California a mortgage on the land, without the consent of Elaine. After Calvert died, the State commenced an action to condemn the subject property. Elaine challenged that action, arguing that Calvert's conveyance was only effective as to his interest in the property.

Issue: Is a mortgage on real property executed by one of two joint tenants enforceable after the death of that joint tenant?

Rule: A mortgage is but a lien on the mortgagor's interest and it does not destroy the unity of title or possession and does not terminate the joint tenancy.

Hawthorne v. Hawthorne (1963)

Facts: A wife (plaintiff) and her husband (defendant) were tenants by the entirety. They bought a fire insurance policy. After their dwelling burned down, the wife sought an equal division of the insurance proceeds.

Issue: Must the proceeds of a fire insurance policy insuring an interest held by a wife and husband as tenants by the entirety be divided at the demand of one of the owners?

Rule: Because an insurance contract is personalty and personalty cannot be held by the entirety, insurance proceeds must be divided upon the demand of one of its recipients.

D'Ercole v. D'Ercole (1976)

Facts: A wife (plaintiff) and husband (defendant) held property as tenants by the entirety. When they separated, the husband exercised his statutorily created paramount rights in the family home, denying the wife her equity in the property.

Issue: Does tenancy by the entirety which is designed by statute to favor the husband, create a constitutionally impermissible classification?

Rule: Tenancy by the entirety, being but one option open to married persons seeking to take title in real estate, is constitutionally permissible.

Mann v. Bradley (1975)

Facts: Prior to divorce, a Aaron Mann (defendant) and his wife held property as joint tenants. The divorce agreement allowed the wife and children to live in the family house until the occurrence of certain events, whereupon it would be sold and the proceeds equally divided. None of the contingencies occurred during the wife's life. Upon the wife's death, the husband claimed to be sole owner by virtue of his right of survivorship. The administrator of the wife's estate sued to quiet title, arguing that the earlier agreement had converted the joint tenancy into a tenancy in common.

Issue: May a joint tenancy be terminated by a mutual agreement, explicit or implicit, of the parties?

Rule: A joint tenancy may be terminated by mutual agreement of the parties, which can be inferred from the manner in which the parties deal with the property.

Duncan v. Vassaur (1976)

Facts: A married couple, Edgar and Betty Vassaur owned property as joint tenants. Betty murdered her husband and then argued that her right of survivorship left her sole owner of the property.

Issue: Does a surviving joint tenant lose her rights to survivorship when she murders her cotenant?

Rule: The murder of a cotenant by the other cotenant is inconsistent with the continued existence of the joint tenancy; thus, the joint tenancy is terminated at the time of the murder and right of survivorship will not be effective.

Centex Homes Corp. v. Boag (1974)

Facts: Centex Homes Corp. (plaintiff) contracted to sell a condominium to the Boags (defendant). When the Boags refused to honor the contract, Centex sued for specific performance.

Issue: Is the equitable remedy of specific performance available for the enforcement of a contract for the sale of a condominium?

Rule: Because damages sustained by a condominium vendor resulting from the breach of a sales contract are measurable, and the remedy at law is wholly adequate, specific performance is not an available remedy.

Dutcher v. Owens (1983)

Facts: A fire began in the commonly held area of a condominium complex. The Owenses sued in tort for property damage sustained while renting a condo from Dutcher. The trial court ruled that Dutcher's liability was pro rata to his ownership interest in the common areas. The appeals court partially reversed and held Dutcher jointly and severally liable.

Issue: Are condominium co-owners jointly and severally liable, or are they liable only for a pro rata portion of damages caused by a fire that originated in an area held as tenants in common?

Rule: The liability of a condominium co-owner is limited to his pro rata interest where such liability arises from those areas held by tenancy in common.

Holbrook v. Holbrook (1965)

Facts: By statute, Oregon abolished joint tenancy. Contemplating divorce, Mr. Holbrook and his wife (plaintiff), agreed to hold land "as joint tenants ... with right of survivorship." Before his death, Mr. Holbrook conveyed "an undivided one-half interest" in the land to his nephew (defendant).

Issue: Where the common law rule of severance has been abolished as well as the common law joint tenancy, what will be the effect of an agreement purporting to create a joint tenancy?

Rule: Where the common law rule of severance has been abolished by statute along with common law joint tenancy, an agreement purporting to create a joint tenancy creates concurrent life estates with contingent remainders in the life tenants, remainder to vest in the survivor.

Porter v. Porter (1985)

Facts: Mary Jane Porter (plaintiff) was married to Denis Porter until 1976, when they divorced. Prior to the divorce, they acquired a house as joint tenants with a right of survivorship. The divorce decree temporarily granted Mary Jane exclusive possession of the house. After Denis Porter's death, the executrix of his estate sought partition, arguing that the divorce decree terminated the survivorship provisions of the original deed.

Issue: Does a divorce decree that temporarily divides possession of jointly held property destroy a joint tenancy with right of survivorship in real estate?

Rule: The mere temporary division of property held by joint tenants, without an intention to partition, will not destroy unity of possession and amount to a severance of the joint tenancy; consequently, a divorce decree that is silent with respect to property held jointly with a right of survivorship does not automatically destroy the existing survivorship provisions.

Brant v. Hargrove (1981)

Facts: The Brants (plaintiffs) were husband and wife, and were joint tenants with rights of survivorship. Prior to his wife's death, the husband, without his wife's consent or knowledge, encumbered his joint tenancy interest.

Issue: Does the granting of a deed of trust lien by a joint tenant on his joint tenancy interest sever the joint tenancy relationship?

Rule: The execution of a deed of trust by one joint tenant does not, in and of itself, operate to sever the joint tenancy.

Lerman v. Levine (1988)

Facts: The Levines (defendants) and Lerman (plaintiff) purchased a home as joint tenants. After relations deteriorated between the parties, Lerman left to reside elsewhere. Lerman sued to recover use and occupancy payments from the Levines.

Issue: Do one or more cotenants who use common property to the exclusion of another cotenant have a duty to account to the excluded cotenant for the benefit received in excess of their fair share?

Rule: When two or more persons hold property as joint tenants or tenants in common, if one of them occupies, receives or uses the property in greater proportion than the amount of his interest, any other party may bring an action for use and occupation against such person and recover such value as is in excess of his proportion. It is not required to show that an ouster occurred.

Massey v. Prothero (1983)

Facts: Massey (plaintiff) was the sister of Prothero (defendant). The two held real property inherited from their parents. Because one of their deceased brothers had failed to pay the taxes, the property was placed for sale at a tax sale. Prothero, without telling his sister, purchased the property at the sale.

Issue: May one cotenant extinguish the rights of others by buying the property at a tax sale?

Rule: A cotenant may not extinguish the rights of the other cotenants by buying the property at a tax sale.

Delfino v. Vealencis (1980)

Facts: The Delfinos (plaintiffs), tenants in common of 99/144 of an undivided interest in property, sought to partition the property with the defendant, who owned the rest of the property.

Issue: May a court order a sale to partition property jointly owned?

Rule: A partition by sale may be ordered only when: (1) the physical attributes of the land are such that a partition in kind is impracticable or inequitable; and (2) the interests of the owners would be better promoted by a partition by sale.

Central Nationall Bank of Cleveland v. Fitzwilliam (1984)

Facts: The Fitzwilliams (defendants), husband and wife, were tenants by the entirety. When the husband failed to satisfy promissory notes owed to the plaintiff Central National Bank, the plaintiff sought to conduct a foreclosure sale to satisfy the lien on the jointly held property.

Issue: When holding property as tenants by the entirety, may either spouse alienate that property absent the consent of the other spouse?

Rule: When property is held as a tenancy by the entirety, one spouse is unable, without the consent or acquiescence of the other, to convey, bind, encumber, sever, or otherwise alienate the property.

In Re Estate of Brown (1988)

Facts: The defendant Brown and his wife owned real property as tenants by the entirety. The defendant intentionally killed his wife.

Issue: Does a surviving tenant by the entirety retain title to real property after intentionally killing his spouse?

Rule: Because the survivor's interest is created by the deed creating the tenancy by the entirety, not the spouse's death, the survivor has a vested estate in fee simple regardless of the manner in which the spouse died.

Strong v. Wood (1981)

Facts: To have a deed cancelled, Strong (plaintiff) sued the administrator of her husband's estate. She claimed she was defrauded when, just prior to their marriage, her husband conveyed title to his farm, keeping a life estate for himself only.

Issue: Is intent to defraud sufficient to find a fraudulent conveyance in contemplation of marriage?

Rule: Fraudulent intent is not sufficient to establish a spouse's right in property transferred prior to marriage. The claimant must also prove the fraudulent effect of the transferor's actions (i.e., reliance).

Kerwin v. Donaghy (1945)

Facts: The plaintiff, the widow of William Kerwin, sued her stepdaughter (defendant) to recover stocks, bonds, and deposits in banks, which had been transferred during William's lifetime to the defendant.

Issue: Does a spouse have an absolute right to dispose of personalty while living without the other spouse's knowledge or consent?

Rule: A spouse has an absolute right to dispose of any and all of his personal property while living, without the knowledge or consent of the other spouse.

Drapek v. Drapek (1987)

Facts: Pursuant to a divorce judgment Celia Drapek was awarded a lump sum payment of $42,024.50 from her husband Mark Drapek based on the judge's determination that Mark's medical degree was part of his estate.

Issue: How is a professional license or degree to be evaluated for purposes of distributing marital assets in divorce proceedings?

Rule: Although the earning capacity of the degree holder may be considered in awarding alimony and dividing property a professional license or degree is not property subject to equitable distribution upon divorce or dissolution. Since assigning a present value to a professional degree would involve evaluating the earning potential created by that degree it is not a marital asset subject to division.

Sawada v. Endo (1977)

Facts: Endo (defendant) was liable for plaintiff's injuries. The defendant and his wife had owned a parcel of real estate as tenants by the entirety, but conveyed the land before trial. Unable to satisfy the judgment from the defendant's personal assets, the plaintiff sued to set aside the conveyance as a fraud on the defendant's judgment creditors.

Issue: Is one spouse's interest in real property held in tenancy by the entirety subject to levy and execution by his individual creditors?

Rule: The interest of a husband or a wife in an estate by the entirety is not subject to the claims of an individual's creditor during the joint lives of the spouses.

Pico v. Columbet (1859)

Facts: The plaintiff and the defendant were tenants in common. The defendant exclusively used the property, profited thereby, and retained the proceeds. The plaintiff sued to recover part of the profits.

Issue: Does a tenant in common have an action against a cotenant who exclusively profited from use of the commonly held property?

Rule: One tenant in common has no remedy against another tenant who profits from his exclusive use of the tenancy and receives the entire profits, unless the plaintiff was ousted from possession (when ejectment may be brought) or unless the defendant acted as bailee of plaintiff's interest by agreement (when the action of account will lie).

McKnight v. Basilides (1943)

Facts: Charles Basilides (defendant) owned property with his wife as tenants in common. Following his wife's death, Basilides exclusively used and profited from the land. Fifteen years later, the wife's legal heir, McKnight, brought suit demanding partition, Basilides claimed sole ownership by adverse possession and that the rents received were his alone.

Issue: May a cotenant of land held as a tenant in common acquire sole ownership of the land by adverse possession?

Rule: A tenant in common may obtain sole ownership of the tenancy by adverse possession only when the cotenants not in possession had actual knowledge that their rights were repudiated.

Riddle v. Harmon (1980)

Facts: Riddle (plaintiff) and his wife were joint tenants. The plaintiff's wife attempted to terminate the joint tenancy by conveying her interest from herself as a joint tenant to herself as a tenant in common. The plaintiff sued Harmon, the executrix of the wife's estate, to quiet title.

Issue: May a joint tenant unilaterally sever the joint tenancy without the use of an intermediary?

Rule: The common law "strawman" device is no longer necessary. A joint tenant may unilaterally sever the joint tenancy without the use of an intermediary device.

Harms v. Sprague (1984)

Facts: Harms (plaintiff) and his brother took title to real estate as joint tenants. Before he died, the plaintiff's brother mortgaged his half interest. The plaintiff filed suit to quiet title and named as defendant Sprague, executor of the brother's estate.

Issue 1: Is a joint tenancy severed when less than all of the joint tenants mortgage their interest in the property?

Rule 1: A mortgage given by one joint tenant does not sever the joint tenancy.

Issue 2: Does such a mortgage survive the death of the mortgagor as a lien on the property?

Rule 2: The property right of a mortgaging joint tenant is extinguished at the moment of his death. Thus, the mortgage does not survive as a lien on the surviving tenant's property.

Wiggins v. Parson (1984)

Facts: Cooper named herself and her sister, Broadhead, joint tenants of a bank account. Later, she added the names of another sister, Parson, and a brother to the account. Cooper removed her own name from the account. Parson withdrew and kept all the money.

Issue: Does the complete withdrawal of funds from a joint tenancy account by one owner terminate the joint tenancy nature of the funds so as to destroy the right of survivorship in the funds?

Rule: The withdrawal of jointly-owned funds by a joint owner and placement of the funds in other persons' names terminates the joint tenancy nature of the money and transforms it into a tenancy in common.

Johnson v. Hendrickson (1946)

Facts: Hendrickson was survived by her second husband and the children from both her marriages. All the survivors had an interest in certain land which descended from her first husband.

Issue: When land is so situated that it cannot be partitioned among the various owners without prejudice to such owners, may a court order the sale of the land?

Rule: Where partition would cause the value of each cotenant's share to be materially less than the corresponding share of the money equivalent that could be obtained for the whole, then the court may order a sale of the property.

Spiller v. MacKereth (1976)

Facts: Spiller and MacKereth owned a building as tenants in common. When their lessee vacated the building, Spiller entered the space and began to use it as a warehouse.

Issue: Is a demand to vacate half of a building or pay half the rental value sufficient to establish an occupying co-tenant's liability for rent?

Rule: In the absence of an agreement to pay rent or of an ouster of a co-tenant, a co-tenant in possession is not liable to the other(s) for the value of his use and occupation of that property. Before an occupying co-tenant can be liable for rent, he must have denied his co-tenant the right to enter. A request that the occupying tenant vacate is not sufficient because he holds title to the whole and may rightfully occupy the whole unless the other co-tenant(s) assert their possessory rights.

Swartzbaugh v. Sampson (1936)

Facts: Swartzbaugh (plaintiff) and her husband owned land as joint tenants. The plaintiff's husband leased part of the land without her consent. The plaintiff sued to cancel the leases.

Issue: Can one joint tenant, who has not joined in a lease executed by her cotenant and another, maintain an action to cancel the lease where the lessee is in exclusive possession of the leased property?

Rule: When one cotenant of a joint tenancy executes a lease with a third party, the lease is a valid contract giving to the lessee the same right to possession of the leased property as the cotenant had.

United States v. 1500 Lincoln Avenue (1991)

Facts: The United States sought civil forfeiture of property containing a pharmacy, which was owned as a tenancy by the entirety by a husband, who was convicted for the illegal distribution of prescription drugs, and his wife, who did not know about or consent to the illegal activity.

Issue: In a tenancy by the entirety, is the government entitled to a forfeiture of an interest in property where one spouse is convicted for the illegal use of the property and the other spouse is completely innocent?

Rule: An innocent owner has a right to full and exclusive possession and use of the whole property during his lifetime, is protected against conveyance of and against a levy upon the property by any creditor of the spouse's former interest, and retains all survivorship rights.

In re Marriage of Graham (1978)

Facts: Mrs. Graham provided seventy percent of her husband's support while he earned an M.B.A. They filed for divorce six years after his graduation.

Issue: Is a graduate degree considered marital property subject to division upon the marriage's dissolution?

Rule: An educational degree is not encompassed by the concept of property and does not constitute marital property.

Elkus v. Elkus (1991)

Facts: Elkus was an opera singer, who during the course of her marriage saw a dramatic growth in her career which correlated to a significant increase in her income. During this time, her husband was highly involved in her career, sacrificing his own career to help her and to take care of their children.

Issue: In a divorce proceeding, does the career and/or celebrity status of a spouse constitute marital property subject to equitable distribution?

Rule: The extent to which the development of an individual's career can be attributed to a spouse's efforts and contributions, is the factor that determines what constitutes marital property subject to equitable distribution.

Marvin v. Marvin (1976)

Facts: Plaintiff and defendant lived together for seven years without marrying. All the property that the couple acquired during this time was in the defendant's name. Plaintiff alleged that the two entered into an oral agreement that entitled her to half the property and to support payments.

Issue: What rights do the partners of nonmarital relationships have in the event that one dies or the couple separates?

Rule: Express contracts between nonmarital partners should normally be enforced. If there is no express contract, an inquiry should be made to determine whether the conduct of the parties demonstrates an implied contract, agreement of partnership or some other tacit understanding between the parties.

Hewitt v. Hewitt (1979)

Facts: The plaintiff and her boyfriend (defendant) lived together as an unmarried couple for fifteen years.

Issue: Does a woman who alleges that she and her boyfriend lived as husband and wife have a claim to an equal share of the profits and property accumulated by the parties during the period of cohabitation?

Rule: Knowingly unmarried cohabitants do not acquire mutual property rights.

CHAPTER 5 LANDLORD-TENANT LAW

I.   LEASEHOLDS
Leaseholds are nonfreehold possessory estates. There are four types of leaseholds:

A.   Term of Years

1. Lasts for a designated period of time.
This type of leasehold requires that both the beginning and ending date either be fixed or computable by formula, so that the term of the tenancy is certain.

2. Duration

   a.   This tenancy can be created for any length of time (e.g., 1,000 years or even 1 day).

   b.   Some states limit duration by statute.

3. Termination
Since both parties know the ending date, this type of tenancy expires automatically, and no notice is required. However, it can be terminated earlier upon the happening of some event or condition.

B.   Periodic Tenancy

1. No Fixed Ending Date
The tenancy will continue from period to period (i.e. renews itself automatically), unless one party terminates the arrangement with proper notice.

2. Duration
The period can be expressly agreed upon or implied by the course of dealings between the parties. If there is no period specified in the lease, the court will examine the following factors:

   a.   The Use of the Property
   Example: If the property in question is a farm with a yearly cycle, then the term will be one year.

b.   The Rental Agreement
Example: If rent is paid monthly, then the period will be one month. However, if annual rent is specified but payable in monthly installments, most courts will determine the period to be one year.

3. Termination requires proper notice.

a.   For a year to year tenancy, six months notice was necessary for termination at common law. For tenancies with a period of less than a year a full period's notice was required for effective termination (e.g., a month's notice for a month-to-month tenancy).

Note: Most modern statutes require only thirty days notice for the termination of any tenancy.

b.   Notice must terminate the tenancy on the final day of the period (i.e., if a month-to-month tenant provided notice of termination on March 24, the termination would not be effective until April 30).

Note: Many states today have relaxed this requirement and, for example, allow a month-to-month tenancy to end after the 30-day notice period has expired.

C.   Tenancy at Will

1. Mutual Right of Termination
This tenancy has no stated duration and may be terminated by either party at any time.

2. Methods of Termination

a.   By the Parties
Notice of termination was not required at common law. Modern statutes, however, give a tenant at will a right to prior notice.

b.   By Implication
Death of one of the parties, conveyance of the property, or assignment of the lease terminates the tenancy.

3. Creation of a Tenancy at Will may occur by express agreement. However, this type of tenancy usually arises by implication.

    a. **Example:** The tenant takes possession of the landlord's apartment without agreement as to the term or period when rent would come due.

    b. However, even if no period is specified, a court may still interpret the arrangement as a periodic tenancy, if some plausible period can be deduced (see above).

D. Tenancy at Sufferance
Arises when a tenant remains in possession after a valid lease has ended. This "holdover tenant" is liable for rent.

1. Right of Election
The landlord has the power to either eject the tenant or bind the tenant to a new term.

2. Duration
Courts are in disagreement as to the nature and duration of the tenancy that is created when the landlord exercises his option to bind the tenant to another term. Some courts hold that the new tenancy is a Term of Years, while others hold that it is a Periodic Tenancy. Furthermore, some conclude that the duration should be measured by the rent computation period of the original tenancy, while others hold that the duration of the original lease (with a maximum of one year) should be the duration of the new tenancy.

3. A holdover may be excused for the following reasons:

    a. De Minimis Holdover.
    Example: The tenant was still packing the morning after the lease expired.

    b. Holdover Without Fault.

    c. Negotiation For Renewal.

II. OBLIGATIONS OF A LANDLORD

A. To deliver possession of the premises

1. Traditional View
A landlord had no duty to deliver actual possession at the beginning of a tenant's lease term.

2. "American" Rule
Landlord is obligated to deliver legal but not actual possession.

3. "English" Rule (followed by most American courts)
Landlord is obligated to provide both legal and actual possession. Under this rule, a tenant may sue a landlord for breach when a previous tenant "holds over."

B. Duty to Maintain and Repair

1. Common Law Approach
Caveat emptor. The premises were provided "as is" and without any implied warranties. Landlords did not have a duty to repair.

2. Exceptions to the Common Law Rule

   a. Short-term lease of furnished premises.

   b. Material misrepresentation by landlord, relied upon by tenant.

   c. Tort liability for latent defect known to landlord.

   d. Building not yet completed when lease was signed.

   e. Liability for common areas.

   f. The landlord was liable if he undertook to make repairs.

3. Covenant of Quiet Enjoyment

   a. A covenant of quiet enjoyment is said to be implied in every lease. The tenant therefore has a right to terminate the lease if his right to quiet enjoyment is interfered with.

   b. Breach of the covenant of quiet enjoyment

      i. Acts by landlord
      The following acts, constituting a breach of the covenant of quiet enjoyment, must be done either by the landlord

or by someone holding under the landlord in order to be actionable. Breaches by third parties such as other tenants are not actionable unless the third party is acting with the express or implied permission of the landlord.

(1) Total actual eviction
The landlord physically ousts the tenant from the entire premises.

Remedies: The tenant is relieved of all rent liability and has the right to sue for damages.

(2) Partial actual eviction
The landlord physically ousts the tenant from a portion of the rented premises.

Remedies: The tenant is relieved of all rent liability and may continue to occupy the remainder of the premises rent-free.

Note: This result is based on the notion that the landlord may not apportion his wrong.

(3) Total constructive eviction
The landlord's acts or omissions make it extremely difficult or impossible for the tenant to use any portion of the premises.

Remedies: The tenant may terminate the lease and sue for damages, but he must abandon the premises within a reasonable time after the landlord's breach of the covenant.

(4) Partial constructive eviction
The landlord's acts or omissions make it extremely difficult or impossible for the tenant to use part of the premises.

Remedies: The tenant's remedies are the same as for total constructive eviction.

    ii. Paramount title

       If a third party holds title to the leased premises that is superior to that of the landlord, the tenant may terminate the lease upon discovery of this paramount title if he has not yet entered into possession of the premises. If the tenant has already taken possession, he may only terminate if the paramount title holder actually asserts his title.

  c. The continued evolution of the implied warranty of habitability has virtually eliminated the usefulness of the covenant of quiet enjoyment in residential leases. However, in commercial leases, the covenant of quiet enjoyment remains a tenant's only avenue of relief.

4. Implied Warranty of Habitability (majority view today)
Landlords leasing urban *residential* property must maintain their premises in a condition that satisfies applicable housing codes and makes the premises safe and habitable.

  a. Applicable to residential but not commercial leases (majority rule), and to both single and multiple dwellings.

  b. The implied warranty may not be waived by the tenant.

  c. Standards are greatly influenced by local housing codes, a substantial deviation from which will violate the warranty.

  d. Multiple immaterial deviations may combine to constitute a material breach.

  e. Conditions that interfere with safety or habitability may constitute a breach even if local housing codes have not been violated.

    i. Conditions existing prior to tenant's occupancy.

      (1) Latent defects
         Tenant is protected by the implied warranty of habitability.

      (2) Patent defects

Some courts and the Second Restatement hold that the tenant waives the warranty by entering the premises, unless the defect made the premises unsafe or unhealthy, or the landlord promised to repair the premises at a later date.

    ii. Conditions that arise after the tenant enters.
The landlord must make all repairs, unless the damages were caused by the tenant, a sudden natural force (tenant may terminate the lease but may not claim damages), or a third party (e.g., a burglar).

    f. Some courts have held that the age of a building and the rent charged may be considered to determine whether the implied warranty of habitability has been breached.

5. Tenant's remedies for landlord's material breach of the implied warranty of habitability

Mnemonic: **4 R's**

    a. **R**escission
Tenant may terminate the lease, vacate the premises, and recover damages. (Some states require that the landlord be given notice and an opportunity to fix the defect, and that the tenant had been current on his rent prior to the defect).

    b. **R**ecover damages
Tenant continues to pay rent and the lease continues.

    c. **R**epair and offset cost of repairs against the rent

    d. **R**ent abatement
Tenant pays rent into an escrow account pending the outcome of the dispute.

6. Various ways of measuring damages for a landlord's breach

    a. Tenant accepts defective premises "as is."
Damages equal actual rent or fair rental value of premises.

    b. Percent reduction.

Damages equal percentage of usage lost multiplied by the rent.

   c.   Actual expenses caused by breach.

   d.   Loss of bargain.
Damages equal fair market value of premises as promised minus fair market value of premises "as is."

III.   OBLIGATIONS OF A TENANT

A.   Payment of rent.

B.   Express promises to repair (no duty to reverse ordinary wear and tear).

C.   Liability for waste.

D.   Reasonable behavior in use of premises.

IV.   LANDLORD'S REMEDIES

A.   Deposit
A landlord may withhold a security deposit if the tenant abandons or misuses the property.

B.   Eviction
A landlord may evict a tenant who has committed a material breach or is holding over.

1. Self Help
Most states have abolished the common law right of a landlord to forcibly regain possession and to seize the chattels of a tenant who has not paid rent. Most states allow self help without the use of force, though case law has limited this option so much that it is rarely of practical benefit to a landlord.

2. Summary Process
A legal procedure whereby a landlord can quickly (usually within 30 days) evict a tenant by proving that the lease had expired, or that the tenant had not paid rent.

C.   Acceleration Clause

A contractual clause requiring a lump sum payment of all rents due on the remainder of the lease term in the event of a breach by the tenant. The tenant may remain on the premises after paying the accelerated damages.

D. Damages
A landlord may recover damages from a tenant who has abandoned the premises or has occupied a leasehold after the leasehold expired. The landlord is entitled to reasonable rent plus special damages caused by the holdover that the tenant could have foreseen.

1. When a tenant "holds over," the landlord may either bind the tenant to a periodic tenancy or evict the tenant.

2. When a tenant abandons the premises the landlord may either accept the surrender of the premises, let the premises remain vacant, or relet the premises on behalf of the tenant. If the landlord accepts a surrender the tenant is released from his rent obligation. If the landlord elects to pursue either of the other options he may sue for damages. Courts are split on the question of a landlord's duty to mitigate damages.

E. Mnemonic: If you don't pay your rent, you're **DEAD**

1. **D**eposit

2. **E**viction

3. **A**cceleration clause

4. **D**amages

V. TRANSFER, ASSIGNMENT, AND SUBLEASE

A. Absent a contractual agreement to the contrary, a landlord may transfer or sell his interest in a leasehold, and a tenant may assign or sublease his interest.

B. Assignment and Sublease

1. A transfer of *all* of a tenant's interest is an assignment. A transfer of *less* than a tenant's complete interest is a sublease.

2. Assignment

    a. Must be for the balance of the lease, under the same terms, and an intent to create a new landlord-tenant relationship must be present.

    b. The assignor (i.e., original tenant) remains contractually liable to the landlord.

    c. The assignee falls into privity of estate with the landlord. Therefore, an assignee will be bound by all covenants that "run with the land."

3. Sublease

    a. A sublessee is only liable to the sublessor (i.e., original tenant). The sublessor remains liable to the landlord.

    b. A sublease does not establish privity; therefore, the sublessee will not be bound by covenants that "run with the land."

    c. Agreements not to assign a lease will generally be enforced, but a landlord may waive the assignment prohibition by his actions.

VI.   LIABILITY OF LANDLORD AND TENANT IN TORT

A.   Liability of a Tenant
A tenant is liable to others for injuries sustained on his leased premises as if he were the owner of the property.

B.   General Duties Owed by an Occupier of Land

1. To Invitee
Duty to inspect property and remedy all hazards.

2. To Licensee
No duty to inspect and remedy hazards but must exercise reasonable care.

3. To Trespasser
No duty.

C.   Liability of a Landlord
A landlord is generally not liable for injuries sustained by third parties on property he has leased (for exceptions see Duties of Landlord above).

VII. NO FAULT TERMINATION OF A LEASEHOLD

A.   Condemnation
Condemnation will terminate a lease when the entire estate (not just part of the estate) is condemned by eminent domain.

B.   Impossibility
The destruction of the premises, through no fault of the tenant, will relieve the tenant of his duties under the lease.

C.   Frustration of Purpose
Strict frustration of the very purpose for which the lease agreement was made allows the tenant to terminate the lease and vacate the premises.

D.   Subsequent Illegality
If the purpose for which the property is leased becomes illegal after the lease is entered into, the lease is rescinded.

CASE CLIPS

Cook v. University Plaza (1981)

Facts: The plaintiffs and University Plaza entered into a "Residence Hall Contract Agreement" that stipulated that the parties did not intend a landlord-tenant relationship. The defendant reserved the right to require a resident to move from room to room.

Issue: Is a contractual agreement between students and a university dormitory a lease or a license?

Rule: The essence of a lease is transfer of possession, while a license is an agreement which merely entitles one party to use property subject to the management and control of the other party. Therefore, an agreement which allows a dormitory to move students from room to room at its discretion is a license because it fails to pass a possessory interest in specific property.

Womack v. Hyche (1987)

Facts: Womack leased property to Hyche for a fixed minimum rent plus funds received from running a fishing camp on the property. Hyche had the option to renew the lease as long as the camp was run for a profit. When friction developed between the two parties Womack instituted a declaratory judgment action to have the lease agreement voided.

Issue: May a lease for a term of years be valid when the renewal clause is so ambiguous as to create uncertainty regarding the duration of the lease?

Rule: Where a renewal clause fails to state with certainty a date on which the lease terminates, the lease is void as a tenancy of years and a tenancy at will results.

Marina Point, Ltd. v. Wolfson (1982)

Facts: The tenants, Stephen and Lois Wolfson, renewed their lease in January, 1974. In October, 1974 the landlord instituted a blanket ban on families with children. When the tenants failed to vacate the premises, the landlord commenced an unlawful detainer action.

Issue: May a landlord of an apartment complex refuse to rent an apartment to a family solely because the family includes a minor child?

Rule: Some states prohibit, by statute, all arbitrary discrimination by business establishments. Therefore, in those states, such a restriction aimed at children as a class is illegal.

Adrian v. Rabinowitz (1930)

Facts: On April 30, 1934, Rabinowitz (defendant) and Adrian (plaintiff) entered into a lease whose term was to begin on June 15, 1934. Rabinowitz's prior tenant failed to vacate voluntarily. Rabinowitz began proceedings against the prior tenant, but Adrian did not take actual possession until July 9, 1934.

Issue: Does a lessor, in the absence of an express undertaking to that effect, have a duty to put the lessee in actual, as well as legal possession of the leased premises at the commencement of the term?

Rule: When the term of a lease is to begin in the future, there is an implied duty owed by the lessor that the premises shall be legally and actually open to the lessee's entry when the time for possession under the lease arrives.

Blackett v. Olanoff (1977)

Facts: The lessor leased premises to be used as a nightclub. The tenants of the lessor's nearby apartment building abandoned their apartments because of loud music and other disturbances emanating from the club. The tenants claimed that the lessor breached their implied warranty of quiet enjoyment. The terms of his lease with the club would have allowed the lessor to correct the disturbing conditions if he had undertaken to do so.

Issue: Does a lessor constructively evict his tenant when he permits a third party to substantially deprive his tenants of quiet enjoyment of the premises?

Rule: Where a lessor fails to eliminate a disruptive condition, which is within his power to eliminate, and which results in the deprivation of the tenant's right to quiet enjoyment, the lessor will be held to have constructively evicted the tenant.

Brown v. Southall Realty Co. (1968)

Facts: At the time a lease was executed Southall, the landlord, knew that several conditions existed upon the premises that violated certain housing regulations. He brought suit to collect unpaid rent, and the tenant defended on the grounds that the lease was illegal and therefore unenforceable.

Issues: Is a lease illegal and therefore unenforceable where the condition of the premises violates housing regulations, and the landlord is aware of the violations at the time the lease is executed?

Rule: An illegal contract (i.e., lease), made in violation of the statutory prohibition designed for police or regulatory purposes, is void and confers no right upon the wrongdoer.

Javins, Saunders and Gross v. First Nat'l Realty Corp. (1970)

Facts: The lessor, First National Realty Corp., sued for possession for nonpayment of rent. The tenants contended that they were equitably excused from paying rent because of nearly 1500 violations of the Housing Regulations of the District of Columbia, arising after their leases were executed.

Issue: Is a tenant's obligation to pay rent independent of the landlord's obligation to comply with applicable housing regulations?

Rule: A warranty of habitability, measured by the standards outlined in the Housing Regulations for the District of Columbia, is implied by operation of law into leases of urban dwellings. Therefore, a tenant's rent liability is dependent upon the landlord's compliance with his responsibilities under the implied warranty of habitability.

Davidow v. Inwood North Professional Group—Phase I (1988)

Facts: The plaintiff sued Dr. Davidow for unpaid rent on medical office space. The doctor argued that defects in the premises made the space unsuitable for use as a medical office.

Issue: Is there an implied warranty by a commercial landlord that the leased premises are suitable for their intended commercial purpose?

Rule: There is an implied warranty of suitability by the landlord in a commercial lease that the premises are suitable for their intended commercial purpose.

Sargent v. Ross (1973)

Facts: The tenant sued the landlord for negligently constructing a stairway from which the tenant's child fell to her death. The defendant asserted that she owed no duty to the child.

Issue: Does a landlord owe his tenants a duty of reasonable care with respect to the safety of the premises?

Rule: The doctrine of landlord tort immunity is abrogated. Hence forth, landlords are liable for injuries caused by their failure to exercise reasonable care.

Trentacost v. Brussel (1980)

Facts: The tenant, Florence Trentacost, was robbed and seriously injured in the hallway of her apartment building. Although the building was located in a high crime area, its front door was not equipped with a lock.

Issue: Is a landlord who provides inadequate security for common areas of rental premises liable for failing to prevent a criminal assault upon a tenant?

Rule: A landlord has a legal duty to take reasonable security measures for tenant protection on his premises. Failure to provide adequate security gives rise to potential liability on grounds of both conventional negligence and the implied warranty of habitability.

Orange County Taxpayers Council, Inc. v. City of Orange (1980)

Facts: The City of Orange enacted a rent control ordinance requiring that the landlord's building be in "substantial compliance" with municipal housing regulations before a rent increase in rent controlled housing would be allowed.

Issue: Is a rent control ordinance that prohibits increases in rent without a certification that a dwelling is in "substantial compliance" with municipal housing regulations arbitrary and unreasonable?

Rule: A requirement that an apartment be in "substantial compliance" with local housing regulations before a lessor can charge higher rent is neither arbitrary nor unreasonable.

Commonwealth Building Corp. v. Hirschfield (1940)

Facts: Hirschfield, through no fault of his own, vacated a leasehold one day after the lease expired. The lease provided that the lessor could collect double rent if the tenant failed to vacate on time.

Issue: May a lessor treat a tenant as a holdover tenant for another complete term when the tenant involuntarily holds over?

Rule: A tenant who, through no fault of his own, involuntarily holds over cannot be bound to a new and complete term by the lessor.

Swann v. Gastonia Housing Auth. (1982)

Facts: The Swans participated in the Gastonia Housing Authority's (GHA) public housing program. When the Swans' landlord refused to renew their lease they contended that the landlord must have good cause, and that they were entitled to a full hearing before the GHA on that issue. GHA, however, refused to deviate from its policy of allowing landlords to refuse to renew a tenant's lease with or without cause.

Issue: Does the Due Process Clause of the Fourteenth Amendment guarantee to tenants, under 42 U.S.C. § 1437, a right to a full and complete hearing by the GHA?

Rule: The due process clause will be invoked when a tenant is evicted pursuant to a state action. In such a case only a showing of good cause will permit a landlord to terminate a tenancy. However, a full-fledged hearing by the GHA is not mandated by the due process requirement of good cause.

Seawall Associates v. City of New York (1989)

Facts: Seawall Associates challenged a city law prohibiting the demolition or conversion of single room occupancy properties and obligating the owners to lease them at controlled rents for an indefinite period. New York City housing officials defended the law on the basis that it was a valid effort to prevent homelessness.

Issue: Do uncompensated affirmative obligations and restrictions on use imposed by the state, which prevent an owner's development of his property, constitute an unconstitutional taking?

Rule: Uncompensated affirmative obligations and restrictions on property development constitute an unconstitutional taking when they drastically interfere with the property owner's right to possess and to exclude, or they deny an owner economically viable use of the property, or do not substantially advance legitimate state interests.

Flynn v. City of Cambridge (1981) Note Case

Facts: A city ordinance prohibited conversion of rent controlled apartments to condominium units. Flynn challenged the ordinance as an unconstitutional taking of property.

Issue: Does an ordinance restricting an owner's use of his property automatically constitute a taking?

Rule: A government action does not constitute a taking when an owner's primary expectation concerning the use of his property is not frustrated and he is assured of a reasonable return on his investment.

Stroup v. Conant (1974)

Facts: As a prospective tenant, the defendant assured the plaintiff that he planned to use the premises for the operation of a variety store. Some time after the lease was executed the landlord discovered that the defendant had opened an adult book store. She filed suit to have the lease rescinded.

Issue: May a lease be rescinded when a prospective tenant misrepresents his proposed use of the premises?

Rule: When a landlord relied on a misrepresentation of the planned purpose for which the premises were leased, the landlord may rescind the lease.

Handler v. Horns (1949)

Facts: Horns leased premises in which he installed equipment used to carry on his trade.

Issue: May a tenant who has installed equipment used to carry on his trade remove the fixtures when his lease expires?

Rule: In the absence of an agreement to the contrary, a tenant may remove whatever he has erected or installed for the purpose of carrying on his trade, provided that it can be severed from the freehold without material injury thereto, and that such removal is effected before he yields possession of the premises.

College Block v. Atlantic Richfield Co. (1988)

Facts: College Block leased land to the Atlantic Richfield Company (ARCO) on the condition that ARCO operate a gas station on that property and pay as rent a minimum monthly amount plus an amount determined by the quantity of gas delivered. When ARCO stopped operating the gas station, it paid College Block all of the minimum monthly payments remaining on the lease. College Block brought suit alleging that ARCO was also responsible for the additional sum it would have received had the gas station remained in business.

Issue: Where rent is based on a minimum payment plus a percentage of the lessee's revenues, does the lease contain an implied in law covenant of continued operation?

Rule: A covenant of continued operation will be implied in commercial leases containing a specified minimum payment plus a percentage of the lessee's revenues only when the guaranteed minimum is not substantial, i.e., when the specified minimum fails to provide the lessor with what was reasonably expected.

Edwards v. Habib (1968)

Facts: Edwards, a month-to-month tenant, notified authorities of her landlord's multiple sanitary code violations. Habib, her landlord, promptly attempted to evict her.

Issue: May a landlord evict a month-to-month tenant for reporting housing code violations to the authorities?

Rule: While a landlord may evict a month-to-month tenant for any legal reason or for no reason at all, he is not free to evict in retaliation for the tenant's report of housing violations to the authorities. However, the landlord is free to evict the tenant after the illegal purpose has dissipated.

United States National Bank of Oregon v. Homeland, Inc. (1981)

Facts: The plaintiff leased commercial space to Homeland, Inc., who subsequently abandoned the premises. The plaintiff succeeded in finding a new tenant for a longer term at a higher rate but the second tenant also defaulted.

Issue: When a lessee of commercial space abandons the premises prior to the expiration of the lease, and the lessor relets the premises for a term extending beyond the expiration of the original lease and at a higher rent, does such reletting constitute a termination of the lease as a matter of law, thus freeing the first tenant from any claim for damages accruing subsequent to the reletting?

Rule: Reletting or attempting to relet by a commercial lessor at a higher rate and for a longer term than provided for in an original lease does not, as a matter of law, bar the lessor's claim for damages against a lessee who abandoned the premises.

Jaber v. Miller (1951)

Facts: The lessee, Jaber (defendant), transferred his lease to Norber & Son "for the remainder of the term of said lease." Norber & Son transferred the lease to Miller (plaintiff), who contended Jaber's transfer constituted a subletting, not an assignment, under the common law.

Issue: Is the intent of the parties determinative when deciding if a transfer of a lease constitutes an assignment or a sublease?

Rule: The intention of the parties governs in determining whether an instrument is an assignment or a sublease.

A.D. Juilliard & Co. v. American Woolen Co. (1943)

Facts: A.D. Juilliard & Co., leased property subject to a covenant obligating the lessee to pay rent, but not restricting assignments. The lease was assigned several times without any covenant requiring the assignor, in the event of default by the assignee, to assume the obligation to pay rent for the unexpired term, American Woolen, one of the companies in the chain of assignments, itself assigned to another party who defaulted. A.D. Juilliard & Co. contended that American Woolen was responsible for payment.

Issue: Is the assignee of a lease of real property liable for the payment of stipulated rent for the entire unexpired term of the lease, notwithstanding that the assignee did not agree to assume such obligation and assigned the lease to another party before the expiration of the term?

Rule: In the absence of an assumption by the assignee of an obligation to pay off the remainder of the lease, the liability of an assignee to the original lessor rests in privity of estate which is terminated by a new assignment of the lease made by the assignee.

Note: The original lessee always remains liable to the lessor, even if he assigns the lease.

Childs v. Warner Brothers Southern Theatres, Inc. (1931)

Facts: Childs leased premises imposing a covenant requiring its consent to an assignment by a lessee. The lessee, with Childs' consent, assigned the lease to Warner Brothers (defendant), Warner Brothers, in turn, attempted to assign the lease without Childs' consent.

Issue: If a lessor executes a lease to a given lessee, and the lease provides that the lessee shall not convey the lease nor sublet the premises without the written consent of the lessor, and thereafter, the lessor consents to an assignment of the lease, can such assignee subsequently make a valid reassignment of the lease without the consent of the lessor?

Rule: If a reasonable construction of a lease leads to the conclusion that a restriction against assignment and subletting operated upon the heirs and assigns of the lessee as well as on the lessee himself, the lessor, by consenting to one assignment, does not waive the restriction.

Sproul v. Gilbert (1961)

Facts: The plaintiffs held grazing privileges upon lands owned by the federal government. The state of Oregon attempted to levy a tax on these privileges pursuant to a statute requiring taxation of property owned by the federal government and held by a person "under lease or other interest less than a fee." The plaintiffs brought an action for declaratory judgment arguing that their grazing privileges could not be classified as "a lease or other interest less than a fee" and therefore were not subject to the type of tax required under the statute.

Issue: Does the granting of grazing privileges on land owned by the federal government constitute a lease agreement or merely a license?

Rule: A lease is a transfer of an interest in land and is characterized by a grant of a right to exclusive possession. A license, by contrast, is a revocable privilege to use land in the possession of another. The exclusiveness of the possessory interest, the character of the land, and degree of control that the lessee exercises over the land are the determinative factors in characterizing an agreement as either a lease or a license. In this case, grazing privileges were found to be a sufficiently possessory interest in the land to constitute a lease.

David Properties, Inc. v. Selk (1963)

Facts: Selk sold property to the defendant corporation, and the defendant allowed him to live on the land for over two months for a price of $1. When Selk failed to quit the premises after the agreed date, the defendant asked him to pay a monthly rent of $300.

Issue: What remedies may a landlord pursue when a tenant holds over after the term of the lease without responding to the landlord's demand that the tenant pay increased rent if the tenant continues in possession?

Rule: The landlord could choose either to claim damages for trespass in the amount of rental value or to bind the tenant to a new lease term.

Note: Courts are split on the duration of a tenancy so created.

Krasner v. Transcontinental Equities, Inc. (1979)

Facts: Kasner brought suit against several defendants for an unauthorized assignment of a lease in which he had a reversionary interest.

Issue: Is a tenant free to assign his leasehold interest in the absence of an express prohibition against assignment incorporated in the lease?

Rule: A lease agreement will be construed strictly against the drafter, usually the landlord, and a tenant will be free to assign the lease unless the lease itself prohibits it.

Kendall v. Ernest Pestana, Inc. (1985)

Facts: An express provision of a lease required the written consent of the defendant lessor before the plaintiff lessee could assign his interest. The defendant refused to consent to an assignment unless the assignee agreed to pay a higher rent.

Issue: May a commercial lessor unreasonably and arbitrarily withhold his consent to an assignment?

Rule: Where a commercial lease provides for assignment only with the prior consent of the lessor, such consent may be withheld only where the lessor has a commercially reasonable objection to the assignee or the proposed use.

Arbenz v. Exley, Watkins & Co. (1905)

Facts: Arbenz and the defendant had a written lease for a period of more than five years. It lacked a seal and therefore was considered a year-to-year tenancy, ending at the close of the calendar year. After the property was destroyed by fire, the defendant, on Oct. 31, 1898, sent Arbenz a letter stating "we have vacated the premises—and hereby surrender possession of same."

Issue: When is a notice of termination effective for a year-to-year tenancy?

Rule: To be an effective notice of termination of a year-to-year tenancy, notice must be given at least three months prior to the term's end and state a specific future date for termination.

Lindsey v. Normet (S.Ct 1972)

Facts: Oregon's Forcible and Wrongful Detainer Statute precluded consideration of a tenant's defenses in a landlord's action to recover possession of the demised premises. Lindsey argued that the statute violated Due Process.

Issue: Is it a violation of constitutional due process to prohibit a tenant, in a summary proceeding, from asserting as an affirmative defense a lessor's violation of the implied warranty of habitability?

Rule: (White J.) Since a tenant can initiate a separate action against a lessor, states can constitutionally restrict the issues to be addressed in summary proceedings.

Warshawsky v. American Automotive Products Co. (1956)

Facts: The defendant's landlord sued for rent due when the defendant failed to pay rent. The defendant asserted as a defense the fact that his use of the premises as set forth in the lease was thwarted because it was contrary to a zoning ordinance.

Issue: May a tenant defend against an action for rent on the grounds that the use to which he had contemplated putting the premises is prohibited by a zoning ordinance?

Rule: Where a lease is restricted to a legal use, a zoning ordinance prohibiting that use is not a defense to an action for rent.

The Liberty Plan Co. v. Adwan (1962)

Facts: The plaintiff lessor notified The Liberty Plan Co. that he would attempt to relet the premises that Liberty had vacated, but would continue to "hold you (Liberty) liable for loss of rent."

Issue: Is a tenant who vacates a leasehold released from liability when the landlord notifies the tenant of his intent to reenter and relet the premises?

Rule: When a tenant wrongfully abandons leased premises, a lessor may give notice to the tenant of his refusal to accept surrender and sublet the premises for the unexpired term.

Sommer v. Kridel (1977)

Facts: On May 19, 1972, the defendant James Kridel abandoned an apartment he had leased for a two-year period. Although the landlord had an opportunity to relet the apartment he chose not to do so. Instead he brought an action for payment of the entire rent that was due under the lease.

Issue: Is a landlord seeking damages from a defaulting tenant under a duty to make reasonable efforts to relet an apartment wrongfully vacated?

Rule: A landlord has a duty to make reasonable efforts to mitigate damages where he seeks to recover rents due from a defaulting residential tenant.

Hannan v. Dusch (1930)

Facts: The defendant, a landlord, entered into a lease with the plaintiff, Hannan. When the lease term was to begin the defendant's prior tenant wrongfully held over. The plaintiff argued that the lease contained an implied covenant obligating the defendant to take legal action to oust the holdover tenant.

Issue: Is a landlord who leases property without any express covenant as to delivery of possession required to oust trespassers and wrongdoers in order to allow for entry by the tenant at the beginning of the term?

Rule: Under the "American Rule," absent an agreement to the contrary, the landlord only has a duty to deliver legal possession and not actual possession. The responsibility of ousting holdover tenants rests with the new tenant.

Note: Case law is divided between the above stated "American Rule" and the "English Rule" which commands the opposite result.

Anderson Drive-in Theatre v. Kirkpatrick (1953)

Facts: Kirkpatrick; leased farmland to the defendant knowing that the defendant planned to erect a drive-in theater. After the lease was executed, the defendant discovered that the land was unsuitable for this purpose. When Kirkpatrick sued to recover rent, the defendant contended that Kirkpatrick breached an implied warranty that the land was fit for the contemplated use.

Issue: Does a lease contain an implied warranty that leased premises are fit for the purposes for which they are let?

Rule: There is no implied warranty that leased premises are fit for the purposes for which they are let.

Chambers v. The North River Line (1920)

Facts: The defendant company's lease contained a covenant obligating it to "maintain the said wharf in its present condition during continuance of this lease." Through no fault of the defendant company, the wharf was destroyed.

Issue: Is a tenant who covenants to "maintain" the premises obligated to rebuild destroyed property and liable for the rent on the lease?

Rule: A tenant who covenants to repair or maintain property is obligated, even if not at fault, to rebuild destroyed property and pay rent.

Barash v. Pennsylvania Terminal Real Estate Corp. (1970)

Facts: When the defendant lessor failed to adequately ventilate Barash's office during evening and weekend hours Barash refused to pay rent, but remained in possession of the leased premises.

Issue: Does a landlord's wrongful failure to supply a continuous flow of fresh air on evenings and weekends to offices leased by a tenant constitute an actual partial eviction relieving the tenant from the obligation to pay rent, or is it a constructive eviction requiring the tenant to abandon the premises before he may be relieved of the duty to pay rent?

Rule: An actual eviction occurs only when the lessor wrongfully ousts the tenant, either by physical expulsion or exclusion. A constructive eviction exists where, though there has been no physical expulsion or exclusion of the tenant, the landlord's wrongful acts substantially and materially deprive the tenant of the beneficial use and enjoyment of the premises. A tenant must abandon the premises to sustain a claim of constructive eviction.

Hilder v. St. Peter (1984)

Facts: The tenant leased an apartment from the defendant Stuart St. Peter that was in a terrible state of disrepair, and despite having ample notice of multiple health code violations the defendant failed to correct the problems. Instead of vacating the premises the plaintiff paid all rents due and then sued for reimbursement of rent paid, together with compensatory and punitive damages.

Issue 1: Does a tenant have to vacate the premises in reliance on the covenant of quiet enjoyment before he can be released from having to pay rent?

Rule 1: The implied warranty of habitability has made reliance on the covenant of quiet enjoyment virtually obsolete in residential leases. It applies to all residential leases and does not require the tenant to move out in order to avoid paying rent.

Issue 2: What remedies are available to a tenant when the landlord has breached the implied warranty of habitability?

Rule 2: The tenant may withhold future rent, seek damages in the amount of rent previously paid, seek damages for discomfort and annoyance, seek punitive damages, or make repairs himself and deduct their cost from future rent.

Jack Spring, Inc. v. Little (1972)

Facts: The lessor sued in a summary proceeding to recover possession of demised premises for nonpayment of rent. The court prohibited the defendant, Little, from presenting evidence of violations of an implied warranty of habitability as an affirmative defense.

Issue: May a tenant assert a landlord's violations of an implied warranty of habitability as a defense in a summary proceeding?

Rule: The Forcible Entry and Detainer Act does not bar presentation of issues that are germane to the lessor's claims in a judicial proceeding, such as violations of an implied warranty of habitability.

Dickhut v. Norton (1970)

Facts: The lessor sued for possession of the demised premises. In defense, the tenant, who had an oral month-to-month lease, answered that the landlord brought suit only because the tenant had earlier notified the authorities of the unsanitary conditions of the premises. The lower court dismissed the tenant's defense as immaterial.

Issue: May a tenant, in an unlawful detainer action, assert as a defense an allegation that the landlord's attempt to terminate the tenancy and evict the tenant was motivated by retaliation for the tenant's complaint to the health authorities of a housing code sanitary violation?

Rule: A landlord cannot terminate a tenancy at will or a month-to-month tenancy as a means of retaliation, simply because a tenant has reported an actual housing code violation.

Pennell v. City of San Jose (S.Ct. 1988)

Facts: A rent control ordinance enacted by the city of San Jose allowed a hearing officer to consider, among other factors, the "hardship to a tenant" when determining whether to approve a rent increase proposed by a landlord.

Issue: Does taking into consideration a tenant's hardship when reviewing a rent increase violate either the Takings Clause, equal protection, or due process?

Rule: (Rehnquist, C.J.) The ordinance does not violate the Due Process Clause because its purpose is to protect tenants from burdensome rent increases, which is a legitimate goal within the police power of the legislature. The Equal Protection Clause is not violated because distinguishing between landlords is rationally related to the purpose of the ordinance. Since there is no record of a rent increase actually being denied because of the ordinance, it is premature to decide whether the ordinance violates the Takings Clause.

Concurring in part, dissenting in part: (Scalia, J.) The ordinance effects a taking of property without just compensation because, while the other factors are rationally related to providing reasonable rents, the tenant hardship factor is aimed at a different social problem, one which the landlords did not cause. Thus, this problem should be borne by the public at large rather than by the landlords. In effect, the city is using rent regulation to establish a welfare program privately funded by those landlords who happen to have "hardship" tenants.

Borders v. Roseberry (1975)

Facts: At the time of the letting of the premises the tenant knew that the landlord, Roseberry, had not reinstalled the gutters used for excess water removal from the premises. Borders, the tenant's social guest, slipped on the ice which had accumulated as a result of the absence of gutters. He sued Roseberry in tort for his injuries.

Issue: May a tenant's social guest sue a landlord for negligence when both the landlord and the tenant knew of the defective condition?

Rule: When a landlord undertakes to make repairs to the premises he is only liable for tortious injury resulting therefrom when the tenant neither knows nor should know that the purported repairs have been negligently made or not made at all.

Kline v. 1500 Massachusetts Ave. Corp. (1970)

Facts: Sarah Kline was criminally assaulted and robbed by an intruder in the common hallway of an apartment house. She sued the defendant corporation in tort for damages.

Issue: Does a landlord have a duty to take steps to protect tenants from foreseeable criminal acts committed by third parties?

Rule: A landlord has the duty of taking protective measures to guard the entire premises and the areas under the landlord's control against the perpetration of criminal acts.

Kulawitz v. Pacific Woodenware & Paper Co. (1945)

Facts: The plaintiff leased space from the defendant in which he operated a furniture store. The lease contained a covenant not to compete, prohibiting the defendant from leasing other space to anyone planning to conduct the same type of business as the plaintiff. The defendant leased space to another who sold several of the same products as the plaintiff, and the plaintiff brought suit for violation of the restrictive covenant.

Issue: Is a tenant whose lease contains a noncompetition clause released from his obligations under the lease when his landlord breaches the agreement?

Rule: When a lessor breaches a noncompetition covenant the tenant is entitled to rescind the lease and is relieved of further rent liability.

Teitelbaum v. Direct Realty Co. (1939)

Facts: By the terms of his lease the lessee was to gain possession of certain premises on July 1, 1938, but the lessor's prior tenant wrongfully held over. The lessee brought suit for damages for failure to deliver possession of the premises.

Issue: Does a lessor have a duty, when the demised premises are wrongfully held by a third person, to take the necessary steps to put his lessee in possession?

Rule: If, at the time a lease begins, possession of the premises is held by a trespasser, there is no implied duty on the part of the lessor to oust the trespasser to enable the tenant to enter.

Franklin v. Brown (1889)

Facts: Franklin leased a furnished dwelling to Brown. The lease had no express covenant of habitability. Due to noxious odors emanating from adjoining premises, of which, neither Franklin nor Brown were aware at the time of the execution of the lease, Brown claimed that the premises were uninhabitable. Brown argued that, because the dwelling was furnished, Franklin impliedly covenanted they were fit for habitation. Franklin brought suit to recover rent payments.

Issue: Does a lessor who leases a furnished dwelling impliedly covenant against external defects detrimentally affecting habitability when the defects were unknown to the lessor at the time of the execution of the lease?

Rule: Absent fraud, an express warranty of habitability, or a covenant to repair, there is no implied covenant that premises are fit for occupation or are in safe condition.

Milheim v. Baxter (1909)

Facts: Baxter leased premises from Milheim who, as owner of the adjoining premises, was aware that the premises were used for "immoral" purposes. Upon discovery of the happenings next door Baxter moved out, claiming wrongful eviction based on a breach of the lease's implied covenant of quiet enjoyment.

Issues: May a tenant be relieved of all responsibility under a lease and recover damages when the landlord breaches the implied covenant of quiet enjoyment?

Rule: Absent a provision to the contrary, all leases contain an implied covenant of quiet enjoyment and any wrongful act willfully done by the lessor justifying the tenant's abandonment of the premises is a breach of said covenant, thereby constituting a constructive eviction.

Johnson v. O'Brien (1960)

Facts: While visiting the defendant's tenant, the plaintiff fell from a stairway sustaining injury.

Issue: Must a lessor, lacking actual knowledge of a latent defect but having information leading him to suspect a danger exists, inform the tenant of the danger?

Rule: When a landlord has information which would lead a reasonably prudent owner exercising due care to suspect that a danger exists on the leased premises at the time the tenant takes possession, and a tenant exercising due care would not discover the defect for himself, the landlord must disclose such information to the tenant.

Bowles v. Mahoney (1952)

Facts: Well after the lease was executed, Mahoney, a nephew of the lessee, was injured by the collapse of a retaining wall. The lessor of the premises, Mrs. Bowles, had built the wall.

Issue: Does a lessor have a duty to repair defects that develop after a lease is executed?

Rule: Absent any statutory or contractual duty, a lessor is not responsible for an injury resulting from a defect which developed during the term of a lease.

Faber v. Creswick (1959)

Facts: The Fabers leased premises from the defendant under a written lease providing that the defendant would "have the house . . . in good order and repair at the beginning of this lease." Mr. Faber was the only signatory to the lease. A few days after moving into the house, Mrs. Faber was injured when she stepped on plasterboard so situated as to look like part of the floor, though it actually concealed a portion of a stairway.

Issue: When a lessor assumes a duty to repair the premises is he liable in tort for injuries to third parties who have the tenant's consent to be on the premises?

Rule: If a landlord negligently performs the duty to repair that he had explicitly assumed, liability in tort arises for proximate consequential injuries suffered by both the tenant and third parties on the premises with the tenant's consent.

Louisiana Leasing Co. v. Sokolow (1966)

Facts: The lessor, Louisiana Leasing Co., included a provision in the lease stating that no ". . . tenant shall make or permit any disturbing noises in the building by himself, his family (etc)" and to so do "shall be deemed a substantial violation" of the lease. The Sokolows, a young couple with two children, resided in an apartment immediately above the Levins. The Levins complained of the noise emanating from the apartment above them and the Louisiana Leasing Co. brought suit to evict the Sokolows.

Issue: Pursuant to a covenant prohibiting noise, may a tenant be evicted because another tenant complains of noise?

Rule: In urban apartment buildings with lease provisions regulating noise a tenant who occupied the premises prior to another complaining tenant cannot be evicted if the noise coming from his apartment is neither excessive nor deliberate.

King v. Conney-Eckstein Co. (1913)

Facts: Conney-Eckstein Co. leased a wharf which the lessor covenanted "to keep in usual repair," King was injured by a loose plank and brought suit against Conney-Eckstein Co.

Issue: Is a lessee liable for injuries caused by defects in the premises when the lessor covenants to repair the premises?

Rule: Lessees who have control or occupancy of premises are liable for injuries caused by the defective or dangerous condition of the premises, where such defective or dangerous condition should have been known to and remedied by the occupying tenant, notwithstanding the lessor's covenant to repair.

Suydam v. Jackson (1873)

Facts: The defendant leased a store from the plaintiff for a three-year term. He subsequently vacated the premises after two years due to a leaking roof. The lease did not contain a covenant to repair. A statute permitted tenants to vacate and escape liability for rent if the premises should "be destroyed or be so injured by the elements ... as to be untenantable."

Issue: May a tenant be released from his responsibility to pay rent by the gradual deterioration of the premises he leased?

Rule: The duty to make ordinary repairs necessitated by normal wear and tear rests with the tenant.

Kennedy v. Kidd (1976)

Facts: Kidd had a periodic oral lease with Kennedy. Kennedy passed away in his apartment but his body was not discovered until a week later. Kidd had to refurbish the premises due to odors that emanated from Kennedy's decomposing body. She filed an action to recover damages from Kennedy's estate.

Issue: Is a tenant liable for all damages to rented premises other than those caused by ordinary wear and tear?

Rule: A lessee is only liable for deterioration or injuries to the premises caused by his own negligence.

Polack v. Pioche (1868)

Facts: The plaintiff leased premises to the defendant that were damaged by a flood. The flood was caused, in part, by an unusual volume of rainwater and, in part, by a third party's interference with the embankment of a reservoir. The lease imposed a general covenant to repair on the defendant, with the exception of "damages by the elements or acts of Providence."

Issue: How is an "act of the elements" defined for the purpose of establishing the relative duties of landlord and tenant.

Rule: An act to which human agency has in any way contributed cannot be considered an "act of the elements."

Melms v. Pabst Brewing Co. (1899)

Facts: Pabst Brewing Co., held a life estate in a quarter acre plot of land. It destroyed the building situated thereon and graded the land down to street level, thereby increasing the value of the property. The reversioners of the estate brought an action for damages for destruction of the building.

Issue: Is a life tenant always guilty of waste when he alters property in such a way that the identity of the property is changed?

Rule: In the absence of any express or implied contract to use the property for a specified purpose, or to return it in the same condition in which it was received, a radical and permanent change in surrounding conditions is always an important consideration when deciding whether a change in the identity of the property implemented by a life tenant constitutes waste.

Sigsbee Holding Corp. v. Canavan (1963)

Facts: The landlord sought to evict Canavan for replacing old cabinets with new ones.

Issue: Under what circumstances will a tenant be held liable for waste?

Rule: A tenant will be held liable for waste if he materially and permanently changes the nature and character of the building, even if he increases the value of the property by doing so.

Mallory Associates, Inc. v. Barving Realty Co. (1949)

Facts: Mallory Associates, Inc. who deposited $65,000 as security, alleged that Barving Realty Co. converted the deposit.

Issue: Is a New York statute addressing the rights and liabilities of landlords and tenants with respect to security deposits applicable when the demised property is not in New York State?

Rule: The New York statute regarding rent deposits is concerned with the security deposit, not the demised premises. Thus, it applies to funds deposited in New York as security under a contract of lease made in New York between corporations created in New York, even though the real property which is the subject matter of the contract is located elsewhere.

Fifty States Management Corp. v. Pioneer Auto Parts Inc. (1979)

Facts: Fifty States Management Corp. and Pioneer Auto Parts Inc., parties of equal bargaining strength, freely negotiated for the inclusion of a clause in their lease whereby the rent for the remainder of the lease term would be accelerated upon breach of tenant's covenant to pay rent. The lease's term was twenty years. Pioneer missed two consecutive monthly rental payments and Fifty States brought suit to collect on the remainder of the payments due under the lease.

Issue: Will equity intervene to prevent enforcement of a provision in a twenty-year lease between commercial parties providing for the acceleration of the rent due for the entire lease term upon the tenant's default in the payment of a monthly rental installment?

Rule: Absent fraud, overreaching or unconscionability, acceleration clauses in commercial leases are enforceable if the sum reserved for liquidated damages is no greater than the amount the tenant would have paid had he fully performed, and the tenant is entitled to possession upon payment.

Jamaica Builders Supply Corp. v. Buttelman (1960)

Facts: A lease between Buttelman and Jamaica Builders Supply Corp. contained a provision which stipulated that certain acts by the tenant were prohibited and would automatically terminate the tenancy and result in forfeiture of rent already paid in advance. When Buttelman held over after the expiration of his lease term the plaintiff corporation instituted summary proceedings to remove the tenant.

Issue: In determining whether a clause in a lease is a condition (requiring the landlord to take affirmative steps to terminate the tenancy) or a conditional limitation (an automatic termination of the lease upon the happening of some event) should the court rely solely on the pertinent clause standing alone?

Rule: When determining whether a clause in a lease is a condition or a conditional limitation courts examine not only the language in the clause itself but also the language of the entire lease in an attempt to ascertain the parties' intent. Because the courts disfavor forfeitures, a clause will be held to be a conditional limitation only if there is a clear and unambiguous intention that when an event happens, the lease, by its terms, comes to an end.

Jordan v. Talbot (1961)

Facts: Jordan, Talbot's lessee, instituted a forcible entry and detainer action when, after falling behind in her rent, Talbot entered her apartment and refused to allow her back in. The lease gave Talbot a right of reentry upon the breach of any condition in the lease.

Issue: Is a landlord's contractual right to reentry a defense to a tenant's action for forcible entry and detainer?

Rule: Regardless of who has the right to possession, a landlord, absent a voluntary surrender of the premises by the tenant, can enforce his right of reentry only by judicial process. A landlord may not reenter the premises by self-help.

Teodori v. Werner (1980)

Facts: The tenant, Werner, asserted that Teodori's breach of their lease's noncompetition clause was a valid defense to actions for ejectment and rent payments due.

Issue: Will a landlord's breach of a lease's noncompetition clause provide a tenant with a defense to the landlord's actions for ejectment and sums due?

Rule: Absent an agreement to the contrary, a tenant's rent obligation and a landlord's promise under a noncompetition clause are interdependent. Therefore, a tenant is relieved from his rent obligation if the landlord materially breaches one of his obligations under the lease.

Marini v. Ireland (1970)

Facts: Because the lease between Marini and Ireland lacked a covenant imposing a duty on the landlord to repair the premises, Marini contended that Ireland could not offset the cost of certain repairs that she had made against her rent.

Issue: May a tenant offset the cost of necessary repairs against rent owed?

Rule: Pursuant to an implied warranty of habitability, if a landlord fails, within a reasonable period of time, to make repairs and replacements of vital facilities necessary to maintain the premises in a livable condition, the tenant may cause the same to be done and deduct the cost thereof from future rents.

Lloyd v. Murphy (1944)

Facts: In August 1941, Lloyd leased to Murphy premises to be used solely for selling new cars and gasoline. Due to the start of the Second World War the government severely restricted sales of new automobiles. Despite Lloyd's willingness to waive the lease restriction, Murphy repudiated the lease.

Issue: What facts must be proved by a tenant seeking to avoid his rent obligation based on the doctrine of commercial frustration?

Rule: To successfully use the doctrine of commercial frustration, a tenant must prove that the risk of the frustrating event was not reasonably foreseeable and that the value of counterperformance by the landlord is totally or nearly totally destroyed.

Albert M. Greenfield & Co., Inc. v. Kolea (1976)

Facts: The plaintiff leased a building to the defendant for the purpose of operating a used car lot and repair shop. The building was subsequently destroyed by fire, and the plaintiff brought an action for rent payments remaining on the lease term.

Issue: Does the common law rule that the lessee must, absent an express provision to the contrary, continue to pay rent even if the leased premises are destroyed retain its viability in today's property law?

Rule: If there is no express allocation of risk within the lease and it is evident to the court that the true subject of the lease was a structure, and not the land upon which it stood, the court should relieve the parties of their respective obligations when the building no longer exists.

Leonard v. Autocar Sales & Service Co. (1945)

Facts: Leonard leased premises to the defendant corporation for a twenty-year term. The state temporarily condemned the premises. The defendant corporation vacated and refused to pay rent.

Issue: Is a tenant liable for rent during the time that the exclusive possession and temporary use of the leased premises has been taken by the government?

Rule: In order for a tenant to be excused from the payment of rent because of the condemnation of the demised premises, it is essential that the estate of the landlord be extinguished by the condemnation proceedings.

Lefrak v. Lambert (1976)

Facts: The Lamberts breached their lease by vacating the demised premises many months before its expiration. Lefrak, contending that a lessor has no duty to mitigate damages when a lessee breaches a lease, sought to recover seventeen months rent, covering the period during which the apartment remained vacant.

Issue: Does a lessor have a duty to mitigate damages when his tenant abandons the premises before the expiration of the lease?

Rule: A lessor must show that he attempted to mitigate damages by making a good faith effort to relet the premises within a reasonable time.

Note: The Appellate Division affirmed this judgment in 1978, but modified it to award the plaintiff damages for the entire seventeen months that the apartment remained vacant. The Appellate Division found it unnecessary to rule on the question of a landlord's duty to mitigate damages because of its finding that Lefrak had in fact made good faith efforts to relet the apartment.

Wright v. Braumann (1965)

Facts: The plaintiff and the defendant entered into an agreement to make a lease, contingent on the plaintiff's completion of a building. The defendant notified the plaintiff, prior to the premises being ready for occupancy, that he would not enter into a lease.

Issue: Does a lessor have a duty to mitigate damages when a lessee breaches a lease agreement?

Rule: A lessor has a duty to mitigate damages by making reasonable efforts to find another tenant.

Pines v. Perssion (1961)

Facts: Perssion agreed to lease a furnished house to Pines and three of his friends. When the lessees took possession of the house they found it uninhabitable. They moved out and sued to recover their deposit.

Issue: Do leases contain an implied warranty of habitability?

Rule: The old rule of no implied warranty of habitability in leases is inconsistent with current conditions and legislative policy. This covenant and a lessee's covenant to pay rent are interdependent.

Berman v. Jefferson (1979)

Facts: Cynthia Jefferson leased an apartment for one year from Berman & Sons Inc. For several months, through no fault of the landlord, she experienced sporadic failures of heat and hot water and consequently withheld a portion of one month's rent.

Issue 1: At what point after a landlord's material breach of the warranty of habitability is a tenant entitled to a rent abatement?

Rule 1: A tenant's obligation to pay rent abates as soon as a landlord is given notice that a violation exists. A tenant is not required to allow a reasonable time for the landlord to make repairs.

Issue 2: How does lack of fault on the part of a landlord impact on a tenant's remedy of rent abatement?

Rule 2: A tenant is entitled to a rent abatement for a material violation of the warranty of habitability whether the landlord is at fault or not.

Feld v. Merriam (1984)

Facts: Plaintiffs Peggy and Samuel Feld were tenants in a large apartment complex. While returning home one evening they were abducted from their parking garage by armed felons. Subsequently, they brought suit against the owners of the complex alleging a breach of a duty of protection.

Issue: Under what circumstances does a landlord have a duty to protect tenants from the foreseeable criminal acts of third persons?

Rule: Absent an agreement, a landlord has no duty to provide protection for his tenants from acts of third parties. However, if a landlord undertakes to provide security services, whether by agreement or voluntarily, he must perform the task in a reasonable manner. The duty is not that of an insurer but of reasonable care under the circumstances.

Habib v. Edwards (1965)

Facts: Habib sued Edwards for possession of premises that were leased to her on a month-to-month basis. He obtained a default judgment but Edwards moved to have it set aside due to excusable neglect of counsel. She also asserted the defense that Habib was merely retaliating because Edwards had previously reported housing code violations present on the property.

Issue: Does a tenant have a constitutional right to inform the authorities of housing code violations that can be asserted as a defense to a lessor's action to repossess?

Rule: A tenant has a constitutional right to inform the proper governmental authorities of violations of law, as well as the correlative right not to be injured or punished by the lessor or anyone else for having availed herself of her basic right to provide such information.

Note: The preceding was a trial court opinion. The case was remanded to the Landlord and Tenant Branch for a new trial. However, at trial the judge excluded evidence of retaliatory intent. The opinion that follows is the disposition of this case on appeal.

Edwards v. Habib (1967)

Facts: Habib sued Edwards for possession of premises that were leased to her on a month-to-month basis. He obtained a default judgment but Edwards moved to have it set aside due to excusable neglect of counsel. She also asserted the defense that Habib was merely retaliating because Edwards had previously reported housing code violations existing on the property.

Issue: Is evidence of a lessor's motive for evicting a tenant admissible?

Rule: In a month-to-month tenancy a notice by a landlord terminating the tenancy need give no reason whatsoever for the termination, and evidence as to the reason for the notice is inadmissible when, by the terms of the lease itself, the landlord may terminate for no reason at all.

Note: For the final disposition of this case, see *Edwards v. Habib* (1968) at p. 114 supra.

O'Callaghan v. Walter & Beckwith Realty Co. (1958)

Facts: O'Callaghan sustained an injury upon the lessor's premises. Her lease contained an exculpatory clause relieving the lessor of all liability for his negligent acts or omissions.

Issue: Is an exculpatory clause invalid in a residential lease?

Rule: An exculpatory clause in a residential lease is enforceable.

Sweney Gasoline & Oil Co. v. Toledo, Peoria & Western Railroad (1969)

Facts: Sweney Gasoline & Oil Co. leased property from the defendant railroad company. The property was damaged by the derailment of the lessor's train. The lease contained an exculpatory clause excluding lessor's liability for property damage caused by its negligence.

Issue: May lessors protect themselves by including exculpatory clauses in their leases?

Rule: Absent a contrary social policy or a social relationship militating against them, exculpatory clauses are enforceable.

Halet v. Wend Inv. Co. (1982)

Facts: Robert Halet brought this suit against Wend Investment Co. and Los Angeles County when his application for an apartment in a rental complex owned by Wend was denied pursuant to an adults-only rental policy. The complex was located on land leased to Wend by Los Angeles County.

Issue: Can an adults-only rental policy be violative of the Fourteenth Amendment, 42 U.S.C. § 1983, or the Fair Housing Act?

Rule: An adults-only rental policy can violate the Fourteenth Amendment and 42 U.S.C § 1983 only if State action is somehow involved in the policy. However, a violation of the Fair Housing Act can occur without State action if the policy leads to significant discriminatory effects.

Samuels v. Ottinger (1915)

Facts: Ottinger assigned his lease with the lessor's consent. The assignee, after paying one month's rent, defaulted on rent due for the next two years. The lessor sued Ottinger to recover the rent.

Issues: Is an original lessee absolved from liability to pay rent by an assignment when the assignee defaults on his obligation to pay the rent?

Rule: The obligation to pay rent remains with a lessee even after he assigns the lease to a third party.

Reid v. Wiessner & Sons Brewing Co. (1898)

Facts: Reid leased certain premises to Miller, who assigned the lease to Wiessner (defendant), who in turn assigned it to Jones. Jones failed to pay the rent due.

Issue: Does an assignee remain liable to a lessor when he is no longer in privity of estate with the lessor?

Rule: In the absence of an independent agreement, the liability of an assignee to the original lessor for rent is founded on privity of estate and such liability continues only so long as that privity exists.

Masury v. Southworth (1859)

Facts: The landlord leased real property to the lessee. The lease provided that the lessee would insure the building. The lessor's interest was assigned to the plaintiff and the lessee's interest was assigned to the defendant, who did not insure the leasehold.

Issue: Is a lessee's assignee bound by a covenant signed by the original lessor and lessee?

Rule: A covenant will bind an assignee if it benefits both parties to a lease, and the two original parties to the lease intended to have the covenant run with the land.

Davis v. Vidal (1912)

Facts: Dallas Brewery agreed to "sublet, assign and transfer" property to Vidal, who defaulted on his rent payments. Dallas Brewery had reserved the right to "reenter and repossess said premises" in the event Vidal failed to pay rent. The original lessor was Antoinette Davis.

Issue: Does a lessor have an action against a transferee who, subject to a right of reentry in the original lessee, assumed the obligations of a lease?

Rule: A sub-lease is created when an original lessee retains a reversionary interest in the demised premises. Since there is neither privity of estate nor privity of contract between the original lessor and the sub-tenant, the original lessor cannot maintain an action for rent against the sub-lessee.

Gruman v. Investors Diversified Services, Inc. (1956)

Facts: Gruman's lease with the defendant corporation prohibited assignment or subleasing of the demised premises without Gruman's consent. Although the premises were abandoned by the defendant before the term's end, the defendant found a suitable sub-tenant. Gruman refused to consent to the proposed sublease.

Issue: Must a lessor, whose lease prohibits assigning or subleasing the premises without his consent, mitigate damages by accepting a suitable subtenant, or can the lessor arbitrarily refuse to accept the proffered subtenant?

Rule: Absent a contractual clause prohibiting a lessor from unreasonably withholding consent, the lessor may arbitrarily refuse to accept a suitable subtenant.

Dress Shirt Sales Inc. v. Hotel Martinique Associates (1963)

Facts: Dress Shirt Sales Inc. leased space from the defendant hotel. It vacated the leased premises prior to the term's end but continued to pay rent. The lease prohibited subleasing without the defendant's consent. The defendant refused to accept a sub-tenant found by Dress Shirt Sales. The two parties reached a settlement and agreed to terminate the lease, whereupon the defendant leased the premises, at a higher rent than he had with Dress Shirt Sales, to the party previously rejected.

Issue: Where no provision to the contrary is in the lease, may a lessor arbitrarily withhold consent to a subletting of the demised premises?

Rule: Unless the lease provides that the lessor's consent shall not be unreasonably withheld, a provision against subleasing without the lessor's consent permits the lessor to refuse arbitrarily for any reason or no reason.

Fetting Manufacturing Jewelry Co. v. Waltz (1930)

Facts: Fetting Manufacturing (defendant) was a tenant for a term of years. It remained on the premises for almost a month after the expiration of its tenancy. Waltz insisted that the defendant, by holding over, acquiesced to a lease for a full year.

Issue: Is a holdover tenant liable for the rent for an entire new term?

Rule: A tenant who holds over becomes, at the lessor's election, either a trespasser in the sense of being wrongfully in possession, or a tenant for another complete term subject to the terms of the original lease.

Mason v. Wierengo's Estate (1897)

Facts: Wierengo informed his landlord, Mason, of his intent to vacate the demised premises upon the expiration of the lease. However, Wierengo died and the premises were not vacated on time. Mason sued Wierengo's estate for the rent of a full new term.

Issue: When a tenant holds over, is the presumption of a renting for another term rebutted by the holdover tenant's intent to vacate on time?

Rule: Absent some express or implied consent on lessor's part to a holding over on new terms, the tenant's intention to vacate on time does not affect the right of the lessor to elect to treat the holding over as a renewal of the lease for a new term.

Margosian v. Markarian (1934)

Facts: Margosian, a tenant at will, was injured by a fall from a defective stairway on the demised premises. Prior to the fall, however, her husband received a notice to quit for nonpayment of rent.

Issue: May a tenant at will maintain a negligence action against the lessor for an injury sustained after the tenant received a notice to quit?

Rule: A tenant at will receiving notice to quit becomes a tenant at sufferance to whom a lessor owes only a duty to neither wantonly nor willfully cause injury.

Gower v. Waters (1926)

Facts: Waters used force to enter the demised premises and regain possession after serving Gower with written notice to quit. Gower, a tenant at sufferance, sued for trespass.

Issue: May a tenant at sufferance maintain a trespass action against his landlord who, using no more force than may be necessary to effect an entrance, enters to dispossess him?

Rule: A landlord may enter a leasehold, using no more force than is necessary, to expel a tenant at sufferance.

Jones v. Taylor (1909)

Facts: Believing he had leased a farm for the year beginning March 6, 1906, Jones (defendant) refused to vacate the farm when requested to do so by the lessor. According to the applicable statute, a holdover tenant was liable for double rent.

Issue: May a tenant use a claim of right as a defense against a forcible detainer action that imposes double rent as a penalty?

Rule: If a tenant in good faith reasonably believed that he had a valid contract giving him the right to remain in possession of the rented premises upon payment of the agreed rent and, therefore, resisted efforts to dispossess him, he is not liable for double rent.

Sigrol Realty Corp. v. Valcich (1961)

Facts: The defendant and others rented waterfront land from Wilmore who sold his interest to Sigrol Realty Corp. The defendant built bungalows on the leasehold which could be removed without injury to either them or the land.

Issue: Do chattels attached to realty remain personalty or become realty?

Rule: Chattels, after attachment to realty, continue to be personalty, or become realty in accordance with the agreement between the chattel owner and the landowner.

In Re Allen Street and First Avenue (1931)

Facts: New York City condemned real property to which the tenant (Ershowsky) had annexed chattels. The tenant and landlord agreed that the annexed chattels, though becoming fixtures, remained the tenant's personalty.

Issue: Must the city, when a tenant and landlord agree to treat an annexed chattel as the tenant's personalty, compensate the tenant for the value of his personalty when the demised property is condemned?

Rule: When a tenant and landlord agree to treat the tenant's annexed chattel as his personalty, the city must, to the extent the value of the real property as a whole is enhanced by the fixtures annexed thereto, compensate the tenant.

Cameron v. Oakland County Gas & Oil Co. (1936)

Facts: Tenant leased real property on which he erected a building for the purpose of operating an oil and gas station. The lease was silent about the ownership of the building at the end of the leasehold.

Issue: Does a structure, regardless of its form or size, built by a tenant in furtherance of his trade or business, remain the tenant's personalty?

Rule: Regardless of their form or size, trade fixtures remain the tenant's personalty, removable by him at the lease's expiration.

Old Line Life Insurance Co. of America v. Hawn (1937)

Facts: The tenant, Ray Hawn, removed structures he erected to further his agricultural business just before proceedings were completed to foreclose on his leasehold.

Issue: May a tenant who is engaged in agriculture on foreclosed land remove structures that were erected by him to further his business?

Rule: When a mortgagor is not prohibited from leasing the mortgaged property, and the land is leased to one who installs trade fixtures for temporary purposes connected with his business, removal of such fixtures without injury to the land is allowed over objections by the mortgagee.

Garner v. Gerrish (1984)

Facts: Garner's lease with Gerrish explicitly stated that Gerrish had the option to terminate the agreement at any time. Garner, assuming he had the power to do the same, brought suit to evict Gerrish.

Issue: Does a lease which grants the tenant the right to terminate the agreement at will create a determinable life tenancy or merely establish a tenancy at will?

Rule: A lease that expressly gives the right to terminate the agreement only to the tenant creates a determinable life tenancy.

Crechale & Polles, Inc. v. Smith (1974)

Facts: The plaintiff leased premises to Smith, the defendant, who, prior to the term's end, requested monthly extensions of the lease. Initially the plaintiff refused to extend the lease but later changed his mind and attempted to hold Smith to a full renewal.

Issue: May a landlord who initially elects to treat a holdover tenant as a trespasser later elect to treat the holdover as a lease renewal?

Rule: When a tenant continues in possession of the premises after the expiration of his lease term the landlord has the option of either treating him as a trespasser or as a tenant under the previous terms. However, having chosen one of the two options, the landlord may not change his mind and pursue the other.

Township of Sandyston v. Angerman (1975)

Facts: By agreement with the National Park Service, the defendants Mr. and Mrs. Angerman had exclusive, private use of a house on public land for a fixed period, though the Park Service reserved the right to terminate the agreement. In lieu of a rent payment the Angermans were obligated to restore the house. Arguing that the defendants were lessees, as opposed to licensees, the plaintiffs sued to collect taxes.

Issue: Does an agreement permitting exclusive use of a publicly owned house for a fixed period of time in exchange for a promise to restore the premises constitute a lease or a license?

Rule: A grant of exclusive possession of property for a fixed period of time constitutes a lease, whereas a license is merely a personal privilege to use the land of another for some particular purpose or in some specific way. A license is therefore a much more tenuous interest than a lease.

United States v. Starrett City Assocs. (1988)

Facts: "Starrett City," the largest housing development in the nation, sought to maintain a racial distribution within the community. It adopted a procedure which caused minority applicants to wait much longer than white applicants for apartments, even though the latter occupied only a small percentage of the applicant pool.

Issue: Do housing policies that disproportionately affect minorities violate the Fair Housing Act?

Rule: The Fair Housing Act does not allow the use of rigid racial quotas of indefinite duration to maintain a fixed level of integration by restricting minority access to scarce and desirable rental accommodations otherwise available to them.

Ernst v. Conditt (1964)

Facts: The plaintiffs original lease with Rogers was renegotiated between the parties to allow the defendant, Conditt, to take over the leased premises from Rogers. The modified lease provided that Rogers would "sublet" the premises to Conditt and be personally liable if Conditt failed to pay the rent.

Issue: Are the words "sublet" and "subletting" conclusive of the construction to be placed on a document when determining if it was a sublease or an assignment?

Rule: When determining if a document is a sublease or an assignment the words actually used by the parties are not dispositive. The parties' intent, gleaned from the whole instrument and the surrounding circumstances, is controlling.

Berg v. Wiley (1978)

Facts: The defendant, pursuant to a lease provision allowing him to retake possession of the premises upon breach of any terms of the lease, locked out the plaintiff, Berg, and relet the premises. The plaintiff subsequently brought an action for wrongful eviction.

Issue: May a landlord resort to self-help to regain possession of leased premises?

Rule: If a tenant claims possession of the premises, and has neither abandoned nor voluntarily surrendered them, then the only course of action open to the landlord is to resort to judicial process.

Note: The above stated approach is not yet the majority position.

Reste Realty Corp. v. Cooper (1969)

Facts: After experiencing serious recurrent flooding and submitting numerous complaints to her landlord, Cooper vacated her leased premises and refused to honor her lease. The plaintiff brought suit to recover the remaining rent due under the lease.

Issue: Does a tenant have the right to vacate the premises when the landlord breaches the covenant of quiet enjoyment?

Rule: Where there is a covenant of quiet enjoyment, express or implied, and it is breached substantially by the landlord, the doctrine of constructive eviction allows the tenant to vacate the premises. However, the tenant must leave within a reasonable time after his right to vacate comes into existence. What constitutes a reasonable time depends largely on the particular circumstances of the case.

Becker v. IRM Corp. (1985)

Facts: The plaintiff, a tenant in an apartment complex owned by the IRM Corp., sustained serious injuries when he fell against a shower door that was made of untempered glass. He sued the defendant in negligence and strict liability.

Issue 1: What is the nature of a residential landlord's liability for injuries sustained by a tenant as a result of a latent defect on the premises?

Rule 1: A landlord engaged in the business of leasing dwellings is strictly liable in tort for injuries resulting from a latent defect in the premises when the defect existed at the time the premises were let to the tenant.

Issue 2: Does a residential landlord owe his tenants a duty of inspection of the premises before they are leased?

Rule 2: A landlord, in the exercise of due care, has a duty to conduct a reasonable inspection of the premises at the time of letting, whether he has knowledge of a defective condition or not.

Cromwell Assocs. v. Mayor and Council of Newark (1985)

Facts: The City of Newark had a rent control ordinance which prohibited rent increases greater than twenty-five percent during any twelve-month period. The plaintiff, an owner of a large apartment complex, claimed that the ordinance denied him a constitutionally mandated fair rate of return.

Issue: Is an ordinance which places a maximum limitation on annual increases, including increases granted pursuant to the hardship provision of the ordinance, constitutionally permissible?

Rule: When the maximum rent increase allowable by a rent control ordinance is insufficient to allow an efficient operator a fair rate of return, the ordinance is unconstitutional on its face.

Chicago Board of Realtors, Inc. v. City of Chicago (1987)

Facts: A group of property owners challenged the constitutionality of an ordinance enacted by the Chicago City Council, which codified the warranty of habitability. The new law established new responsibilities for landlords and gave more legal rights to tenants.

Issue: What are some relevant economic and policy concerns at issue when dealing with landlord/tenant ordinances?

Rule: (Posner, J.) A strong case can be made for the unreasonableness of the ordinance. The implication is that the initial consequence will be to reduce the resources landlord have to devote to improving the quality of housing, higher rents as well as The increased cost to landlords will result in higher rents, largely hurting the people the ordinance was intended to help, the poor, and newer tenants.

Note: The majority opinion, which dealt with a constitutional analysis of the ordinance, was not included in a casebook.

CHAPTER 6 NUISANCE

I. **NATURE OF A NUISANCE**
    A nuisance is an interference with a person's use and enjoyment of his land (private nuisance), or an interference with a right common to the general public (public nuisance).

    Examples: Offensive odors, loud noises, improper or unlawful uses of land.

    A. Interest Protected
        A person's use and enjoyment of his property (trespass only protects possession).

    B. Intent Requirement
        Nuisance liability can arise either from intentional acts which unreasonably interfere with another's use and enjoyment of land or from negligent, reckless, or ultrahazardous conduct.

II. **PUBLIC NUISANCE**
    An interference with a right that is common to the general public or community.

    Examples: Blocking a public highway, polluting a municipal beach, violating a local statute, engaging in illegal activities.

    A. Elements

        1. Injury is to the public at large.

        2. Harm must be substantial.
           Unlike trespass, where nominal damages are awarded even if no harm is done, a nuisance action requires proof of actual damages.

    B. If an individual plaintiff wants to recover damages that he suffered from a public nuisance, he must show that he suffered a different kind of harm than the public (not just more of the same harm).

        Example: The defendant blocks a road, delaying all commuters, and the plaintiff suffers a heart attack because of his irritation.

III. PRIVATE NUISANCE
A substantial and unreasonable interference with another's use or enjoyment of his land.

A. Elements

1. The plaintiff must have a possessory interest in the land.
A person who is residing with his friend cannot sue a factory that pollutes his friend's lawn. However, a tenant has a sufficient possessory interest.

2. The interference must be substantial.

a. A nominal injury is not enough.

b. Whether an interference is substantial is determined by its effect on an average person. An extra-sensitive individual does not recover.

Example: The plaintiff cannot stand cats. No nuisance will be found if the defendant, his neighbor, acquires three cats.

3. The defendant's interference must either be intentional and unreasonable or negligent, reckless, or ultrahazardous.

a. In assessing reasonableness a court will balance the harm to the plaintiff against the benefits of the defendant's conduct.

Example: The defendant's oil refinery may cause pollution, but oil is a necessary commodity.

b. The Restatement (2d) suggests an alternative test, providing that plaintiffs should also be reimbursed for a substantial interference if the interference is unreasonable, and greater than one should be required to bear without compensation.

B. To determine whether or not an activity constitutes a private nuisance, the court will consider the following factors:

1. The character of the neighborhood (i.e., is the defendant's activity appropriate to its surroundings?).

2. Land values.

3. The nature of the parties.

4. The type of nuisance.

    a. Nuisance "per se"
       Illegal no matter where it is done.

       Example: A factory spills toxic chemicals.

    b. Nuisance "per accidens"
       Nuisance only because of surroundings.

       Example: An oil refinery in the middle of a residential neighborhood.

IV. REMEDIES
A plaintiff has three possible remedies against a nuisance:

A. Abatement by Self-Help
In some cases a plaintiff is allowed to use minimal force to cure the nuisance himself if the defendant refuses to do so.

B. Injunction
An injunction will only be granted if the plaintiff succeeds in proving that his injuries outweigh the benefit to the community from the defendant's activity (balancing test).

C. Damages

    1. Temporary
    Compensation for past harm. The plaintiff must bring successive actions if the interference continues.

    2. Permanent
    Compensation for past and future harm. The plaintiff needs to bring only one action. Generally permanent damages are awarded in cases where the nuisance will be permanent but an injunction is not issued.

D. Mnemonic: **AID**

    1. **A**batement by self-help

2. Injunction

3. Damages

V.   DEFENSES

A.   "Coming to the nuisance"
This is really a variation on the "assumption of risk" doctrine.

1. Old Rule
The presence of the defendant's enterprise in an area prior to the plaintiff's arrival constituted a complete defense to a nuisance action, even if the defendant's activity substantially interfered with the plaintiff's use and enjoyment of his land.

2. Restatement (2d)
"Coming to the nuisance" is only one factor to look at in the balancing test.

B.   Conduct of Others
When several parties combine to produce a nuisance, each party is liable only for the damages it actually caused.

C.   Contributory Negligence
Only applies if the plaintiff claims that the defendant negligently created the nuisance.

D.   Legislative Authority
Compliance with local zoning laws and regulations is persuasive, though not conclusive, evidence that an activity was not a nuisance.

CASE CLIPS

Rose v. Chaikin (1982)

Facts: The Roses sought to enjoin the defendants from operating a noisy windmill in a residential area.

Issue: Can noise alone constitute a private nuisance?

Rule: Noises that injuriously affect the health and comfort of ordinary people to an unreasonable extent can, considering all the circumstances, constitute a private nuisance.

Boomer v. Atlantic Cement Co. (1970)

Facts: Individual property owners brought suit against the Atlantic Cement Company requesting damages and an injunction. They alleged that in the course of its operation the cement plant was emitting dirt, smoke, and vibrations which were causing injury to their property.

Issue: Must a court grant an injunction whenever substantial damage results from the operation of a nuisance?

Rule: If the court, after balancing the equities, determines that an injunction would impose a grossly disproportionate economic loss on the enterprise that is creating the nuisance, it may allow the enterprise to pay permanent damages to the aggrieved property owners in lieu of an injunction.

Spur Indus., Inc. v. Del E. Webb Development Co. (1972)

Facts: Del E. Webb Development Co. developed a huge tract of land for residential purposes and subsequently sued Spur Industries in a nuisance action to enjoin further operation of its large cattle feedlot located nearby. The plaintiff alleged that the odors emanating from the feedlot constituted both a public and a private nuisance to the people living in their newly constructed homes. Del E. Webb further alleged that the odors were substantially hurting sales.

Issue 1: When the operation of a business is lawful in the first instance, but becomes a nuisance by reason of the encroachment of a nearby residential area, may the business be enjoined from further operation?

Rule 1: A change in the composition of the area surrounding a business may cause the business to become a nuisance subject to being enjoined from further operation.

Issue 2: Is a developer of a new residential area in a previously agricultural one required to indemnify the operator of a business which has been enjoined from further operation due to the actions of the developer?

Rule 2: A developer who, with foreseeability, converts a previously agricultural or industrial area into a residential one, thereby necessitating an injunction against a lawful business, must indemnify the owner of the business for a reasonable amount of the cost of moving or shutting down.

Bove v. Donner-Hanna Coke Corp. (1932)

Facts: Bove bought land near an industrial area and built a residence there. Subsequently the defendant built a coke oven across the street which Bove sought to enjoin as a private nuisance.

Issue: Although a particular enterprise, claimed to be a nuisance, began operations after a residence was built, must the enterprise be enjoined when the residence was built in an area suited for and already used for industrial purposes?

Rule: Equity will not issue an injunction when the complainant claims that her peace and comfort have been disturbed by a situation which existed, at least to some extent, at the very time complainant bought her property and where it was foreseeable that the condition would worsen.

Morgan v. High Penn Oil Co. (1953)

Facts: The plaintiffs brought suit against the High Penn Oil Company, alleging that its oil refinery was a nuisance because it emitted noxious gasses in close proximity to the plaintiffs' property.

Issue: For a claim of nuisance to be actionable, must the alleged tort-feasor, if conducting a legal enterprise, have behaved negligently?

Rule: A nuisance exists when a person's conduct substantially interferes with another's interest in the use and enjoyment of his land, whether such interference is the result of negligent conduct or not.

Estancias Dallas Corp. v. Schultz (1973)

Facts: The air conditioning unit of the defendant's apartment complex produced such high levels of noise that the Schultzes, owners of adjoining property, brought suit for injunctive relief.

Issue 1: When facts constituting a private nuisance are found by the judge or jury, must there be a further balancing of the equities involved?

Rule 1: Before injunctive relief can be granted the court must balance the injury to the defendant or the general public if an injunction is issued against the injury to the complainant if an injunction is denied.

Issue 2: Under what circumstances will a court, after balancing the equities, refuse to enjoin a private nuisance?

Rule 2: An injunction prohibiting a nuisance will be denied only when it is found that the continued operation of the nuisance is *strictly necessary* for the benefit of others.

CHAPTER 7 PRIVATE LAND-USE ARRANGEMENTS

I. EASEMENTS

A. Definition

An easement is a nonpossessory interest in another's land. Easements benefit one parcel of land, the *dominant* tenement, and burden another, the *servient* tenement.

1. Affirmative Easement

   Entitles the easement holder to enter the servient tenement for a specified purpose.

2. Negative Easement

   Entitles the holder to compel the possessor of the servient tenement to refrain from using his property in a specified manner.

3. Easement Appurtenant

   Benefits the holder in his use and enjoyment of a particular parcel of land.

4. Easement in Gross

   The benefit to the holder is personal and independent of his use and enjoyment of a particular parcel of land.

5. Profit

   A right to enter another's land to remove its product, such as minerals or crops.

B. Creation

An easement may be created in any of the following ways:

1. Easement by Express Grant

   a. A written conveyance may expressly grant or reserve an easement, but it must be reasonably clear regarding the scope of the easement. Express easements must comply with the statute of frauds.

   b. Expressly granted easements will be valid if the parties unambiguously include the following elements:

    i. Location

    ii. Dimensions

    iii. Special uses allowed or disallowed

2. Easement by Implication
In order for an easement by implication to arise, the dominant and servient estates must have been owned by the same person at some earlier time.

Requirements:

a. The use, claimed to be an easement by implication, must have existed prior to the time when the two estates were severed from each other.

b. It must also have been apparent and continuous prior to the severance.

c. Lastly, it must be reasonably necessary for the use and enjoyment of the dominant tenement.

Note: When the original owner claims that he impliedly reserved an easement at the time of severance a showing of strict necessity is required, whereas a lesser showing of necessity is required when a grantee claims an implied easement.

3. Easement by Necessity
Will arise only if the two parcels of land were, at one time, owned by the same person. No prior use is required, but a showing of strict necessity is mandatory.

Example: A parcel of land is so situated that it is impossible for the owner to have access to a road without a right of way across someone else's property.

4. Easement by Prescription

a. An easement by prescription will arise when the claimant's use is open, notorious, and continuous for the period of time required by the statute of limitations. The statute of limitations will begin to run when the servient tenement's owner gains a cause of action against the adverse user.

b. Easements by prescription are "close relatives" of adverse possession, and similar rules regarding the disability and tacking doctrines will apply.

5. Mnemonic: **E**asements **I**ncorporate **P**eople's **N**eeds

   a. **E**xpress Grant

   b. **I**mplication

   c. **P**rescription

   d. **N**ecessity

C. Scope of Easements

   1. Prior location, dimension, and special uses determine the scope of implied and prescriptive easements.

   2. The scope of an easement by necessity is strictly confined to the necessity.

   3. Easements may be enlarged by prescription.

   4. Reasonably foreseeable normal changes in use will be permitted if the resultant increased burden on the servient tenement is not unreasonable.

   5. The servient tenement's owner may grant an identical easement to a third party if the granted easement is not inconsistent with the original easement holder's interest.

D. Transfer of Easements

   1. An easement appurtenant automatically passes to the new owner upon conveyance of either the dominant or the servient tenement, unless the parties agree otherwise.

   2. If the servient tenement is subdivided or conveyed in whole or in part, the burden of an easement appurtenant remains with those

portions of the property, subdivided or conveyed, that are subject to the easement.

3. Except for commercial easements, an easement in gross is generally not alienable.

E.   Termination of Easements
Easements may be terminated in the following ways:

1. Written release

2. Prescription

3. Abandonment
The holder must manifest an intent by conduct (not words alone) to permanently discontinue using the easement.

4. Merger (i.e., common ownership of the servient and dominant tenement).

5. When the purpose for the original creation of the easement no longer exists.

6. When creating document prescribes conditions governing the easement's duration.

7. Forfeit (i.e., the servient tenement's burden dramatically increases and cannot be alleviated).

8. When the easement is by necessity and the necessity no longer exists.

9. Estoppel (i.e., the owner of the servient tenement changes his position in reliance on the words or conduct of the easement holder).

II.   LICENSE

A.   Generally
A license is a privilege or right of a licensee to enter or use the property of the licensor.
Elements:

1. The creation of a license is not subject to the statute of frauds.

2. A license is traditionally inalienable.

3. A licensor may revoke a license at will by an express or implied manifestation of an intent to so do.

4. A licensee may surrender a license at will.

B. Revocation by Operation of Law
A license will be revoked by operation of law if:

1. The licensor dies.

2. The licensor conveys the subject property.

3. The licensee attempts to transfer the license.

C. Irrevocable Licenses

1. When an easement is improperly created (e.g., orally) and the holder made substantial expenditures in reliance on the invalid easement, a license results. A licensor will be estopped from revoking a license so created to the extent necessary to protect the licensee's reliance interest.

2. A license coupled with an interest is irrevocable to the extent necessary to protect that interest.

    Example: A licensee has a chattel on the licensor's land. The licensor cannot revoke the license in an attempt to prevent the licensee from entering his land to reclaim the chattel.

D. Public Events
Paying an entry fee (e.g., to play golf) or buying a ticket to an event (e.g., to the movies) creates a revocable license. If a license is improperly revoked by a licensor, the licensee may sue for breach of contract but he will not have any remedies under the laws of property.

III. REAL COVENANTS

A. Generally

A covenant running with the land (i.e., a real covenant) is a contract between two landowners, binding the successor in interest of each, that restricts one owner's use of his land (the burdened estate) in a manner benefiting the other's land (the benefited estate). Covenants may be either affirmative or negative.

B.   Requirements for a covenant to run with the land.

1. Running of the Burden

   a.   The statute of frauds must be satisfied.

   b.   The promise between the original parties must be enforceable.

   c.   The original parties must have intended that the promise bind their respective successors in interest.

   d.   A buyer of the burdened estate must have notice of the covenant prior to acquiring his interest.

   e.   The covenant must "touch and concern" the land.

      i.   A covenant "touches and concerns" a particular parcel of land if the burden or benefit imposed by the covenant is intimately tied to the land.

      ii. The covenant must "touch and concern" both the burdened and benefited estates in order for the burden to run with the land. However, some courts will allow a burden to run with the land even if the benefit is in gross.

   f.   There must be both horizontal and vertical privity of estate.

      i.   Horizontal privity exists when the covenant is incident to a conveyance of an interest in the burdened property. Horizontal privity is absent if two property owners simply agree to restrict the use of their respective property.

      ii. Vertical privity exists when the present owners of the burdened and benefited property have a certain relationship to their predecessors in interest. In order for a burden to run with the land, an assignee must acquire the entire interest in the estate.

Example: An assignee acquiring a life estate from his predecessor in title, who held a fee simple absolute, does not comply with the vertical privity requirement.

2. Running of the Benefit

   a. The statute of frauds must be satisfied.

   b. The promise between the original parties must be enforceable.

   c. The original parties must have intended that the benefit run to subsequent assignees.

   d. Notice is *not* required for the benefit to run.

   e. The covenant must "touch and concern" the land.
      It is sufficient that the covenant "touch and concern" only the benefited land.

   f. There need only be vertical privity of estate.

      i. There must be privity of estate between the assignee and the original promisee. However, the assignee need not succeed to the identical estate of his predecessor in interest.

      ii. Horizontal privity is not required.

3. The remedy for breach of a covenant is *damages.*

IV. EQUITABLE SERVITUDES

A. Generally
   An equitable servitude is an equitable interest of one property owner (the benefited estate) in the land of another (the burdened estate). Privity is not required to create an equitable servitude.

B. Elements

For an equitable servitude to bind a subsequent purchaser, the following requirements must be met:

1. Compliance with the statute of frauds.
   However, negative equitable servitudes may be implied in cases of restricted residential subdivisions, carried out pursuant to a general scheme.

2. The parties creating the servitude must intend to benefit a particular parcel or parcels of land.

3. The promisor's successor in interest must have notice, actual or constructive.

4. The burden must "touch and concern" the burdened estate.

C. Termination
   Equitable servitudes may be terminated in any of the following ways:

   1. Release

   2. Prescription

   3. Merger (i.e., the burdened and benefited parcels become commonly owned.)

   4. Abandonment
      The beneficiary must, by conduct, manifest an intent to permanently discontinue using the servitude.

   5. Government action (e.g., condemnation)

   6. Conditions change to such an extent that the purpose of the servitude is no longer furthered by its continued existence.

D. Unenforceable Equitable Servitude
   The following may prevent enforcement of an equitable servitude:

   1. Laches (delay in bringing suit).

   2. Plaintiff is estopped.

3. Plaintiff has unclean hands (plaintiff has himself committed a violation of a similar servitude).

4. The servitude's purpose is against public policy.

5. Plaintiff has tolerated similar violations of the servitude.

E.   General Scheme Doctrine
When a developer subdivides a tract of land, putting restrictive covenants on some, but not all, of the parcels, implied reciprocal servitudes arise. The grantees of each of the plots of land so subdivided may enforce the restrictive covenant against each other, whether the covenant was expressly in their deed or not, provided that the following conditions are met:

1. The subdivision was carried out pursuant to a general scheme.

2. The grantees seeking enforcement purchased their lots in reliance on their right to enforce the restrictive covenant.

3. The grantee against whom enforcement is sought had actual or constructive notice that the land may be subject to a restrictive covenant.

F.   Equitable servitudes are enforced through *injunctive* relief.

CASE CLIPS

Mitchell v. Castellaw (1952)

Facts: A grantor conveyed two of her three lots and, without using terms of art, reserved an express easement on one of the lots conveyed. Castellaw, the grantor's devisee, sued to establish the easement's validity.

Issue: Are words of inheritance or other words of art essential to a valid reservation of an appurtenant easement?

Rule: Neither words of inheritance nor other words of art are essential to the valid reservation of an appurtenant easement, even one of unlimited duration.

Willard v. First Church of Christ Scientist (1972)

Facts: Petersen bought land which was subject to an easement reserved for the benefit of the defendant, a third party to the transaction. He then sold the land to Willard with no mention of the easement in the deed. Willard subsequently brought suit to quiet title.

Issue: May a grantor reserve an easement for the benefit of a third party?

Rule: A grantor's intent is dispositive in the interpretation of his conveyance. Therefore, if there is enough evidence to indicate that the grantor intended to reserve an easement for the benefit of a third party the easement will be upheld.

Note: Jurisdictions are split on this issue with some courts adhering to the old common law rule that a grantor may not reserve an easement for the benefit of a third party.

Midland Valley Railroad Co. v. Arrow Indus. Mfg. Co. (1956)

Facts: Midland Valley Railroad Co. and Arrow Industrial Mfg. Co. both acquired their land from a common grantor. The grant to the plaintiff Midland Valley Railroad Co. conveyed by deed "a strip of land for a right of way" located across land now owned by the defendant corporation. The defendant corporation asserted that the grant created an easement rather than an estate in fee. Pursuant to Oklahoma statute every estate conveyed by deed was in fee simple, unless limited by express language.

Issue: Is an estate in land conveyed by deed without language of express limitation an estate in fee simple or merely an easement?

Rule: The intent of the parties to a conveyance, gleaned from the four corners of the granting instrument, is the controlling factor in deciding whether the conveyance is an estate in fee simple or an easement. Where it appears that the intent of the parties was to convey a described strip of land, rather than a right of way over a strip of land, the conveyance is considered a fee estate rather than an easement.

Baseball Publishing Co. v. Bruton (1938)

Facts: Baseball Publishing Co. and Bruton executed a writing granting the plaintiff company the "exclusive right and privilege to maintain" a sign on the wall of Bruton's building. Bruton later refused to honor the agreement and the plaintiff corporation brought suit for specific performance.

Issue: May a contract to give a license be enforced by a court of equity through the granting of specific performance?

Rule: In the absence of fraud or estoppel, there cannot be specific performance of a contract to give a license because a license is revocable at will and conveys no interest in land. However, when a writing gives one the "exclusive right" to maintain a sign on another's property for a term of years, an easement in gross arises and specific performance may be granted.

Stoner v. Zucker (1906)

Facts: The defendant had a license from the plaintiff to build, use and maintain an irrigation ditch on the plaintiff's land. After the defendant spent $7,000 building the ditch, the plaintiff revoked the license.

Issue: Is an executed parol license revocable at the will of the licensor, when it has already involved the expenditure of money, and when the very nature of the license is one of continuous use?

Rule: Where a licensee enters under a parol license and expends money, or its equivalent in labor, in the execution of the license, the license is irrevocable and will continue for so long a time as its nature requires.

Marrone v. Washington Jockey Club (S.Ct 1912)

Facts: After buying an admission ticket, Marrone was forcibly prevented from entering a racetrack. He brought a suit for trespass.

Issue: Is an admission ticket a conveyance of an interest in property?

Rule: (Holmes J.) An admission ticket does not by itself convey an interest in property, but rather is a revocable license. Therefore, the plaintiff does not have an absolute right, enforceable at equity, to enter upon the property, and his only remedy is to sue for breach of contract.

Finn v. Williams (1941)

Facts: Finn's land was entirely surrounded by Williams' land, from which it was originally severed, and by land owned by third parties. From the date of severance, Finn had a permissive right of ingress and egress over the land of a third party. He brought suit in order to establish his right of way over Williams' land by virtue of an easement by necessity, created at the time of severance.

Issue: Where an owner of land conveys a parcel thereof, which has no outlet except over the grantor's retained land or land owned by third parties, does an easement by necessity arise, and if so, may it lie dormant through several transfers of title?

Rule: Where an owner conveys a parcel of his land which has no outlet except over the grantor's retained land or that of third parties, an easement by necessity arises over the grantor's remaining land. Although this easement may lie dormant through several transfers of title, it still passes with each transfer as appurtenant to the dominant estate and may be exercised at any time by the title holder of the dominant estate.

Granite Properties Limited Partnership v. Manns (1987)

Facts: The plaintiff sold a lot to the Mannses, while retaining two lots on either side of the Mannses' property. The plaintiff had used driveways situated between its land and that of the Mannses, which had been there before the land was sold to the Mannses. The plaintiff therefore argued that an implied easement over the driveways had arisen due to the plaintiff's prior use.

Issue: For an easement to be implied from a prior existing use, must the use be one that was absolutely necessary to the grantor's beneficial enjoyment of his land?

Rule: For an easement to be implied from a prior existing use, the use need only be reasonably necessary.

Lunt v. Kitchens (1953)

Facts: Under license from Lunt's predecessor in title, the Kitchenses used a driveway for a period of time satisfying the statutory period for adverse claims. However, the Kitchenses never communicated to Lunt's grantor their intent to repudiate the license and claim the driveway under color of right.

Issue: Where a landowner consents to the use of his land by another, will a prescriptive easement arise after passage of the statutory period?

Rule: If a landowner consents to the use of his land by another, the right created is a license and the presumption of adversity will not arise through mere conforming use by the licensee. A prescriptive easement can only arise from a license when the licensee openly renounces the license and uses the property under a claim of right.

Dartnell v. Bidwell (1916)

Facts: Bidwell claimed a prescriptive easement over Dartnell's land. Prior to the expiration of the statutory period, Dartnell notified Bidwell in writing that she did not acknowledge Bidwell's right of way across her property. She subsequently brought an action for trespass. Bidwell argued, in defense, that the writing was not sufficient to interrupt the running of the statutory period.

Issue: Is an owner's acquiescence essential to the creation of a prescriptive easement and if so, may the owner interrupt the running of the statutory period by actions that fall short of actual entry and ousting of the adverse claimant?

Rule: An owner's acquiescence is one of the essential elements in the creation of a prescriptive easement. In this context acquiescence is understood to mean passive assent, submission, or consent by silence. Therefore, an owner may interrupt the running of the statutory period by demonstrating his nonacquiescence. A notice in writing served or delivered to the adverse claimant is sufficient for this purpose. No physical intrusion by the owner is required.

Note: Most courts no longer require acquiescence as an element in establishing a prescriptive easement. Consequently, a protest alone will not block a prescriptive easement.

State ex rel. Thornton v. Hay (1969)

Facts: The Oregon State Highway Commission sought to enjoin William and Georgianna Hay, the owners of a tourist facility at Cannon Beach, from constructing fences or other improvements in the dry-sand area contained within the legal description of their ocean-front property.

Issue: Does a state have the power to limit the record owner's use and enjoyment of his dry-sand area property by whatever boundaries the area may be described?

Rule: When dealing with a large region which ought to be uniformly treated, the "doctrine of custom" allows the state to equitably protect the public's interest in the privately owned dry-sand area of ocean beaches.

S.S. Kresge Co. v. Winkelman Realty Co. (1952)

Facts: Appurtenant to one of several lots acquired by Winkelman Realty Co. was a prescriptive easement for ingress and egress over the plaintiff's lot. Winkelman Realty substantially increased the burden of the easement relative to the use made during the prescriptive period.

Issue: May the use of an easement originally established by prescription be substantially changed in nature or increased over that use which served to create the easement?

Rule: A prescriptive right acquired by a particular use of the property cannot justify an added use in connection with the dominant estate in a manner greatly different from that employed under the original use.

Sakansky v. Wein (1933)

Facts: Wein, owner of the servient estate, proposed to erect a building with an eight foot high clearance over Sakansky's right of way, and to lay out a new way for Sakansky's use. Sakansky sued to enjoin the construction of the building.

Issues: Where a general easement with a definite location is conveyed, may a court defer to the requirements of reasonableness to alter the terms of the easement?

Rule: In defining the scope of an easement, the rule of reason is applied to provide a detailed definition to rights created by general words, and it may not be used to compel the easement holder to abandon a right of way, even if continued use of it is unreasonable.

Miller v. Lutheran Conference & Camp Ass'n (1938)

Facts: The plaintiff Frank C. Miller acquired an easement in gross that granted him an exclusive right to use a lake for recreational purposes. He subsequently assigned a 1/4 interest in the easement to his brother. Prior to the brother's death, he and the plaintiff were business partners who jointly operated and proportionately shared the receipts from recreational activities on the lake. The assignee's executors licensed the defendant to use the lake and collect receipts from such use. The plaintiff thereupon sought an injunction against the defendant's use of the lake.

Issue 1: Can an easement in gross be established by prescription?

Rule 1: As long as all of the requirements for a prescriptive easement are met, an easement in gross can be established by prescription.

Issue 2: Are easements in gross assignable and/or divisible?

Rule 2: An easement in gross is assignable when the parties to its creation manifest a clear intent that it be so. Furthermore, an easement in gross is divisible as long as the beneficiaries make common use of the easement.

Lindsey v. Clark (1952)

Facts: By deed, the Clarks had an easement for a right of way on the south side of the Lindseys' lot. The Clarks mistakenly used a strip of land on the north side of the Lindseys' lot to gain access to their land. The Lindseys instituted a suit to enjoin the Clarks from using the north side strip.

Issues: May an express easement be abandoned by mere non-use of the easement?

Rule: To constitute abandonment of an easement, there must be acts or circumstances clearly manifesting an intention to abandon (in addition to non-use).

Gallagher v. Bell (1986)

Facts: The Gallaghers and the Bells acquired their respective property from a common grantor. Subsequently the two parties covenanted that the Gallaghers, in return for an easement across the Bells' property, would contribute to the cost of certain improvements that were required. The Gallaghers then sold their property to Deborah Camalier, agreeing to indemnify her for any financial outlays that the Bells would demand of her in relation to the covenant. The Bells later brought suit against the Gallaghers when the Gallaghers refused to honor the covenant. The Gallaghers defended on the ground that their covenant with the Bells ran with the land and, having sold the property, they were no longer bound by the covenant.

Issue 1: What conditions must be satisfied in order for the burden of a covenant to run with the land?

Rule 1: In order for the burden of a covenant to run with the land three conditions must be met. The covenant must "touch and concern" the burdened land, the original parties to the covenant must have intended that the covenant run with the land, and there must be privity between the parties, such that the person claiming the benefit or being subjected to the burden is a successor to the estate of the original person so benefited or burdened.

Issue 2: Can an original covenantor escape the burden of a covenant that runs with the land by conveying his burdened estate to a third party?

Rule 2: The continuing liability of an original covenantor on a covenant of the type involved here will end upon his conveyance of the burdened property if the parties so intended.

Neponsit Property Owners' Ass'n, Inc. v. Emigrant Indus. Savings Bank (1938)

Facts: The Neponsit Property Owners' Association sought to enforce a covenant requiring owners of lots on a certain tract of land to pay an annual fee for the general upkeep of the area. The defendant argued that such a covenant cannot run with the land and therefore was not binding on successors to the original purchasers.

Issue 1: Does an affirmative covenant to pay money for use in connection with, but not upon, the land which is purportedly subject to the burden of the covenant run with the land?

Rule 1: One of the requirements for a covenant to run with land is that it must "touch" or "concern" the land. This requirement is satisfied if the covenant, in its effect, substantially alters legal rights which otherwise would flow from the ownership of land and which are connected with the land. Whether a particular covenant is sufficiently connected with the use of land to run with the land is generally a question of degree.

Issue 2: Does a property owners association, which technically owns no interest in property, have standing to enforce a covenant that runs with the land?

Rule 2: In order to give deference to function over form, the court may recognize a corporate entity, created solely for the purpose of advancing the common interests of the property owners, as having standing to bring suit to enforce a covenant that runs with land.

Eagle Enterprises, Inc. v. Gross (1976)

Facts: The plaintiff's predecessor in title included a covenant in all the deeds of a subdivision requiring lot owners to purchase water from it. The deed stipulated that the covenant run with the land. Gross, a subsequent purchaser of one of the lots, refused to comply.

Issue 1: Will an affirmative covenant run with the land if it does not touch and concern the land?

Rule 1: In order to run with the land, an affirmative covenant must touch and concern the land, i.e., it must relate in a significant degree to the ownership rights of the parties.

Issue 2: Will an affirmative covenant without a time limitation run with the land?

Rule 2: An affirmative covenant that lacks an outside time limitation and purports to bind all future owners, regardless of the use to which the land is put, creates a burden in perpetuity that is an undue restriction on alienation. It is therefore unenforceable.

Tulk v. Moxhay (1848)

Facts: Tulk, the plaintiff, sold land with a covenant requiring the vendee, his heirs and assigns to keep the land in an "open state, uncovered with any buildings." The defendant eventually acquired the property through a deed that was silent about the covenant, but he had actual notice of the covenant's existence.

Issue: Will a party who had notice of a restrictive covenant be permitted to use land in a manner inconsistent with the terms of the covenant?

Rule: If a restrictive covenant is attached to property by the owner, no one purchasing with notice of that covenant can stand in a different situation from the party from whom he purchased.

London County Council v. Allen (1914)

Facts: Allen covenanted with the plaintiff that he would not improve his lots, on which the plaintiff planned to build roads. Subsequently, Allen's assignee breached the covenant.

Issue: Where a benefit is in gross, will equity enforce the running of a burden as an equitable servitude?

Rule: A covenantee must have land for the benefit of which the covenant is created, both at the time of the creation of the covenant and afterwards, for the burden of the covenant to run with the land at equity.

Whitinsville Plaza, Inc. v. Kotseas (1970)

Facts: When selling a portion of his property the defendant covenanted not to use his remaining land in competition with the grantee. Whitinsville Plaza, Inc. succeeded to the grantee's interest and sought an injunction when the defendant breached the covenant.

Issue: Does the benefit of a covenant not to compete run with the land?

Rule: Reasonable covenants against competition may run with the land when they serve a purpose of facilitating orderly and harmonious development for commercial use.

Sprague v. Kimball (1913)

Facts: Kimball conveyed several contiguous lots, and included in all but one deed restrictive covenants for the mutual advantage and protection of all the lot owners. Sprague, an owner of a restricted lot, sought to enforce the covenant as to the unrestricted lot.

Issue: Must an equitable servitude be evidenced by a writing to be enforceable?

Rule: As a property interest, an equitable servitude must be evidenced by some sufficient instrument in writing. Otherwise it is unenforceable.

Sanborn v. McLean (1925)

Facts: The lot owned by the McLeans (defendants) originally belonged to an individual who, at one time, owned all the other lots comprising the immediate neighborhood, 53 of the 91 lots which he eventually sold were burdened with restrictive covenants expressly providing that all structures be built for residential purposes only. The deed held by the defendants, however, had no such express restriction.

Issue 1: May a grantor, who burdens certain lots with reciprocal negative easements, convey other lots of the same original tract without the restrictions?

Rule 1: If the owner of two or more lots, so situated as to bear the relation, sells one with restrictions of benefit to the land retained, the servitude becomes mutual, and, during the period of restraint, the owner of the lots retained can do nothing that is forbidden to the owners of the lots sold.

Issue 2: Is the existence of a visible uniform plan of use sufficient to give a purchaser of a lot in a subdivision constructive notice of land use restrictions?

Rule 2: When a purchaser's visual examination of the premises clearly indicates that lots are occupied in strict accordance with a general plan, he has constructive notice that a reciprocal negative easement may exist and is under a duty to make certain inquiries.

Snow v. Van Dam (1935)

Facts: In 1907 the grantor conveyed part of his land to be subdivided with restrictions limiting construction to residential units. In 1919 he conveyed the remainder of his land with similar restrictions. The defendant Van Dam acquired a lot in the common grantor's last conveyed subdivision and built a commercial establishment which the prior purchasers in the first subdivision sought to enjoin, claiming a violation of the restrictions.

Issue: When a grantor divides property into two subdivisions with common restrictions on use, can purchasers in one subdivision enjoin later purchasers in the separate subdivision from using their land in a manner which violates the common restrictions?

Rule: If there is a scheme of restrictions existing when the sale of lots begins which includes both the prior purchasers' land and the grantor's remaining unsold land, the prior purchasers acquire a right to enforce the restrictions against subsequent purchasers. However, the individuals seeking to enforce the restrictions must bear the burden of proving the existence of a scheme of restricted usage.

Shelley v. Kraemer (S.Ct. 1948)

Facts: Shelley's property was impressed with a restrictive covenant prohibiting occupancy or ownership of his house by blacks.

Issue: Does the Equal Protection Clause of the Fourteenth Amendment prohibit judicial enforcement by state courts of restrictive covenants based on race or color?

Rule: (Vinson CJ.) The granting of equitable judicial enforcement of restrictive covenants that deny property rights available to other members of the community, is prohibited by the Equal Protection Clause of the Fourteenth Amendment.

McMillan v. Iserman (1983)

Facts: The defendant owned a lot in a subdivision subject to restrictive covenants, which also allowed three-fourths of the subdivision's property owners to amend the restrictions at any time. After letting his land for the purpose of a group home for the mentally impaired, the deed restrictions were amended to exclude this type of use.

Issue 1: Are amended deed restrictions enforceable when they impose a harsher restriction than any imposed in the original deed restrictions, and when they become effective after a lot owner has detrimentally relied on the absence of such restrictions?

Rule 1: Although amended deed restrictions may be more restrictive than those contained in the original deed restrictions, they are inapplicable to a lot owner who has, prior to the amendment, committed himself to a certain land use which the amendment seeks to prohibit, provided the lot owner both justifiably relied on the existing restrictions (i.e., had no notice of the proposed amendment), and will be prejudiced if the amendment is enforced as to his lot. **Issue 2**: Are restrictive covenants discriminating against the mentally impaired unenforceable as against public policy?

Rule 2: Deed restrictions prohibiting residential facilities for the mentally handicapped are manifestly against the public interest and unenforceable as against public policy.

Joslin v. Pine River Development Corp. (1976)

Facts: A subdivision's restrictive covenants limited the type and number of buildings that could occupy a lot owned by the defendant corporation.

Issue: Are restrictive covenants to be strictly construed, so that no restrictions may be implied from those expressly stated in order to permit the free use of land?

Rule: The policy of strictly construing restrictive covenants is no longer operative. Rather, in giving the covenant effect, courts must consider the surrounding circumstances as well as the conduct and intent of the parties.

Suttle v. Bailey (1961)

Facts: The original grantor placed restrictive covenants in all of the grantees' deeds to lots in a subdivision. However, he retained the right to alter or annul the covenants. The plaintiffs, owners of two of the lots in the subdivision, sought to enforce one of the restrictions against the defendants, owners of two adjoining lots.

Issue: Does a general reservation by the grantor of the power to dispense with restrictive covenants make the covenants personal?

Rule: A reservation by the grantor of a right to amend or annul restrictive covenants makes the covenants personal between the grantor and his individual grantees. Therefore, the covenants do not run with the land, and one grantee may not enforce a covenant against another.

Rhue v. Cheyenne Homes, Inc. (1969)

Facts: Pursuant to a restrictive covenant, a subdivision required that all buildings be approved by an architectural control committee. There were, however, no specific standards to guide the committee's determinations. Cheyenne Homes, Inc. sought an injunction prohibiting Leonard Rhue from moving an architecturally nonconforming house into the subdivision.

Issues: Are restrictive covenants that mandate the approval of an architectural control committee of all buildings erected or placed on a lot in a subdivision enforceable, if no specific standards are contained in the covenant to guide the committee?

Rule: So long as the intention of a covenant is clear, a covenant mandating the prior approval of an architectural control committee as to the appropriateness of erecting or placing a building on a lot is enforceable, even absent specific guidelines for the committee, when a refusal to grant approval is reasonable, made in good faith, and is neither arbitrary nor capricious.

Cowling v. Colligan (1958)

Facts: A subdivision's restrictive covenants limited all the lots to residential use, Colligan owned a lot on the subdivision's border, which was bordered on both sides by commercial establishments. Cowling and other owners of lots brought suit to enjoin Colligan from using her property for business purposes.

Issue: When conditions substantially change in the surrounding area of a subdivision, will restrictive covenants be nullified as to border lots if the interior lots still benefit from the covenants?

Rule: If the benefits of the original plan for a restricted subdivision can still be realized for the protection of the interior lots, the restriction is enforceable against border lots, notwithstanding that such lot owners are deprived of the most valuable use of their lots due to changes in the surrounding area.

Waldrop v. Town of Brevard (1950)

Facts: Grantor conveyed a portion of his land to the defendant. The deed expressly waived any right to sue the defendant over the use made of the land and granted the defendant the right to use the land as a garbage dump. Thirty-five to forty homes were later built on the grantor's remaining land. Waldrop, one of these homeowners, sued the defendant alleging that the garbage dump was a nuisance.

Issue: Will changed conditions justify the non-enforcement of a covenant?

Rule: Changed conditions may, under certain circumstances, justify the nonenforcement of restrictive covenants. However, the type of covenant between the grantor and the Town of Brevard may be viewed as granting the Town an easement over the remaining property of the grantor. In the case of a duly recorded easement, changed conditions will not prevent its enforcement

Noone v. Price (1982)

Facts: The Noones owned a house which was located at the top of a hill. The defendant's house was located directly below, at the bottom of the hill. Both the defendant and her predecessor allowed a retaining wall located on their property to deteriorate, allegedly causing damage to the Noones' property due to lack of lateral support.

Issue: Is a landowner strictly liable for damage caused to an adjacent landowner's property when the damage is the result of his removal of lateral support?

Rule: An adjacent landowner is strictly liable for acts and omissions on his part that result in the withdrawal of lateral support (sufficient to support the land in its natural state) to his neighbor's property. If, however, land in its natural state could support a building and lateral support is withdrawn, the adjacent owner is liable for damage to the land and the building. But, if an adjacent owner provides sufficient support for land in its natural state and the land subsides as a result of the added weight of a subsequently built structure, then in the absence of negligence, there is no liability whatsoever on the part of the adjoining landowner.

Armstrong v. Francis Corp. (1956)

Facts: By artificially draining water from its land, the Francis Corp. caused damage to downstream owners.

Issue: Does a landowner have an absolute right to drain surface water from his land?

Rule: A landowner is legally privileged to make a reasonable use of his land even though the flow of surface waters is altered thereby and causes some harm to others, but he incurs liability when his harmful interference with the flow of waters is unreasonable.

Evans v. Merriweather (1842)

Facts: Evans purchased land directly upstream from Merriweather. He diverted water to such an extent that Merriweather did not receive any.

Issue: To what extent may riverbank proprietors use the water flowing on their land?

Rule: A riparian owner may use all the water necessary to meet his domestic needs, but, where he uses water for a commercial use or irrigation, his consumption is limited to a reasonable use.

Stratton v. Mt. Hermon Boys' School (1913)

Facts: The defendant, located upstream from Stratton's property, diverted a large quantity of water for use in a boys' school. The school was located on another estate owned by the defendant which was not adjacent to the stream. The diversion caused a substantial diminution in the natural flow of water through Stratton's property.

Issue: Must a riparian owner confine his use of water to the benefit of his land adjoining the water course?

Rule: A riparian owner may divert water out of the watershed or to a disconnected estate only if such diversion causes no actual injury to downstream owners.

Coffin v. Left Hand Ditch Co. (1882)

Facts: The plaintiff claimed ownership of water that came from the same source as Coffin's water. Coffin tore out a part of the plaintiffs Jam in order to have more of the water flow to his property. The plaintiff brought an action for damages and an injunction.

Issue: Does a landowner who appropriates water before another, whose land receives water from the same source, obtain a right to that amount of water from that time forward?

Rule: The first appropriator of water from a natural stream for a beneficial purpose has a prior right to that water to the extent of that appropriation.

Prather v. Eisenman (1978)

Facts: Prather and other plaintiffs were domestic well owners who drew water from the same aquifer as the defendants, who owned an irrigation well. The defendant's well impaired the ability of the plaintiffs to pump water.

Issue: May a landowner appropriate without limit subterranean water found under his land?

Rule: A landowner may appropriate subterranean waters found under his land, but he cannot extract them in excess of a reasonable and beneficial use upon the land he owns. If the natural underground supply is insufficient for all owners, each is entitled to a reasonable proportion of the whole and has precedence over agricultural and commercial users.

United States v. Causby (S.Ct 1946)

Facts: The path of government planes at an airport near Causby's land diminished the value of his business property. Causby argued that the frequent overflights by army and navy aircraft constituted a taking of his land within the Fifth Amendment.

Issues: Within the meaning of the Fifth Amendment, is a compensable servitude imposed on property by frequent and regular flights of U.S. planes at low altitudes in the adjacent airspace of a landowner?

Rule: (Douglas J.) When they are so low and so frequent as to be a direct and immediate interference with the enjoyment and use of land, direct flights over private land by U.S. planes constitute a taking.

Dissent: (Black J.) The solution of problems precipitated by novel technological advances should be developed by Congress and should not come about through the application of rigid constitutional restraints formulated and enforced by the courts.

Prah v. Maretti (1982)

Facts: Prah's house was heated by solar energy. The defendant began construction on a house which, when fully built, would cast a shadow on Prah's solar collectors.

Issue: Does an owner of a solar-heated residence state a cause of action when he asserts that his neighbor's proposed construction of a residence interferes with his access to sunlight?

Rule: The law of private nuisance is applicable to claims for relief from unreasonable interference with access to sunlight.

Southwest Weather Research, Inc. v. Rounsaville (1958)

Facts: Rounsaville sought to enjoin an alleged trespass by "cloud seeding" airplanes owned by the defendant corporation. The cloud seeding was carried out in an attempt to suppress hail.

Issue: Do a landowner's property rights encompass the benefits of natural rainfall?

Rule: A landowner is entitled to that precipitation from clouds over his own property which nature may provide. Consequently, the enjoyment of, or entitlement to, the benefits of nature are protected by the courts if interfered with improperly or unlawfully.

Stanton v. T.L. Herbert & Sons (1919)

Facts: In his grant of land to Stanton the grantor reserved a right to remove sand from Stanton's property. The grantor assigned his right to two other parties. Stanton brought suit to enjoin the defendants from removing the sand.

Issue: Is an incorporeal hereditament (a profit a prendre) assignable and divisible?

Rule: A profit a prendre, though assignable, is not divisible and an attempted division destroys the reservation.

Martin v. Music (1953)

Facts: Music granted Martin an easement to construct and maintain a sewer line under his land. In return, Martin granted Music an easement that allowed him to hook up to the sewer line. Subsequently, Music sold his property to several grantees, each of whom wanted to hook up to the sewer line. Martin brought an action for a declaration that the right to use the sewer line was personal to Music, and that Music's grantees did not acquire this right from him.

Issue: May a dominant estate be divided, thereby increasing the burden on the servient tenement?

Rule: A dominant estate may be divided or partitioned, and the owner of each part may claim the right to enjoy the easement as long as no additional burden is placed upon the servient estate.

Loch Sheldrake Associates v. Evans (1954)

Facts: The plaintiff's grantor reserved a right to draw water from a lake that he conveyed to the plaintiff. He then conveyed this right, along with other property, to the Evanses. The Evanses drew water from the lake in large quantities, and for purposes not encompassed by the grantor's original reservation. The plaintiffs brought suit requesting damages and an injunction.

Issue: May water rights, not appurtenant to any particular parcel of land, be used by their owner in any manner or at any location?

Rule: Water rights duly granted by deed, not appurtenant to any particular parcel of land, may be used by the owner at any place or in any manner, so long as he does not interfere with or impair the rights of others.

Henley v. Continental Cablevision (1985)

Facts: The plaintiffs' predecessors in title were granted the right to construct and maintain electric, telephone, and telegraphic service for five lots and to grant easements for those purposes. They, in turn, conveyed easements to electric and telephone companies to provide those services. Subsequently, Continental Cablevision acquired licenses from both those utilities to use the easements for the purpose of transmitting television programs.

Issue: Are easements in gross apportionable?

Rule: Where a grant of an easement in gross excludes the grantor's participation in the rights granted, divided use of the rights granted is presumptively allowable.

Ricenbaw v. Kraus (1953)

Facts: Ricenbaw's predecessor in title was orally granted permission to construct a drain on the land of the predecessor in title of the defendant. The defendant attempted to revoke the license.

Issues: Is a license revocable at will?

Rule: A mere license, whether created by deed or parol, is revocable at will, except where the license is executed and where, by reason of expenditures by the licensee on the strength of the license, it would otherwise be inequitable to permit the licensor to effect a revocation. In such a case a court of equity may rule that the license became an easement by virtue of the financial outlays of the licensee undertaken in reliance upon the apparent validity of an otherwise invalid parol easement.

Campbell v. Great Miami Aerie No. 2309 (1984)

Facts: Campbell's and defendant's adjoining property was once owned by a common grantor. The sewage system serving both pieces of property was located on Campbell's property. When each party purchased its respective property the placement of the sewage system was not known to either of them. Alleging trespass, Campbell sued for damages and a permanent injunction to prevent the defendant from using his sewage facilities. The defendant claimed that he had an implied easement.

Issue: Where a sewage system serving adjoining properties previously owned by a common grantor is located on one parcel, does the other parcel retain an implied easement upon severance of the two parcels?

Rule: In order for an implied easement to arise there must have been a severance of the unity of ownership of an estate. The easement shall have been long continued and obvious before the separation. The easement must be reasonably necessary to the beneficial enjoyment of the land, and the servitude shall be continuous. Absent actual or constructive notice of the easement by the party sought to be charged with knowledge of it, no implied easement arises.

Krzewinski v. Eaton Homes, Inc. (1958)

Facts: The Krzewinskis bought a lot from Eaton Homes, Inc. pursuant to a plat which showed their lot abutting a through street. Eaton Homes refused to complete the street and the Krzewinskis sought specific performance.

Issue: Where a vendee buys a lot with reference to a plat that shows that the property abuts a planned street, does an implied easement for the use of the road arise?

Rule: Where a deed describes the lot conveyed by reference to a plat, the grantee acquires an implied easement to use the road that extends to the whole street shown so far as it was owned by the grantor when the deed was executed.

Hester v. Sawyers (1937)

Facts: The defendant built, used and maintained a road that traversed the plaintiff's land. His tenants, visitors, and those doing business with him had used the road daily and openly without interruption or objection from anybody, and without obtaining anybody's permission. He claimed that he had established a prescriptive easement over the plaintiff's land.

Issue: May an easement be acquired by prescription?

Rule: An easement by prescription arises where the user makes open, uninterrupted, peaceable, notorious, and adverse use of another's land under a claim of right, which use continues for a period of years set by the statute of limitations and is with the knowledge or imputed knowledge of the owner.

Shanks v. Floom (1955)

Facts: The predecessors in title to Shanks and Floom orally agreed to build a common driveway on the medial line of their adjacent properties. The Shanks brought suit to enjoin the defendants from using the common driveway.

Issue: Is it necessary to show that there was a heated controversy or ill will to establish the required hostility for a prescriptive easement?

Rule: All that is required to fulfill the hostility requirement of a prescriptive easement is that the use be inconsistent with the rights of the title owner and not subordinate or subservient thereto.

Kanefsky v. Dratch Construction Co. (1954)

Facts: Kanefsky bought a lot from the defendant. The deed included a portion of a common driveway, but the grantor reserved an easement in the driveway and retained title to a narrow strip of land parallel to it. The defendant sold his interest and the successor in title used the driveway to transport a developer's equipment.

Issue: May the owner of a dominant tenement extend an easement to benefit other land owned by him?

Rule: An easement cannot be extended by the owner of the dominant tenement to benefit land to which it was not originally appurtenant.

Cameron v. Barton (1954)

Facts: When he conveyed his land, the original grantor created an easement over the lot subsequently acquired by the plaintiff. Over time, the defendant's use of the dominant tenement changed and, consequently, so did the nature of the easement.

Issue: Does normal change in the use of a general easement of a right of way constitute an unacceptable deviation from the terms of the original grant?

Rule: In ascertaining, in the case of an easement appurtenant created by conveyance, whether additional or different uses of the servient tenement required by changes in the character of the use of the dominant tenement are permitted, it is assumed that the parties to the conveyance contemplated a normal development of the use of the dominant tenement.

Glenn v. Poole (1981)

Facts: The Pooles had a prescriptive easement across the plaintiff's land. Originally, it was used for hauling operations conducted by horse drawn wagons and by light trucks. When the Pooles' business changed, they increased their use of the road.

Issue: Does the use made during the prescriptive period permanently fix the scope of an easement obtained by prescription?

Rule: The use made of a prescriptive easement may change over time to accommodate normal developments in accord with common experience, provided the variations in use are not substantial and are consistent with the general pattern formed by the adverse use.

Pasadena v. California-Michigan Land & Water Co. (1941)

Facts: A municipal water vending service had easements from various property owners to lay water pipes. A private competitor, the defendant, received permission from the owners of the servient estates to lay its pipe in the same areas where the municipal company held its easements. The plaintiff sued to enjoin the defendant water company's installation of its equipment.

Issue: Is the owner of a servient estate prohibited by law from granting an easement over the exact parcel of land that is already subject to an easement granted to a third party?

Rule: Where the easement is founded upon a grant, only those interests expressed in the grant and those necessarily incident thereto pass from the owner of the fee. The owner of the servient estate may make any use of the land, including a transfer of his rights to a third party, that does not unreasonably interfere with the easement.

Carr v. Bartell (1043)

Facts: By deed, the predecessors in title to Carr and the defendant, Bartell, created an easement for a common driveway, 105 feet long, on the medial line of their respective lots. With the permission of Carr's predecessor in title, the defendant erected a fence on the driveway which extinguished the easement. Also, Carr's predecessor built a barn that encroached on a part of the way.

Issue 1: May an easement be extinguished by a use inconsistent with the continued use of the easement?

Rule 1: A use that is inconsistent with the continued use of an easement, when performed over a significant period, evinces an intent to abandon the easement and thereby extinguishes the easement.

Issue 2: May an easement be extinguished by adverse possession when the initial adverse use was by permission?

Rule 2: Where a use adverse to the use of an easement was by permission of the easement holder, the easement cannot be defeated under a claim of adverse possession and use.

Abbott v. Bob's U-Drive (1960)

Facts: Abbott leased premises to the defendant who created two corporations. Although both corporations were in possession of the demised premises, the defendant assigned the lease to one corporation only. The lease contained a covenant mandating arbitration of disputes arising from the lease.

Issue: Is a party who is neither the lessee nor a formal assignee bound by covenants running with the land?

Rule: When a person other than the lessee is in possession of leased premises and is paying rent to the lessor, there is a presumption that j the lease has been assigned to the person in possession and such implied assignment is effective to form the basis for the running of covenants in the lease so as to burden or benefit the assignee.

Thruston v. Minke (1870)

Facts: Thruston and the defendant were tenants in common of a plot of land upon which stood a hotel. Thruston leased his interest in an undeveloped portion of the land to the defendant. The lease contained a covenant prohibiting certain uses of the demised portion. Subsequently, Thruston conveyed his reversionary interest in the demised premises and assigned the covenants in the lease.

Issue: Where a lessor sells his interest in demised premises burdened by a covenant benefiting his retained land, may he nevertheless enforce a lease restriction?

Rule: Where a lessor has included a covenant in a lease which benefits other land owned by him, the covenant does not run with the land. Consequently, the lessor, even after divesting himself of all interest in the demised premises, can enforce a lease restriction that benefits his retained land.

Burton v. Chesapeake Box & Lumber Corp. (1950)

Facts: Burton's lease contained a covenant requiring the lessee to insure against fire loss, but it contained no covenant obligating Burton to use the insurance proceeds to rebuild. Burton's lessee conveyed his interest in the lease to the defendant.

Issue: Does a covenant in a lease requiring the lessee to insure against fire loss, when not coupled with a covenant requiring the lessor to rebuild, run with the land?

Rule: A bare covenant to insure without a reciprocal obligation from the lessor to rebuild does not run with the land.

Gerber v. Pecht (1954)

Facts: The defendant, Pecht, assigned his lease. Subsequently, his assignee assigned the lease with the plaintiff's consent. The second assignee defaulted.

Issue: Does the subsequent assignment by a lessee's assignee relieve the lessee of his obligations under the lease?

Rule: The subsequent assignment of a lease by a lessee's assignee relieves the lessee of his obligations under the lease only if the second assignment constitutes a material and prejudicial variation in the terms of the lessee's lease.

Neal v. Craig Brown, Inc. (1987)

Facts: Neal subleased the defendant's property but the two parties did not have a written agreement. Neal wished to renew the lease as the original lessor would have had the rights to do under the original lease.

Issue: Does a sublessee obtain the sublessor's rights to renew a lease?

Rule: A sublessee may not exercise an option to renew granted to his sublessor in the original lease or demand such a renewal from the original landlord.

Keppel v. Bailey (1834)

Facts: The Kendalls, lessees of an ironworks, joined a joint stock company with the plaintiffs and others. They agreed to bind themselves and their successors to using a certain railroad. Bailey, with notice of this agreement, acquired the Kendalls' interest and attempted to use another railroad.

Issue: May one bind his successors to a covenant entered into with third parties with whom he has no privity of estate?

Rule: Absent privity of estate between a covenantor and covenanted neither can bind their successors to their covenant.

Wheeler v. Schad (1872)

Facts: Wheeler's predecessor in title conveyed land and water rights to the defendant's predecessor. Six days later, they agreed to jointly build and maintain a dam. When the dam was damaged, the defendant refused to contribute to its repair.

Issue: When covenanting parties not in privity of estate enter into a covenant concerning land, does the covenant run with the land?

Rule: For a covenant to run with the land, it is necessary that it touch and concern the land. A covenant imposing a burden on the land can only be created where there is privity of estate between the covenantor and covenantee, and a promise made after a conveyance does not satisfy the privity requirement.

Carlson v. Libby (1950)

Facts: The plaintiff's predecessor in title conveyed an easement to the defendant's predecessor in title but reserved a right for itself and its successors to use the railroad siding constructed on it.

Issue: Is a covenant that materially affects the value of the land in question a real or personal covenant?

Rule: If a covenant touches the land involved to the extent that it materially affects the value of that land, it is a real covenant running with the land, if it is in accord with the intent of the parties.

Petersen v. Beekmere, Inc. (1971)

Facts: The defendant, a community association, sought to compel the plaintiff, a subsequent purchaser with notice, to comply with a covenant requiring owners and their grantees to contribute to the maintenance of a lake in a subdivision.

Issue: May an affirmative covenant be enforced in equity?

Rule: An affirmative covenant is enforceable in equity as an equitable servitude against a subsequent grantee who takes with notice.

Oliver v. Hewitt (1950)

Facts: Oliver included an anti competition covenant in a recorded deed between himself and the defendant's predecessor in interest. Subsequently, the defendant, having actual and constructive notice of the existence of the agreement, leased the premises to Boyd, who also had constructive notice. Neither the deed to the remote grantee nor Boyd's lease referred to the covenant. Boyd entered into competition with Oliver.

Issue: Is a personal covenant enforceable in equity against a subsequent purchaser with notice?

Rule: A personal covenant will be held valid and binding in equity upon a purchaser taking the estate with notice.

Rodgers v. Reimann (1961)

Facts: The plaintiff's grantor sold a lot to the defendant, whose deed contained a restrictive covenant. The plaintiff sought to enforce the covenant.

Issue: Is a prior grantee entitled to enforce a covenant inserted in a deed from his grantor to a subsequent grantee?

Rule: To be entitled to enforce a covenant between his grantor and a subsequent grantee, a prior grantee must show that the covenant in the subsequent grantee's deed was intended to benefit the prior grantee's land and that the subsequent grantee entered into the covenant with notice of both the restriction imposed on the land he is purchasing and the extent to which others may enforce it.

Kell v. Bella Vista Village Property Owners Ass'n (1975)

Facts: The plaintiffs, landowners in a planned community, contended that an assessment covenant was invalid for vagueness and indefiniteness.

Issue: Is an assessment covenant containing a formula to calculate the assessment invalid as a restraint on alienation?

Rule: Assessment covenants that contain a formula for calculating the amount of, and purposes for, an assessment are valid and binding if applied alike to all units of a subdivision and are not restraints on alienation.

Osborne v. Hewitt (1960)

Facts: Due to changes in the surroundings, the Osbornes sought the nullification of a subdivision's restrictive covenants.

Issue: When substantial change occurs in an area surrounding a subdivision with restrictive covenants, will the covenants be nullified when the benefits they were intended to secure are still realizable?

Rule: Restrictive covenants on a subdivision will be enforced, notwithstanding change in the surrounding area, if the change in the character of the neighborhood is not such as to make it impossible to secure, in a substantial degree, the benefits sought to be realized through the adherence to the restrictive covenants.

Barrows v. Jackson (1953)

Facts: Contrary to a restrictive covenant prohibiting the sale to or occupancy of her house by blacks, Jackson sold to a black.

Issue: Can a restrictive covenant that prohibits a homeowner from selling his home to blacks be enforced at law by a suit for damages against a co-covenantor who allegedly broke the covenant?

Rule: The awarding of damages by a state court for the breach of a restrictive covenant that prohibits the sale of property to blacks constitutes state action under the Fourteenth Amendment. Hence, it is an unconstitutional denial of equal protection of law.

Penthouse Properties, Inc. v. 1158 Fifth Avenue, Inc. (1939)

Facts: The defendant organized cooperative apartments pursuant to an agreement that required a shareholder to gain approval from either the directors or shareholders before selling shares. Without approval, the plaintiff sold her shares.

Issue: May a corporation established to build cooperative apartments restrain alienation of the corporation's shares and the apartment's leases?

Rule: Pursuant to a restrictive plan under which cooperative apartment houses have been constructed and stock sold, restrictive covenants in a corporation's certificate and leases that restrain alienation of the corporation's shares or of an apartment's lease are valid and enforceable.

Weisner v. 791 Park Avenue Corp. (1959)

Facts: A corporation was formed pursuant to a plan of cooperative organization. Pursuant to provisions in its by-laws and leases, the defendant corporation rejected Weisner as an assignee of a lessee.

Issue 1: Does a lessee in a cooperative apartment have a duty to attempt to secure the other tenants' approval of his prospective assignee?

Rule 1: An assignment of a proprietary lease by a lessee of a cooperative apartment does not impose a duty on the assignor to secure the corporation's approval of the assignment.

Issue 2: Does a cooperative have an absolute right to restrain the transfer of a stockholder's interest in the corporation?

Rule 2: Absent discrimination based on race, religion, ancestry, or national origin, owners of cooperatives may restrain the alienation of the corporation's shares and leases.

Lauderbaugh v. Williams (1962)

Facts: Contrary to an agreement entered into by the plaintiff and other landowners requiring future purchasers to be members of the Lake Watawga Association, the plaintiff deeded her land to a non-member.

Issue: Is an agreement among landowners that restrains alienation based on lack of membership unreasonable?

Rule: A restrictive covenant that lacks standards of admissibility to the association is an unreasonable restraint on alienation.

Gale v. York Center Community Cooperative, Inc. (1960)

Facts: Gale, a cooperative member of the defendant corporation, wanted to withdraw, but the defendant required twelve months to approve the sale.

Issue: May a cooperative housing association partially restrain the alienation of its member's property?

Rule: When accepted social and economic considerations are advanced by a restraint on alienation, the utility of the restraint outweighs the injurious consequences flowing from it to the public, and such a restraint is valid and enforceable.

Justice Court Mutual Housing Cooperative, Inc. v. Sandow (1966)

Facts: The defendants are shareholder-tenants of the plaintiff cooperative housing corporation. The corporation's by-laws reserved the power to promulgate rules and regulations. For seven years the defendants' daughters played musical instruments in their apartment. Following a complaint by adjoining tenants the plaintiffs restricted the playing of musical instruments to before 8:00 P.M. and "by any one person" in excess of ninety minutes a day.

Issue: After purchasers take possession, may a cooperative housing corporation adopt a rule regulating the mode of living of its shareholder-tenants?

Rule: A new regulation established under a cooperative housing corporation's reserved power to promulgate rules must be reasonable and cannot be arbitrary.

Green v. Greenbelt Homes, Inc. (1963)

Facts: Pursuant to the terms of a mutual ownership contract, a cooperative housing corporation terminated the contract between itself and the plaintiff.

Issue: Under a proprietary lease, may a member's use of a cooperative dwelling unit be terminated by the corporation when the lease's terms are breached by the member?

Rule: If an issue arises concerning the rights of a member to occupy a dwelling unit after proof of her misconduct, members of a cooperative corporation are held to be lessees rather than owners, and the restrictions on the use of a cooperative dwelling unit are covenants between the members and the corporation, the breach of which gives the corporation the right to terminate a mutual ownership contract.

Dick v. Sears-Roebuck & Co. (1932)

Facts: The plaintiff conveyed a lot opposite his business with a covenant not to compete. A subsequent grantee, whose deed contained a similar covenant, leased the premises to the defendant. The defendant's lease did not refer to the covenant and the defendant's business entered into competition with the plaintiffs.

Issue: Does the burden of a covenant not to compete run with the covenantor's land?

Rule: Because a covenant not to compete restrains the use to which land may be put in the future as well as in the present, and may likely affect its value, it touches and concerns the land and therefore runs with the covenantor's land if reasonable and consistent with the parties' intent.

Shell Oil Co. v. Henry Ouellette & Sons Co. (1967)

Facts: When conveying a portion of its land, the defendant corporation covenanted not to use his remaining land in a manner competitive with his grantee's use of the conveyed parcel. A subsequent grantee leased land to Shell Oil, which erected a gas station. The defendant granted Mobil Oil Co., who planned to open a gas station, an option to buy part of its remaining land.

Issue Does the benefit of a covenant not to compete inure to a lessee of a subsequent grantee of the covenantor?

Rule: A covenant not to compete is personal and does not inure to the benefit of remote or successive grantees.

Note: This case represents a minority view. Since this decision Massachusetts has modified its position.

Werner v. Graham (1919)

Facts: After subdividing his land, the grantor placed similar restrictions in all the deeds to his lots. He failed, however, to state in the deeds that he intended a general restrictive development plan. The grantor quitclaimed his interest in plaintiff Werner's lot, effectively removing any restriction on it.

Issue: May parol evidence be admitted to show either the existence of a general plan of development or some other expression of a grantor's intent to benefit the lots of a subdivision?

Rule: Any evidence of an intent to create a servitude outside of the deed is immaterial.

Note: This case represents a minority position.

Manning v. New England Mutual Life Insurance Co. (1987)

Facts: A state law stipulated that any restriction imposed before 1962 will be unenforceable unless a notice of the restriction is recorded before January 1, 1964. The Commonwealth Restrictions, drafted in the 1850's, affected properly on Boylston Street. No notice of the Commonwealth Restrictions was recorded.

Issue: Is a statute which renders unenforceable ancient restrictions unless they are recorded within a certain time period unconstitutional?

Rule: A statute requiring the recordation of ancient restrictions within a reasonable time is constitutionally valid.

Malley v. Hannah (1985)

Facts: Each of the parties acquired their property through a chain of title derived from a single original owner. The restrictive covenant in defendants' chain of title limited residential construction to single-family homes.

Issue: What must be shown to enforce a restrictive covenant?

Rule: A restrictive covenant is enforceable if the owner of the dominant estate derived the property from the original grantor who received the benefit, and the owner of the servient estate derived that property from the original grantee who took it subject to the covenant. Furthermore, the original grantor must have intended that the covenant run with the land.

Merrionette Manor Homes Improvement Ass'n v. Heda (1956)

Facts: As assignee of the benefit of certain covenants, a homeowner's association with no legal title to realty in a subdivision sued to enforce a burden imposed on Heda's (a purchaser with notice) dwelling unit.

Issue: Does an association of homeowners organized as a nonprofit corporation, whose membership consists of the owners of real property within an area subjected to planned and uniform restrictive covenants, have sufficient interest to bring suit to enjoin alleged violations of these covenants?

Rule: Regardless of privity of contract or estate, a homeowner's association may equitably enforce covenants in a deed against purchasers with notice.

Pratte v. Ralatsos (1955)

Facts: The plaintiff contracted with the defendant's predecessor in interest, requiring him to keep a jukebox on his premises. With notice of this contract the defendant refused to honor it.

Issues: Are easements in gross enforceable in equity against a subsequent purchaser with notice?

Rule: As against subsequent purchasers with notice, easements in gross are enforceable equitable servitudes.

Jones v. Northwest Real Estate Co. (1925)

Facts: Pursuant to a restrictive covenant governing architectural designs, the plaintiff grantor of a subdivision rejected Jones' building plans. Nevertheless, Jones began construction based on his plans.

Issue: Is a restrictive covenant giving the grantor power to approve or reject architectural designs valid in a subdivision subject to a general plan of development?

Rule: An architectural approval covenant is enforceable if the intent of the parties is clear and the restriction is reasonable.

Rick v. West (1962)

Facts: Restrictive covenants required a tract of land to be used for residential purposes only. By the terms of these covenants, the plaintiff reserved the right to modify the covenants in case of "special unforeseen conditions," provided the "spirit and intent" of the covenants is maintained. The defendant, owner of a half acre tract, refused to release the plaintiff from the covenant when he desired to sell fifteen acres to a hospital.

Issue: May restrictive covenants mandating a general plan of development be abandoned by a grantor who reserves the right to modify the covenants?

Rule: A limited reserved right by the grantor to modify restrictive covenants does not alone justify abandonment of a general plan of development when the restriction is not outmoded and still affords real benefit to the grantees.

Maranatha Settlement Ass'n v. Evans (1956)

Facts: The plaintiff sold lots of a subdivision allowing the "grantee and his immediate family only" the use of a pool. Evans, a subsequent purchaser, was denied use of the pool.

Issue 1: Will the language of a granting clause alone determine the extent of the interest granted?

Rule 1: The intent of the parties, as determined by a fair interpretation of the language employed and consideration of all attendant circumstances, determines the extent of the property interest granted.

Issue 2: Do easements appurtenant to the dominant estate automatically pass to the transferee?

Rule 2: The use of an easement appurtenant to the dominant estate passes to a subsequent purchaser.

Van Sandt v. Royster (1938)

Facts: Under the plaintiff's house was a sewer drain that flooded his cellar. The document which originally conveyed his land did not expressly reserve an easement for the passage of sewer pipes under his property. Therefore, upon discovery of the leakage, he brought an action to enjoin the defendants from using the underground sewer drain.

Issue: In order to establish an easement by implied reservation in favor of the grantor must the easement be one of strict necessity?

Rule: If land may be used without an easement, but cannot be used without disproportionate effort and expense, strict necessity is not a requirement for finding an implied easement by reservation.

Maioriello v. Arlotta (1950)

Facts: The defendant built a wall on her property that partially blocked light and air from entering the plaintiff's home.

Issue: Will an implied easement of light and air arise absent an absolute necessity?

Rule: Absent an absolute necessity, an implied easement of light and air cannot be created.

Parker & Edgarton v. Foote (1838)

Facts: After the defendant built an edifice on his own land which blocked the plaintiff's light, the plaintiff, whose windows were unobstructed for twenty-four years, claimed an easement by prescription to light.

Issue: May an easement of light be acquired by prescription?

Rule: In the case of light, since there is neither an adverse user nor any use whatsoever of another's property, no foundation is laid to support a presumption of adverse use against a rightful owner. Therefore, a prescriptive easement to light cannot arise.

Romans v. Nadler (1944)

Facts: By occasionally trespassing on Nadler's land to clean his gutters and paint his house, the plaintiff claimed a prescriptive easement on Nadler's land.

Issue: Will sporadic and occasional use satisfy the element of continuity needed to establish a prescriptive easement?

Rule: Since the requirement of continuity essential to establishing a prescriptive easement depends on the nature and character of the right claimed, sporadic and occasional use will not constitute continuous use.

Crimmins v. Gould (1957)

Facts: The defendant held an express appurtenant easement to use a road owned by Crimmins. In order to service a nearby nondominant parcel that he owned, the defendant extended Crimmins' road so that it joined a road that the defendant built through the nondominant parcel that connected with a public road.

Issue: May an express easement appurtenant be extinguished?

Rule: Where the burden of the servient estate is increased through changes in the dominant estate which increase the use and subject it to use of property to which it is not appurtenant, an easement will be extinguished if the unauthorized use cannot be severed and prohibited.

Bang v. Forman (1928)

Facts: The defendants held an express easement appurtenant granting them beach access. They subdivided their three lots to which the easement was appurtenant into twenty-six, granting all beach access.

Issue: May a grantee of a dominant estate increase the burden on the servient estate beyond that contemplated at the time the easement was created?

Rule: Where land is granted to which an easement is appurtenant, the right is appurtenant to every part of the dominant estate subsequently conveyed, provided the servient estate is not burdened to a greater extent than was contemplated at the time the easement was created.

Geffine v. Thompson (1945)

Facts: Thompson's predecessor in interest granted the defendant's predecessor in interest an easement to lay and maintain a gas pipeline over Thompson's land. The defendant owned no land to which the easement was appurtenant.

Issue: Is an easement in gross assignable?

Rule: An easement in gross is assignable if it is consistent with the parties' intent and requires virtual exclusive possession of the land, i.e., where an easement in gross is necessary to the operation of an entity, it is appurtenant to the entity and therefore assignable.

Hopkins The Florist, Inc. v. Fleming (1942)

Facts: The grantor, Fleming's predecessor in interest, exacted an easement from the grantee, plaintiff's predecessor in interest, prohibiting the grantee from using his land in any manner that would block the grantor's southerly view. Fleming subsequently moved the house's location on the lot so that instead of facing the south, the house now faced the north. The plaintiff sought a declaration that Fleming no longer had a valid easement.

Issue: May an express appurtenant easement to a right of view be extinguished through abandonment?

Rule: An act inconsistent with the continued use of an easement to a right of view may constitute abandonment and thereby extinguish the easement.

Union Nat'l Bank v. Nesmith (1921)

Facts: On adjoining lots, J. and T. Nesmith constructed buildings which shared a common entrance, stairway, and landings by which the only access to the upper stories of each building was possible. The plaintiff, T. Nesmith's successor in title, proposed to demolish his building. The defendant claimed an easement in the building.

Issue: May a servient estate owner voluntarily destroy a building in which the dominant estate owner has an easement?

Rule: An easement is lost when the servient building is intentionally destroyed by the owner of the servient estate.

Note: This rule is recognized in Massachusetts only.

Crosdale v. Lanigan (1892)

Facts: The defendant allowed the plaintiff to build a retaining wall on the defendant's land which, after it was completed, the defendant proposed to tear down.

Issue: Does a license become irrevocable when a licensee expends money and labor on the faith of a parol license?

Rule: A parol license to do an act on the land of the licensor is revocable at the option of the licensor, even if the intention was to confer a continuing right and money is expended by the licensee upon the faith of the license.

Gorton v. Schofield (1942)

Facts: The defendant's predecessor in title excavated his land and erected a retaining wall to provide lateral support for the plaintiff's land. Subsequently, the wall fell into disrepair and the plaintiff's land subsided. The plaintiff sued in equity to compel the defendant to rebuild the wall.

Issue: Does the burden of providing lateral support to an adjacent owner's land in its natural condition run with the land?

Rule: The burden of providing lateral support to an adjacent owner's land in its natural condition is one of continued support and runs against the servient land.

United States v. Willow River Power Co. (1945)

Facts: Willow River Power Co., a riparian landowner, claimed that the U.S. (defendant) had appropriated its property by impounding the water to improve navigation.

Issue: Does the government effectuate a taking when it diminishes a riparian owner's land use in order to improve navigation?

Rule: As against the U.S. government, a riparian landowner on a navigable stream has no appurtenant property right to the stream's natural level.

United States v. Louisiana (S.Ct. 1985)

Facts: Louisiana argued that if the Mississippi Sound qualifies as a historic bay, then it contains inland waters, and the State owns the lands submerged underneath its waters. The Government argued that the Sound in large part does not contain inland waters, and therefore the United States owns these lands.

Issue: How is a body of water determined to be a historic bay?

Rule: (Blackmun, J.) Four factors must be considered in determining whether a body of water is a historic bay: (1) the exercise of authority over the area by the claiming nation; (2) the continuity of this exercise of authority; (3) the acquiescence of foreign nations; and (4) the vital interests of the coastal nation, including elements such as geographical configuration, economic interests, and self-defense.

United States v. Louisiana (S.Ct. 1988)

Facts: As directed by the Court in its 1985 opinion, the Special Master filed a Supplemental Report concluding the disagreements relating to the

Mississippi Sound. The state of Mississippi intervened in the litigation noting exceptions to this report, relating to the "seaward boundary" of Mississippi at two points. These areas concern only a region located to the south of the Mississippi Sound.

Issue: Can a state extend a suit dealing with rights to a certain body of water to cover disputes over additional bodies of water?

Rule: (Blackmun, J.) When the litigation concerns the ownership rights in the seabed of a certain body of water, then any exceptions which do not relate to those waters may be overruled at the Court's discretion; they must then be brought under a separate claim.

Phillips Petroleum Co. v. Mississippi (S.Ct. 1988)

Facts: The disputed tracts are non-navigable tributaries to the Jourdan River, a stream flowing into the Gulf of Mexico. The tracts are affected by the tides. Phillips traces its title to these areas back to pre-statehood Spanish land grants.

Issue: Did the State of Mississippi, when it entered the Union, take title to lands lying under waters that were influenced by the tide running in the Gulf of Mexico, but were not navigable?

Rule: (White, J.) Under the public trust doctrine, the states own all lands under waters subject to the ebb and flow of the tide.

Dissent: (O'Connor, J.) The public trust doctrine grants to the states ownership rights only to land underlying navigable bodies of water and their borders, bays, and inlets.

Tucker v. Badoian (1978)

Facts: The defendant made physical changes to his land which caused the plaintiff's land to flood.

Issue: Is a landowner who improves his land and thereby causes water to accumulate on adjacent land liable for damages to the adjacent landowner?

Rule: Pursuant to the common enemy rule, there is no liability on one who improves his land thereby causing another's land to flood absent proof that he caused water, which might otherwise have been absorbed or might otherwise have flowed elsewhere, to be artificially channeled and discharged onto the other's land.

Von Henneberg v. Generazio (1988)

Facts: Generazio built a berm on his land which prevented water from draining from Von Henneberg's land and caused that land to flood.

Issue: Does the reasonable use doctrine apply to Generazio's actions?

Rule: The reasonable use doctrine holds that a landowner incurs liability when his harmful interference with the flow of surface waters is unreasonable.

Meeker v. City of East Orange (1909)

Facts: The defendant used its groundwater for purposes unconnected with the beneficial use and enjoyment of its land, thereby causing Meeker's land to become arid and untillable.

Issue: Does a landowner have an absolute right to appropriate all percolating water under his land?

Rule: There are correlative rights in percolating underground waters. Thus, no landowner has an absolute right to withdraw water from the ground to the detriment of other owners and each landowner's use of such waters is limited to reasonable uses.

Ferguson v. City of Keene (1968)

Facts: Although flight paths did not cross over her land, Ferguson claimed that the noise from the defendant's airport damaged her land and made her life unbearable, thereby constituting a taking for which she should have been compensated.

Issue: Does an action for inverse condemnation lie where noise from a city-owned airport damages nearby land, even if no flight paths cross over the land?

Rule: Where a flight path does not cross directly over property no taking of the property results, even when the enjoyment of the property is diminished by noise emanating from a nearby airport.

Holbrook v. Taylor (1976)

Facts: The Taylors owned land adjacent to the Holbrooks. From 1944 to 1970 the Holbrooks had allowed a road, running through their property, to be built and improved by successive owners of the adjoining property, including the Taylors. The Taylors filed suit to establish their right to use the road as an irrevocable license.

Issue: When a licensee makes substantial expenditures to a roadway over another's land on the faith of the license, and the licensor consents to or tacitly approves of such use, is the licensor estopped from revoking the license?

Rule: The right of revocation of a license is subject to the qualification that where the licensee has exercised the privilege given him and erected improvements on the faith or strength of the license, it becomes irrevocable and continues for so long as the nature of the license calls. In effect the license becomes a grant through estoppel.

Shepard v. Purvine (1952)

Facts: Plaintiffs were close friends and neighbors of the defendants. The parties entered into an agreement, but plaintiffs did not insist upon a deed, accepting defendants' word as they would a written instrument.

Issue: When an individual enters into an agreement with a close friend, is it negligent not to insist upon a formal transfer of rights?

Rule: When one makes an oral agreement with a close friend or neighbor, the license promptly acted upon is just as valid and binding, and irrevocable as a deeded right of way.

Henry v. Dalton (1959)

Facts: Henry filed suit when the respondent revoked his license.

Issue: Is a license revocable where the intention is to confer a continuing right, and money has been expended by the licensee upon the faith of the license?

Rule: A parol license to perform an act on the property of a licensor is revocable at his option.

Othen v. Rosier (1950)

Facts: The plaintiff Albert Othen could only enter and exit his property by traveling across a roadway on the defendant's land, which the defendant also used. The common grantor of both parcels first conveyed the defendant's parcel and then, more than two years later, conveyed the plaintiffs. The plaintiff claimed that the common grantor impliedly reserved an easement for himself, and consequently he, as the successor in interest, also held an easement.

Issue 1: What are the requirements that must be met before an easement can be said to have been created by implied reservation?

Rule 1: Before an easement can be held to have been created by implied reservation it must be shown that (1) there was a unity of ownership of the alleged dominant and servient estates; (2) the easement is a necessity, not a mere convenience; and (3) the necessity existed at the time of severance of the two estates.

Issue 2: Can a prescriptive easement arise when both the owner and the claimant use a roadway?

Rule 2: In order for a prescriptive easement to be created the claimant must be using the roadway under a claim of right. Use of a roadway by both the owner and the adverse claimant is sufficient evidence that the claimant's use of the roadway is merely permissive, and not under a claim of right.

Matthews v. Bay Head Improvement Ass'n (1984)

Facts: One of Bay Head's neighboring communities instituted this suit because its residents were prohibited form gaining access to the ocean and the beachfront in Bay Head, which was controlled and supervised by the Association.

Issue: What are the rights of the public to use non-municipality owned beaches?

Rule: The public must be given access to and use of privately-owned beaches as is reasonably necessary. The public's rights on private beaches are not co-extensive with the rights enjoyed in municipal beaches, but private landowners may not in all instances prevent the public from exercising its rights under the public trust doctrine. Where a beachfront property is controlled by a quasi-public body, membership must be open to the public at large.

Brown v. Voss (1986)

Facts: The plaintiff, Brown, had an express easement of a right of way over the defendant's land. Having acquired a parcel adjoining his previously owned land, the plaintiff sought to extend the easement to benefit his new property as well.

Issue: Does the owner of a servient estate have the right to enjoin the owner of a dominant estate from extending the easement to benefit an additional estate to which it is not appurtenant?

Rule: Although the act of extending the scope of the easement for the benefit of a nondominant estate constitutes a misuse of the easement, a court of equity may decline to issue an injunction when the servient estate suffers no increase in burden and no damages.

Petersen v. Friedman (1958)

Facts: The plaintiff sought to perpetually enjoin Friedman from violating an express easement of a right to light, air, and unobstructed view created in 1942, and to compel him to remove certain television aerials and antennae from his roof.

Issue: May an easement of light, air, and view be enforced when, at the time the easement was created, the obstructions in question were not yet invented?

Rule: If the language of an easement clearly prohibits any use of the servient land that is in violation of the terms of the easement, and is not restrictive of only those uses to which the land was being put at the time the easement was created, then the owner of the servient estate may be enjoined from making any use of his land that is inconsistent with the terms of the easement.

Southern California Edison Co. v. Bourgerie (1973)

Facts: The defendants purchased a tract of land from the Bank of America, which retained a portion of the tract adjacent to the defendants' land. Both the defendants' land and the land retained by the bank were subject to a restrictive covenant prohibiting use of the property as an electric transmission station. The Southern California Edison Co., a public utility, sought condemnation of the portion of the tract owned by the bank for the purpose of erecting an electric substation.

Issue: When property that is subject to a restrictive covenant is condemned through the power of eminent domain, must the con-demner compensate not only the owners of the condemned property but also the landowners who benefit directly from the restrictions?

Rule: Building restrictions constitute property rights for purposes of eminent domain proceedings, and the condemnor must compensate a landowner who is damaged by a violation of the restriction.

Caullett v. Stanley Stilwell & Sons, Inc. (1961)

Facts: A developer conveyed one acre to the plaintiff, inserting a clause in the deed that 'The grantors reserve the right to build or construct the original dwelling or building on said premises." The plaintiff brought suit to quiet title, arguing that such a covenant cannot run with the land.

Issue 1: Where a burden is placed on land and the corresponding benefit is personal to one of the parties, does the burden run with the land?

Rule 1: Where a benefit is clearly personal to the grantor, and not enhancing or otherwise affecting the use or value of any retained land, the covenant does not run with the land.

Issue 2: Can a covenant be enforced as an equitable servitude where the benefit is in gross and neither affects retained land of the grantor nor is part of a neighborhood scheme of similar restrictions?

Rule 2: Since the existence of a dominant estate is essential to the validity of the servitude granted, a benefit purely personal to the grantor does not burden the conveyed premises but only obligates the grantee personally.

Crane Neck Assoc, Inc. v. New York City/Long Island County Services Group (1984)

Facts: The defendant State facility leased property for the purpose of housing eight severely retarded adults in violation of a covenant restricting buildings to single family dwellings. The plaintiffs sought an injunction prohibiting the continuation of the lease.

Issue: May a court of equity refuse to enforce a restrictive covenant on public policy grounds?

Rule: If enforcement of a restrictive covenant would be contrary to public policy, a court may decline to enforce it. A court may impair private arrangements, so long as it is reasonably necessary to further an important public purpose, and the measures taken to impair the private arrangement are reasonable and appropriate to effectuate that purpose.

Western Land Co. v. Truskolaski (1972)

Facts: Western Land Co. subdivided a 40 acre tract of land and sold the lots subject to a covenant restricting the area to single family dwellings. Almost thirty years later, after considerable change in the character of the surrounding neighborhood, Western Land Co. attempted to build and operate a supermarket in violation of its own restrictive covenant. Homeowners in the subdivision brought suit to enjoin Western from building the supermarket.

Issue: Will restrictive covenants be enforced when the area in the vicinity of the restricted area undergoes considerable change?

Rule: As long as the original purpose of the covenants can still be accomplished, and substantial benefit continues to inure to the restricted area by their enforcement, courts will enforce restrictive covenants even when the surrounding area changes.

Laguna Royale Owners Association v. Darger (1981)

Facts: The Dargers owned a condominium unit in a 78 unit community apartment complex. A provision of the Subassignment and Occupancy Agreement required the approval of the Owners Association prior to an assignment of any interest. In violation of the agreement, the Dargers assigned 3/4 of their interest to three other couples. The Owners Association brought an action to have the assignment declared invalid.

Issue: Does an owners association of a condominium complex have an, absolute right to withhold approval of an owner's assignment of his interest?

Rule: In exercising its power to approve or disapprove transfers or assignments, an owners association must act reasonably, exercising its power in a fair and nondiscriminatory manner. It may withhold approval only for reasons rationally related to the protection, preservation, and proper operation of the property, and for the purposes of the association as set forth in its governing instruments.

Nahrstedt v. Lakeside Village Condominium Ass'n, Inc. (1992)

Facts: Nahrstedt, a Lakeside resident, and owner of three cats, sued the Association over its restriction against the ownership of pets.

Issue: Under what circumstances is an equitable servitude enforceable?

Rule: The enforceability of equitable servitudes is a mixed issue of law and fact and can only be resolved in the context of the specific facts of a case. Restrictions are enforceable when they prohibit conduct which interferes with or has a reasonable likelihood of interfering with the rights of other owners to the peaceful and quiet enjoyment of their property.

O'Buck v. Cottonwood Village Condominium Ass'n (1988)

Facts: The Association removed all television antennas from the roof, prohibited their reinstallation, and made cable available to all of the units for $10 per month per set. The O'Bucks, who owned 4 television sets, objected.

Issue: Under what circumstances will a homeowners association's restrictions be reasonable?

Rule: When a rule set down by a homeowners association does not infringe upon significant interests, the rule will be deemed reasonable.

Trustees of the Prince Condominium Trust v. Prosser (1992)

Facts: The homeowners association sued a unit owner who refused to pay monthly charges until his claim for loss of an assigned parking space was offset.

Issue: May a unit owner refuse to pay a monthly assessment because he asserts a grievance?

Rule: The fact that a unit owner has a grievance, does not permit him to refuse to pay monthly charges.

Duffey v. Superior Court (1992)

Facts: The Duffeys and others complained to their homeowners association about their neighbors' proposed erection of a patio cover that would block their ocean views. The association, in turn, joining the neighbors as parties, sued for a declaratory judgment, asking the court to determine whether the covenants prohibited the patio cover.

Issue: Should homeowners associations be permitted to name objecting neighbors in a lawsuit?

Rule: The notion of naming objecting neighbors in a lawsuit is incongruous with the purpose of homeowners associations, as the associations are responsible for enforcing a development's restriction, whether or not an individual's neighbors approve of his proposed activity. Thus, objecting neighbors may not be named in a lawsuit.

CHAPTER 8 PUBLIC INTERESTS IN LAND

I.   **EMINENT DOMAIN**
     Eminent domain is the power of the state and federal governments to take private property.

A.   The government may regulate the use of property. However, when the regulation goes too far, the act constitutes a taking and requires an exercise of the power of eminent domain.

B.   The power of eminent domain is limited by the Fifth Amendment's takings clause.

     1. The taking must be for a public use.

     2. Just compensation must be provided to the property holder.

II. **PROCEDURE TO EFFECT A TAKING**

A.   Condemnation
     A judicial proceeding brought to obtain title and compute the compensation due.

B.   Inverse Condemnation

     1. Often the state will restrict a landowner's use of property through regulation without exercising its power of eminent domain and without paying compensation. The landowner may nevertheless bring suit and attempt to force the state to obtain title and pay just compensation.

     2. There exists no set formula by which plaintiffs can argue that a taking has been effectuated. Nevertheless, courts consider several factors.

         a. The action does not benefit the public.
             The government action must directly promote a legitimate public use to be a valid exercise of the police power. If not, the state must compensate for past injury and cannot continue the activity even if compensation is given.

         b. The magnitude of the injury to the owner is too great. If the owner suffers too great a loss, the ordinance constitutes a taking regardless of the public benefit. In such a case, the state can only conduct the activity if compensation is given.

III.   PUBLIC USE REQUIREMENT

A.   The state may only take land for public use even though the property's owner is compensated. The concept of "public use" is by nature ill-defined; nevertheless, the courts have established guidelines in this area.

   1. Promoting a private use of land is not a legitimate government objective, regardless of how valuable that use is to the private parties.

   2. However, courts may permit an exercise of eminent domain which benefits certain private parties if the predominant purpose behind the action is public in nature.

B.   When a taking is rationally related to remedying a social or economic ill, the state need not actually possess and use the property.

IV.   REGULATORY TAKINGS

A.   Even if the public use requirement is met, when a regulation or ordinance exceeds constitutional limitations a taking has occurred and the owner is entitled to compensation. There are three tests to determine if a taking has occurred:

   1. Physical Invasion Test
   Has the land been physically invaded? (e.g., a government-built dam floods the owner's land).

   2. Prevention of Harm Test
   The benefit to the public from prohibiting a particular use of land is balanced against the extent of harm to the adversely affected owner. When the balance tips in the public's favor, no taking has occurred even if the owner's use or the value of the land is greatly impaired.

   3. Reasonable Return or Diminution in Value Test

When an owner can no longer realize a reasonable return on his investment, a taking occurs regardless of the public benefit.

B. Temporary Takings
If a regulation or ordinance is held to be an unconstitutional taking, an owner shall be compensated for the loss incurred during the period in which the regulation or ordinance was enforced.

V. JUST COMPENSATION

A. Just compensation is determined by the fair market value of the property at the time of the taking.

B. Value is computed based on the "highest and best use" to which the property can conceivably be put.

C. The state is not required to pay "substitution cost" (the expense to the owner of relocating where the cost of other property which can satisfy the owner's unique needs is higher than the market value of the land in question).

D. When payment of market value would be manifestly unjust to the owner or the public, or the value is too difficult to discern, substitution value may be required.

VI. ZONING

A. Regulating Land Use
The state may regulate land use by using the police power subject to the due process, equal protection and taking clauses. Zoning is the principal means of land-use regulation.

B. Under a state's zoning enabling act, the zoning power is delegated to local governments who develop a comprehensive plan responsive to the community's needs.

1. Local legislatures enact zoning ordinances.

2. Building departments enforce the ordinances.

3. A board of adjustment or board of zoning appeals is empowered to hear appeals of the building department's actions.

      a. However, the power to determine whether a proposed variance promotes the public welfare cannot be delegated without specified guidelines and standards intended to govern such decisions.

      b. The board must expressly consider all relevant factors when adjudicating variances.

C.   Cumulative Use Schemes
Most zoning ordinances establish a number of zoning categories and place each zoning district into one of those categories. The categories progress from most to least restrictive. The most restrictive category might allow only single homes. The next category may allow single home and apartment construction. Each successive category permits the activities from the more restrictive categories as well as additional uses, from commercial to heavy industrial. The modern trend is to reject cumulative use schemes on the grounds that the least restrictive districts result in an undesirable mixture of residential and industrial uses.

VII. TYPES OF ZONING

A.   Use or Area Zoning
The municipality is divided into districts in which only specified land uses are permitted (e.g., residential, commercial, or industrial).

B.   Spot Zoning
An ordinance allowing a deviation from a district's general restrictions for an individual's plot. An ordinance excepting a parcel from a comprehensive plan will be invalidated when the parcel's owner, but not the general community, is benefited.

C.   Floating Zones
A zone is established but not mapped. The zone is said to "float" over the entire community.

    1. A landowner may request that the zone be applied to his land.

    2. If the request is approved, the zone becomes anchored to a particular parcel.

D.   Cluster Zones

If the overall density of a district remains constant, the size and width of individual lots may be reduced, designating the space saved for common use.

E.   Planned Use Developments (PUDs)
     A developer submits a plan to the local authority that includes both residential and commercial uses.

F.   Density Controls
     Density controls are not concerned with use of the land (contrast with use restrictions). The controls regulate population and building construction such as:

     1. Minimum lot size

     2. Setback requirements mandating unbuilt land surrounding a structure

     3. Minimum square footage

     4. Height limits

G.   Contract or Conditional Zoning
     In exchange for a developer's promise to comply with conditions prescribed by it, the legislature will rezone a particular parcel so that its use may permissibly deviate from a district's restrictions.

VIII. EXCEPTIONS TO THE COMPREHENSIVE PLAN

A.   Nonconforming Use
     A use that existed prior to a zoning ordinance's enactment that does not conform to the new rules is a nonconforming use that will be permitted to continue indefinitely provided that:

     1. The use is not abandoned or terminated.

     2. The nonconforming use is not significantly changed.
        Example: a nonconforming grocery store cannot become a nonconforming auto garage

     3. The building or lot size is not expanded.

Note: Some statutes require amortization of nonconforming uses whereby the owner is granted a grace period during which the nonconforming use must be phased out.

B. Special Use Permits
    Uses that serve large numbers of people (e.g., schools) require special permits due to the problems (e.g., traffic) attending their anticipated use.

    1. A special permit is required even if the districts already permit schools, etc.

    2. The special use will generally be located within the district to minimize its attending problems.

C. Variance
    A variance is a deviation from the literal restrictions of a zoning ordinance. A variance will be granted if:

    1. The owner can show that an unnecessary hardship would result from the ordinance's enforcement.

    2. The need for a variance is unique to the applicant's parcel.

    3. The variance will not be adverse to the neighborhood's general welfare if it is granted.

D. Validity of Zoning Ordinances

    1. A zoning ordinance may be found invalid if:

        a. The ordinance violates the constitutional limits on police power. Early cases established the permissible aims of the police power as "public health, safety, morals, or general welfare." Recent cases have expanded this formulation to include other objectives such as community character.

            i. Approved Objectives:

                (1) Protecting residential districts

                (2) Family values

(3) Aesthetics

    ii. Impermissible Objectives:

        (1) Preventing population growth

        (2) Preventing progress and development

        (3) Precluding certain groups (unless shown to directly promote a government objective)

  b. The ordinance is beyond the local government's authority under the state's enabling act. The state's enabling act specifies those objectives the state may promote through zoning.

  c. It discriminates as to a particular parcel.

2. Due Process

  a. Procedural due process is required only if the zoning decision is administrative (i.e., a decision not taken by an elected body).

  b. Adoption of the comprehensive plan is a legislative duty.

  c. Unlike legislative acts, no presumption of validity attaches to a zoning board's action.

  d. An administrative action (e.g., denying a variance application), will only be valid if the landowner was provided with:

    i. Adequate notice;

    ii. A public hearing;

    iii. Written findings of fact and conclusions of law;

    iv. Preservation of the record for use on appeal;

    v. An impartial tribunal (i.e., its members may not have a pecuniary interest in the subject matter before the tribunal).

e. A zoning ordinance violates substantive due process only if it bears no rational relationship to permissible state objectives. Consequently, if the zoning ordinance's purported objective falls within the state's police power, it will not violate substantive due process.

3. Equal Protection
An ordinance is invalid if it constitutes exclusionary zoning.

a. The rational relation test is applied to zoning ordinances that differentiate between classes of people.

b. If the discrimination is based on a suspect classification or infringes on a fundamental right, the strict scrutiny test is triggered.

4. Takings

a. Even if rationally related to the exercise of the police power, a zoning ordinance depriving land of virtually all its economic use may constitute a taking and require just compensation.

b. Official map statutes

i. A community may adopt an official map designating areas of planned development.

ii. If privately held land reserved by the official map for future community use is developed by its owner, the community need only compensate him for the land's unimproved value.

iii. Official map statutes must, however, grant such exceptions as are necessary to provide the owner a reasonable return on his investment prior to the community's expansion.

CASE CLIPS

Village of Euclid v. Ambler Realty Co. (S.Ct. 1926)

Facts: The Village's zoning law designated certain areas as residential districts and excluded businesses of all sorts from these areas. The value of the Ambler's land, located in such a district, was substantially diminished.

Issue: Is a zoning ordinance which creates residential districts, from which all business and trade is excluded, and which therefore may reduce the value of property in such districts, invalid as an unreasonable deprivation of property without Due Process?

Rule: (Sutherland, J.) A zoning ordinance is unconstitutional only when its provisions are clearly arbitrary and unreasonable, having no substantial relation to the public health, safety, morals or general welfare. An ordinance which establishes residential districts in which all business is excluded is not unreasonable and does benefit the public.

Nectow v. City of Cambridge (1928)

Facts: A zoning ordinance limited a portion of the plaintiff's land to residential use. Because of the character of the district, no practical use could be made of P's land.

Issue: Must a zoning ordinance's application bear a substantial relation to the public health, morals, safety, and welfare?

Rule: (Sutherland, J,) An ordinance restricting a citizen's land is unconstitutional if it does not promote the health, safety, convenience, and general welfare of the public.

Durant v. Town of Dunbarton (1981)

Facts: Durant requested that the defendant planning board approve her subdivision plan. The planning board rejected her plan for three reasons: (1) potential disruption of natural watercourses; (2) potential sight distance problems from the driveways exiting onto a state highway; and (3) potential problems with subsurface septic systems. Durant brought suit, arguing that the board did not have the authority to deny the plan for these reasons.

Issue: Does a planning board have broad discretionary authority to approve or disapprove subdivision plans?

Rule: The scope of a planning board's discretionary authority to approve or reject a subdivision plan is quite broad, and it may require an applicant's plan to conform with conditions favorable to health, safety, convenience, or prosperity.

State ex rel. Miller v. Manders (1957)

Facts: Pursuant to Wisconsin's Official Map Law, Miller's request for a building permit was rejected. Miller brought suit to compel issuance of the permit.

Issue: When a city denies a landowner a building permit because of anticipated municipal growth, has the owner's property been taken without just compensation?

Rule: Provided the statute allows a permit to be granted if the applicant would be substantially damaged by its denial, an exercise of the police power, pursuant to an Official Map Law, does not constitute a taking without compensation.

Lomarch Corp. v. Mayor and Common Council of City of Englewood (1968)

Facts: New Jersey's Official Map Act allowed municipalities to freeze a landowner's attempt to develop designated land for one year while the municipality decided if it would purchase the land or not. Lomarch (plaintiff) applied for approval for a subdivision plan. Plaintiff was notified that the land had been reserved for park land acquisition, Lomarch challenged the statute.

Issue: Is an Official Map Act that mandates a one-year restriction on an owner's use of his land an unconstitutional taking?

Rule: An official Map Act that prohibits development of private property until a municipality decides whether to purchase the land constitutes a temporary taking for which just compensation must be made.

Hawaii Housing Auth. v. Midkiff (S.Ct. 1984)

Facts: After determining that the housing market was malfunctioning due to oligopolistic ownership of realty, Hawaii's legislature passed an act permitting the State to transfer title to specified real estate from large landowners to their tenants or others.

Issue: Does the Public Use Clause of the Fifth Amendment permit the use of eminent domain when such exercise is rationally related to a legitimate public purpose?

Rule: (O'Connor, J.) Reducing the concentration of fee simple ownership is a legitimate public purpose. In order to further this objective, a state may exercise its power of eminent domain to take title in real property from lessors (with just compensation) and transfer it to lessees.

City of Los Angeles v. Gage (1954)

Facts: Gage conducted a plumbing supply business on his property. In 1946 the City rezoned the area under a new ordinance. The new zoning designation for Gage's district did not permit the use to which he put the property. The new zoning ordinance required the discontinuance of nonconforming uses within five years. Five years after the ordinance was passed, the City (plaintiff) brought suit for an injunction to command defendants to discontinue their nonconforming use of the property.

Issue: Does a zoning ordinance requiring the discontinuance of a nonconforming use within a reasonable time deprive an owner of due process?

Rule: Use of a reasonable amortization scheme is a valid exercise of the police power.

Stone v. City of Wilton (1983)

Facts: The Stones owned land which was zoned for multi-family dwellings. With the intention of developing a multi-family housing project, the Stones (plaintiffs) secured funding, paid an architect to draw up plans and plats, and applied for a permit. In 1980, the city council rezoned the district to single-family residential, and denied the plaintiff's application. The Stones brought suit to challenge the validity of the ordinance and recover damages for expenses incurred.

Issue: Will efforts and expenditures made toward a construction project, with the expectation that a district will not be rezoned to prohibit such construction, create in the owner a vested right in completing the construction?

Rule: It is impossible to fix a definite percentage of the total cost which establishes vested rights. It depends on the type of project, its location, ultimate cost, and principally the amount accomplished under conformity. Each case must be decided by considering these factors.

Fasano v. Board of County Commissioners of Washington County (1973)

Facts: Fasano (plaintiff) objected to a change in the zoning of his neighborhood, contending that the change did not conform to the comprehensive plan.

Issue: Must a change in zoning conform with the comprehensive plan?

Rule: In order to alter a zoning classification, the party seeking the change must prove that such change is in conformance with the comprehensive plan.

Baker v. City of Milwaukie (1975)

Facts: In 1968 the City adopted a zoning ordinance which allowed within the plaintiff's district the construction of 39 units per acre. In November 1969, the City adopted a comprehensive plan, which allowed 17 units per acre in the plaintiff's district. Subsequently, an application was made for a building permit for the construction of a 102-unit apartment on property adjacent to the plaintiff's land. This complex would result in 26 units per acre. Baker brought suit to compel the City to conform its zoning ordinances to its comprehensive plan.

Issue: Once a city enacts a comprehensive plan, is it bound to effectuate it by conforming both pre-existing and subsequent zoning ordinances to the plan?

Rule: Upon passage of a comprehensive plan, a city is obligated to effectuate that plan and conform prior conflicting zoning ordinances, as well as subsequent ones, with the plan.

Green v. Hayward (1976)

Facts: A tract of land's location on the map accompanying the comprehensive plan was zoned for agricultural use. When a local company applied to have the area rezoned in order to build a bark-processing plant, the Board of County Commissioners (defendant) approved an application to rezone it for industrial use. Local residents challenged the action, contending that it did not conform with the plan.

Issue: Is a map which constitutes a part of a comprehensive plan the controlling land use document?

Rule: The relationship between the text and the maps within a particular comprehensive plan must be determined from the plan document itself considered as a whole. Hence, the map is not controlling.

Application of Devereux Foundation, Inc. (1945)

Facts: A zoning ordinance prohibited the use of land as a home for the mentally ill. Nevertheless, the Board of Adjustment granted a variance, stating that "the circumstances of this case warrant the granting of an exception." The residents of the suburban section opposed the variance.

Issue: On what basis may a Board of Adjustment grant a variance to the applicable zoning ordinance?

Rule: A zoning ordinance may be set aside only where a literal enforcement of its provisions would result in practical difficulties or unnecessary hardships that are substantial, serious and compelling.

Collard v. Incorporated Village of Flower Hill (1981)

Facts: Collard's predecessor in title applied for a rezoning of the land. The Village granted approval subject to certain conditions expressed in covenants restricting the use of the land. One condition provided that no structures could be altered without the consent of the local legislature. Without stating reasons, the Village rejected plaintiff's application to alter the structures.

Issue: May a municipality condition rezoning upon the execution of a private declaration of covenants restricting the use to which the parcel sought to be rezoned may be put?

Rule: Rezoning of a particular piece of property subject to conditions is permissible, as long as the conditions are reasonable and part of a comprehensive plan designed to promote the welfare of the community.

Cheney v. Village 2 of New Hope, Inc. (1968)

Facts: The local legislature amended the town's zoning ordinances to allow a PUD (Planned Unit Development) in a previously zoned, low-density district. Pursuant to the amendments, a planning commission was empowered to regulate the PUD's internal development.

Issue 1: May a local legislature amend a comprehensive zoning plan to allow new uses of specified areas which the prior plan did not permit?

Rule 1: A comprehensive zoning plan, once passed by the local legislature, may be changed by the passage of new ordinances, provided that the legislature passes the new ordinance with some demonstration of sensitivity to impact it will have on the community as a whole.

Issue 2: May the legislature devolve to a planning commission the power to regulate a PUD's internal development?

Rule 2: A planning commission may be invested with the power to regulate the internal use of a particular district. The exercise of such power must, however, strictly accord with the applicable zoning ordinance.

Frankland v. City of Lake Oswego (1973)

Facts: The City of Lake Oswego (defendant) enacted a PUD ordinance requiring, as part of the final plan, detailed architectural sketches of the type of buildings planned, their prospective locations, and their general height and bulk characteristics. The plaintiff's, adjoining property owners, challenged the construction of the buildings, contending that they were not built according to the plan submitted to the City.

Issue: Is a developer who fails to comply with the submitted sketches in noncompliance with the approved final plan and the zoning ordinance that authorizes the construction of PUDs?

Rule: Once approved in the final plan, a developer is bound to construct a PUD in accordance with the submitted sketches.

City of Eastlake v. Forest City Enterprises, Inc. (1976)

Facts: Forest City Enterprises, Inc. (plaintiff) contended that the City's (defendant) charter provision, requiring any change in land use agreed to by the City Council by a 55% vote in referendum, was invalid.

Issue: Does a city charter provision requiring proposed land use changes to be ratified by 55% of the voters violate the due process rights of owners who apply for zoning changes?

Rule: Since zoning is within the scope of legislative power, and since this power is reserved by the people to themselves, the referendum process does not violate the Due Process Clause when applied to a zoning ordinance.

Pennsylvania Coal Co. v. Mahon (S.Ct 1922)

Facts: A state statute forbade the mining of coal in such a way as to cause subsidence under certain structures. Pennsylvania Coal (defendant) owned the rights to mine underneath Mahon's house. Mahon claimed that the statute abolished this right.

Issue: Does a regulation based on the police power that destroys existing property and contract rights constitute a taking?

Rule: (Holmes, J.) While property may be regulated to a certain extent, if the regulation goes too far, it will be recognized as a taking. There must be an exercise of eminent domain and compensation to sustain it.

Dissent: (Brandeis, J.) The legislature has the power to prohibit by statute such activities which seriously threaten the public welfare, even if such regulation deprives the property owner of an existing right.

Penn Central Transportation Co. v. City of New York (S.Ct. 1978)

Facts: New York City's Landmarks Preservation Law restricted the extent to which designated buildings and sites—here, Grand Central Terminal—may be altered.

Issue: As part of a comprehensive program to preserve historic landmarks and historic districts, may a city place restrictions on the development of individual historic landmarks—in addition to those imposed by applicable zoning ordinances—without effecting a "taking" requiring the payment of "just compensation?"

Rule: (Brennan, J.) A landmark restriction does not constitute a taking as long as it preserves for the property owner the opportunity to achieve a reasonable return on his investment.

Dissent: (Rehnquist, J.) The evidence is unclear as to whether the property owner can yet realize a reasonable return. We would therefore remand to the lower court for a determination of this issue.

Keystone Bituminous Coal Ass'n v. De Benedictis (S.Ct. 1987)

Facts: To prevent subsidence, the state prohibited coal miners from mining more than 50% of the coal beneath any building.

Issue: Is a law that prohibits coal miners from mining more than 50% of the coal underneath a building an unconstitutional regulatory taking without compensation?

Rule: (Stevens, J.) A statute, designed to serve a legitimate public interest, that does not unduly interfere with investment backed expectations, or make it impossible to profitably engage in business, does not effect a regulatory taking.

Dissent: (Rehnquist, C.J.) This case is indistinguishable from *Pennsylvania Coal*.

Nollan v. California Coastal Commission (S.Ct 1987)

Facts: The Nollans (plaintiffs) owned beachfront property a quarter of a mile from a public beach. The state would not allow the plaintiffs to build on their land unless they granted an easement for the public to pass through a portion of their land.

Issue: Is a state's conditioning of a grant of a building permit upon the transfer to the public of an easement across the property an unconstitutional taking?

Rule: (Scalia, J.) Unless a permit condition is reasonably related to a legitimate public need, a building restriction is not a valid regulation of land use but a taking without compensation.

Dissent: (Brennan, J.) First, the majority demands a degree of exactitude that is inconsistent with our standard for reviewing the rationality of a state's exercise of its police power for the welfare of its citizens. Second, even if the nature of the public access condition imposed must be identical to the precise burden on the access created by appellants, this requirement is plainly satisfied.

First English Evangelical Lutheran Church of Glendale v. County of Los Angeles (S.Ct 1987)

Facts: Pursuant to an Interim Ordinance, the plaintiff church was denied use of its property because it was within an interim flood protection area. The plaintiff sued to recover damages arising from the period during which it lost the use of the land, but the lower courts limited the remedies to declaratory relief or possibly mandamus.

Issue: Does the Just Compensation Clause require compensation as a remedy for "temporary" regulatory takings?

Rule: (Rehnquist, J.) Where a government ordinance has already worked a taking of all use of property, then a subsequent invalidation of the ordinance, and thus the conversion of the taking into a "temporary" one, is not sufficient to meet the demands of the Just Compensation Clause.

Dissent: (Stevens, J,) A regulatory program which adversely affects property values does not constitute a taking unless it destroys a major portion of the property's value. The court should consider how the owner's use of the property is affected, as well as the duration of the restrictions.

Village of Arlington Heights v. Metropolitan Housing Development Corp. (1977)

Facts: The defendant refused to rezone a district from single family use to multiple-dwelling units for low income groups.

Issue: Does a decision refusing to rezone violate the Fourteenth Amendment if it has a racially discriminatory effect?

Rule: To be unconstitutional, a zoning board's refusal to rezone in order to permit low income housing must entail a discriminatory purpose, not merely a racially disproportionate impact.

Village of Belle Terre v. Boraas (S.Ct 1974)

Facts: Belle Terre's (defendant) zoning ordinance limited all land use in the Village to one-family dwellings. The ordinance also defined "family" as any number of related people "living and working together" but not more than two unrelated people.

Issue: Pursuant to the police power, may a zoning ordinance limit the number of unrelated persons who may live together in a single-family dwelling?

Rule: (Douglas, J.) A zoning ordinance restricting the number of unrelated people who may live in a single-family house is not an unconstitutional infringement of First Amendment rights because it bears a rational relationship to permissible state objectives.

Dissent: (Marshall, J.) Such an ordinance violates prospective tenants' First Amendment freedom of association and constitutionally guaranteed right to privacy.

Moore v. City of East Cleveland (1977)

Facts: East Cleveland's (plaintiff) housing ordinance limited a dwelling's occupants to members of a single "family," but excluded certain members of the extended family from the definition of "family."

Issue: Does a housing ordinance prohibiting members of an extended family from cohabitating violate the Due Process Clause of the Fourteenth Amendment?

Rule: An ordinance prohibiting members of an extended family from cohabiting violates Due Process if not tailored to serving an important government interest.

City of Cleburne v. Cleburne Living Center, Inc. (S.Ct. 1985)

Facts: The City's zoning ordinance required group home facilities for the mentally retarded to obtain a special permit, but other group facilities were not so required. The City denied a permit to the Cleburne Living Center's proposed facility.

Issue: May a zoning ordinance require a special permit for a group home for the mentally ill when other care and multiple-dwelling facilities are not required to obtain a special permit?

Rule: (White, J.) A density regulation applied to group homes for the mentally retarded but not to other care facilities and multiple-dwelling units is invalid under the Equal Protection Clause unless the ordinance is shown to be rationally related to a legitimate government purpose.

Southern Burlington County NAACP v. Township of Mount Laurel (1983)

Facts: The admitted goal of Mount Laurel's zoning ordinance was to maintain favorable local tax rates by excluding those people who would require extensive municipal services such as education. The effect of this ordinance was to shut out people of less than middle income. Mount Laurel rezoned pursuant to a court decree in Mount Laurel I, the township was forced to rezone under a court decree. Despite the town's act of rezoning, the ordinance failed to provide a realistic opportunity for the construction of low income housing.

Issue: May a court require a municipality to adopt inclusionary zoning devices?

Rule: Where a municipality's obligation to afford a realistic opportunity for the construction of its fair share of the region's lower income housing needs cannot be satisfied by removal of restrictive barriers, inclusionary devices keyed to the construction of lower income housing are constitutional and within the zoning power of a municipality.

Associated Home Builders v. City of Livermore (1976)

Facts: The defendant's initiative zoning ordinance prohibited issuance of further residential building permits until local educational, sewage disposal, and water supply facilities complied with specified standards. The plaintiffs, an association of contractors, brought suit to enjoin enforcement of the ordinance.

Issues: Is a zoning ordinance that temporarily and impartially restricts immigration into a community subject to strict scrutiny analysis?

Rule: An exclusionary ordinance is valid when it is reasonably related to the welfare of the region affected.

Hadacheck v. Sebastian (S.Ct. 1915)

Facts: The Chief of Police of the City of Los Angeles (defendant) enforced against a brickmaker (plaintiff) an ordinance prohibiting the operation of brick kilns within certain districts.

Issue: Does an ordinance promulgated pursuant to the police power prohibiting the operation of a lawful business constitute a taking?

Rule: (McKenna, J.) A necessary and lawful business that is not a nuisance, per se, can be made so by legislative action and such exercise of the police power, if neither arbitrary nor discriminatory, does not constitute a taking.

Mayor & Council of New Castle v. Rollins Outdoor Advertising, Inc. (1983)

Facts: Defendant Rollins' predecessor in title began to use a piece of property for advertising purposes prior to the enactment of any zoning law. Rollins obtained title and used the property for the same purpose. Subsequently, an amendment to a zoning law forced the elimination of this nonconforming use through a gradual amortization of its value.

Issue: Does an ordinance which compels the termination of a nonconforming use after a specified period of time, but against the will of a landowner and without compensation, constitute an unconstitutional taking of private property?

Rule: The forced termination of a nonconforming use through amortization (allowing the use to continue only for a specified period of time to allow the owner to recoup the investment) is an unreasonable exercise of the police power. The state may eliminate an otherwise lawful activity only through eminent domain.

Krause v. City of Royal Oak (1968)

Facts: The City of Royal Oak enacted a zoning ordinance in 1957 which zoned the plaintiff's land for single-family residential use. The plaintiff brought suit in 1966 to restrain the City from enforcing the ordinance, contending that the property could be more profitably used for multiple-family apartments.

Issue: Is a land-use ordinance invalid if it deprives a property owner of the best economic use of the land?

Rule: As long as a land-use ordinance preserves part of the land's value by allowing for some uses, then a deprivation of the best economic use of that property is not a sufficient reason to invalidate the ordinance.

People ex rel. Skokie Town House Builders v. Morton Grove (1959)

Facts: Because of a noncumulative zoning ordinance, the village of Morton Grove (defendant) refused to grant Skokie Town House Builders (plaintiff) a permit to build residences in a non-dwelling unit district. A noncumulative zoning ordinance excludes most future residences from commercial and industrial districts.

Issue: Do noncumulative zoning ordinances, which exclude future residences from commercial and industrial districts, violate due process?

Rule: The enactment of noncumulative zoning ordinances is, where the exclusion bears a substantial relationship to the preservation of the public health, safety, or general welfare, a valid exercise of the state's police power.

City of Renton v. Playtime Theatres, Inc. (S.Ct 1986)

Facts: A city zoning ordinance prohibited adult movie theaters from locating within 1000 feet of any residential zone, church, park, or school. Playtime Theatres brought suit on grounds that the ordinance was unconstitutional.

Issue: Does a zoning ordinance that prohibits adult movie theaters from locating within 1000 feet of any residential zone, church, park, or school violate the First Amendment?

Rule: (Rehnquist, J.) A zoning ordinance designed to serve a substantial government interest that does not unreasonably limit alternative avenues of communication is, if content neutral, a valid time, place, and manner regulation of speech.

Dissent: (Brennan, J.) The ordinance selectively imposes limitations on the location of a movie theater based exclusively on the content of the films shown there.

Simon v. Needham (1942)

Facts: A zoning by-law prescribed a minimum area of one acre for house lots in the residential district in which plaintiff's land was located. The plaintiff challenged the validity of the by-law.

Issue: May a city require that all houses in a district be on a minimum area of one acre?

Rule: A zoning ordinance is valid where the interests of the public require such action and where the means employed are reasonably necessary for the accomplishment of the purpose.

Puritan-Greenfield Improvement Ass'n v. Leo (1967)

Facts: Leo (defendant), whose property abutted a commercial lot and faced a heavily traveled road, was granted a variance to use the property as a dental and medical clinic. The plaintiff challenged the issuance of the variance on the grounds that the defendant had not demonstrated "unnecessary hardship or practical difficulties."

Issue 1: To obtain a use variance based on hardship, must the hardship be unique to the property for which the variance is sought?

Rule 1: A use variance may not be granted unless the landowner's plight is due to unique circumstances and not to general conditions in the neighborhood that may reflect the unreasonableness of the zoning.

Issue 2: May a board of zoning appeals grant a variance on the ground of unnecessary hardship absent substantial evidence that the property cannot be reasonably used in a manner consistent with the existing zoning?

Rule 2: A use variance should not be granted unless the board of zoning appeals finds on the basis of substantial evidence that the property cannot yield a reasonable return or be put to proper economic use in a manner consistent with existing zoning.

Kotrich v. The County of Du Page (1960)

Facts: Salt Creek Club's application for a special use permit was denied by the zoning board but approved by the county board of supervisors (defendant). The plaintiffs, who are adjacent property owners, challenged the defendant's authority to grant special use permits because the enabling act did not provide for such permits.

Issue: May a county board of supervisors provide special use permits absent explicit statutory authorization?

Rule: A residual category of those special uses which cannot be included in the customary classifications without distortion is permissible as a means of implementing the powers conferred by the statute.

Kuehne v. City of East Hartford (1950)

Facts: The City of East Hartford (defendant) granted a landowner's application to change his lot from residential to business use. The plaintiff challenged such action as constituting "spot zoning,"

Issue: May a zoning authority give to a single lot or small area privileges not extended to other land in the vicinity?

Rule: Action by a zoning authority which gives privileges to a single lot or small area which are not extended to other land in the vicinity is against sound public policy and invalid if not done in furtherance of a general plan properly adopted for and designed to serve the best interests of the community as a whole.

Rodgers v. Village of Tarrytown (1951)

Facts: The Village of Tarrytown (defendant) amended its zoning ordinance by creating a floating zone. The boundaries of the new type district were not delineated in the ordinance but were to be fixed by amendment of the official village building zone map, at such times as such class of zone is applied to properties.

Issue: May a local legislature amend its zoning ordinance by creating floating zones?

Rule: A legislature may create floating zones if they are in accord with the comprehensive zoning plan and benefit the community as a whole.

Sylvania Electronic Products, Inc. v. City of Newton (1962)

Facts: Sylvania Electronic Products, Inc. sought a rezoning of his property from residential to light manufacturing. To induce the city to rezone, the plaintiff agreed to place restrictive covenants on its land and give the city an option to buy a dominant estate. Sylvania subsequently challenged the restrictions.

Issue: May a zoning authority rezone on the express condition that the owner impose restrictions on his land?

Rule: If not contrary to the best interests of the community, a zoning authority may rezone on the express condition that the owner impose restrictions on his land.

Village of Arlington Heights v. Metropolitan Housing Development Corp. (1977)

Facts: The defendant refused to rezone a district from single family use to multiple-dwelling units for low income groups. By effecting a racially discriminatory impact, the plaintiff contended that the defendant's decision violated the Fair Housing Act.

Issue: Is a finding that an action has a discriminatory effect, without a concomitant finding that the action was taken with discriminatory intent, sufficient to support the conclusion that the action violated the Fair Housing Act?

Rule: Under some circumstances, a violation of the Fair Housing Act can be established by a showing of discriminatory effect without a showing of discriminatory intent.

Southern Burlington County NAACP v. Township of Mount Laurel (1975)

Facts: The admitted goal of Mount Laurel's zoning ordinance was to maintain favorable local tax rates by excluding those people who would require extensive municipal services such as education. The effect of this ordinance was to shut out people of less than middle income.

Issue: May a developing municipality make it physically and economically impossible to provide low and moderate income housing in the municipality for the various categories of persons who need and want it, thereby excluding such people from living within its confines because of the limited extent of their income and resources?

Rule: A developing municipality cannot foreclose the opportunity for low and moderate income people to obtain housing. A municipality must bear its fair share of the burden arising from regional development; to this end, its land use regulations must make realistically possible an appropriate variety and choice of housing.

Jordan v. Village of Menomonee Falls (1966)

Facts: Jordan (plaintiff) was required to pay a fee or dedicate a portion of his land to the defendant Village in order to obtain permission to subdivide the land. The Village's ordinance was enacted to insure adequate open spaces and that sites for public uses would be properly located. The plaintiff claimed that the ordinance was unconstitutional.

Issue: Does a village requirement that a subdivider pay a fee or dedicate a portion of the land to the village in order to obtain permission to subdivide constitute an unconstitutional taking of private property for a public purpose?

Rule: The required dedication of land for a fee is a valid exercise of police power, not a taking, if the evidence reasonably establishes that the burden cast on the subdivider is specifically and uniquely attributable to his activity.

Contractors & Builders Ass'n v. City of Dunedin (1976)

Facts: In response to population growth, the City of Dunedin (defendant) enacted an ordinance that imposed connection charges (i.e., fees paid only by new users of the City's sewer and water systems). The ordinance failed to restrict use of the money so collected to expansion needs. The plaintiffs, an association of building contractors, contended that the fees constituted a tax, which only the legislature can impose.

Issue: May a municipality raise capital to expand public services by imposing connection charges?

Rule: Raising expansion capital by setting connection charges, which do not exceed a pro rata share of reasonably anticipated costs of expansion, is permissible where expansion is reasonably required, if the use of the money collected is limited to meeting the costs of expansion.

Construction Indus. Ass'n of Sonoma County v. City of Petaluma (1975)

Facts: The City of Petaluma (defendant) passed an ordinance which restricted the number of new housing units to 500 per year, but the restriction was applicable only to projects of five or more dwellings. The plaintiffs challenged the ordinance as unconstitutional.

Issue: Is a zoning plan that limits the growth of a community an arbitrary and unreasonable exclusionary device violative of due process?

Rule: An exclusionary zoning ordinance is valid if it bears a rational relationship to legitimate state interests.

Golden v. Planning Board of Town of Ramapo (1972)

Facts: Pursuant to its zoning authority, D adopted a growth-control plan that designated subdivisions a special use requiring a permit.

Issue: May a local community implement a sequential development and timed growth ordinance whereby development is conditioned on the provision of specified services and facilities?

Rule: Where it is clear that the existing physical and financial resources of a community are inadequate to furnish the essential services and facilities which a substantial increase in population requires, there is a rational basis for "phased growth," and hence such an ordinance is not violative of the federal or state constitutions.

Claridge v. New Hampshire Wetlands Board (1984)

Facts: The Claridges (plaintiffs) were denied a permit to fill their property and build upon it because the state found it to be a valuable ecological resource. The plaintiffs contend that the denial constituted a taking and required just compensation.

Issue: Does a regulation that precludes development of property constitute a compensable taking of property?

Rule: Only where an owner's substantial, justified expectations concerning the property are thwarted and the burden of the state's action being cast on that property owner is unreasonably onerous, does a regulation that prevents development of property constitute a taking.

State ex rel. Stoyanoff v. Berkeley (1970)

Facts: Berkeley was denied a building permit on grounds that the proposed residence did not conform to certain aesthetic standards established in the town's zoning ordinance.

Issue: Is the imposition of aesthetic standards on proposed buildings by a zoning ordinance unreasonable as an arbitrary exercise of police power?

Rule: When the basic purpose to be served is that of the general welfare of persons in the entire community by preserving property values, the use of aesthetic standards in zoning ordinances is not arbitrary or unreasonable.

Figarsky v. Historic District Commission (1976)

Facts: The plaintiffs' land was located within the Norwich historic district. When the building commissioner ordered the plaintiffs to conduct certain needed repairs on a building on the land, they instead applied for a permit to demolish the building. The plaintiffs were denied the permit on the grounds that it was in a historic district.

Issue: Does preservation of a historical area or landmark fall within the meaning of general welfare and, consequently, the police power?

Rule: Because aesthetic considerations have a definite relation to the public welfare, land use regulations based, in part, on well defined aesthetic considerations are a valid exercise of the police power.

People v. Stover (1963)

Facts: The city enacted an ordinance prohibiting clotheslines in the front or side yards abutting a street. When the Stovers (defendants) were charged with violating the ordinance, they contended that the ordinance was invalid.

Issue: Are aesthetic considerations alone sufficient to justify exercise of the police power?

Rule: Reasonable legislation designed to promote aesthetic ends alone is a valid and permissible exercise of the police power.

Hoffmann v. Kinealy (1965)

Facts: The City of St. Louis enacted a zoning ordinance which required the discontinuance of pre-existing nonconforming uses after a specified number of years. When the City notified the plaintiffs to cease using their property because it was not permitted under the ordinance, the plaintiffs challenged the ordinance as unconstitutional.

Issue: Does a zoning ordinance requiring the amortization of pre-existing nonconforming uses deprive owners of vested property rights and thereby constitute a taking?

Rule: The termination of an owner's previously lawful nonconforming use of his property pursuant to an "amortization" ordinance constitutes the taking of private property for public use without just compensation.

Jenad, Inc. v. Village of Scarsdale (1966)

Facts: The Village of Scarsdale (defendant) passed an ordinance which required subdivides either to set aside park land or, in lieu of park land within the subdivision, to pay money into a common fund to be used to purchase park land.

Issue: Can a village authorize its planning board to require that the subdivider allot some land within the subdivision for park purposes or instead, at the option of the village planning board, pay the village a fee in lieu of such allotment?

Rule: Since new subdivisions create or add to a village's need to provide park land, a village reasonably exercises its police power when it requires subdividers either to set aside park land or to pay an equalization fee.

Williamson County Regional Planning Commission v. Hamilton Bank (S.Ct. 1955)

Facts: A county zoning ordinance reduced the number of residential units that plaintiff could build on its land. The Commission had the power to grant variances to the ordinance. Tennessee law allowed a property owner to bring suit to obtain just compensation. The plaintiff, without having pursued either of these options, brought suit in Federal District Court.

Issue: When can a plaintiff bring suit alleging that a government regulation constitutes a "taking" of property?

Rule: (Blackmun, J.) A plaintiff cannot claim that a regulation violates the Just Compensation Clause until (1) the appropriate government entity has reached a final decision on the regulation's application to the property at issue, and (2) the property owner has used the procedures provided by the State for seeking just compensation.

Berman v. Parker (1954)

Facts: The District of Columbia Redevelopment Act permitted the taking of private property by eminent domain and the transfer of it to private interests to develop for private use. The plaintiffs, seeking to enjoin the condemnation of their property, challenged the constitutionality of the Act.

Issue: Pursuant to the police power, may Congress use its power of eminent domain to gain title to private property and then transfer title to private interests?

Rule: If a legitimate public purpose is present, Congress may, by exercise of its power of eminent domain, take title to private property and transfer it to private interests for development for private use.

Miller v. City of Tacoma (1963)

Facts: The City of Tacoma condemned a blighted area of the city to further urban renewal. The plaintiff, whose land was within the affected area, claimed that the action was unconstitutional.

Issue: Are urban renewal laws constitutional?

Rule: Urban renewal laws are for a public use and are constitutional. Hence, the expenditure of public funds pursuant to such a law is for a public purpose, and the exercise of eminent domain is valid.

Courtesy Sandwich Shop, Inc. v. Port of New York Auth. (1963)

Facts: To stimulate the economic well-being of the Port of New York, the Port Authority was authorized to condemn property for any activity functionally related to the construction of the World Trade Center. The plaintiff claimed that the law violated the Constitution.

Issue: Is the condemnation of property valid for no other purpose than the raising of revenue for the completion of a public use project?

Rule: If subordinated to a primary purpose, property may be condemned for the production of revenue needed to build a public use project.

Poletown Neighborhood Council v. City of Detroit (1981)

Facts: The City's legislature condemned a residential neighborhood with the intention of conveying it to General Motors as the site for a proposed factory. The Neighborhood Council challenged the action.

Issue: Can a city condemn private land for the purpose of allowing an important local company to construct a plant and thus increase employment and improve the city's economy?

Rule: Where the condemnation power is exercised in a way that benefits specific and identifiable private interests, a court will inspect with heightened scrutiny the claim that the public interest is the predominant interest being advanced. Such public benefit must not be speculative, but must be clear and significant to render the condemnation legitimate. In this case, Detroit had demonstrated that the benefit to the people of the city is significant and warrants the condemnation.

City of Oakland v. Oakland Raiders (1982)

Facts: The owners of the Oakland Raiders football team planned to move the team to Los Angeles. The City of Oakland attempted to acquire the team through eminent domain in order to keep it in the city.

Issue: Can a city prove that its exercise of eminent domain to acquire a sports team from its private owners serves a valid public use?

Rule: The operation of a sports franchise may be an appropriate and valid municipal function. Therefore, if a valid public purpose can be demonstrated, a city may acquire a sports team through eminent domain.

United States v. Fuller (S.Ct. 1973)

Facts: The government condemned Fuller's lands, which were adjacent to and being used in conjunction with certain government lands under revocable grazing permits issued by the government. In order to use the lands for grazing, Fuller had made certain improvements. Fuller challenged the Government's measurement of the land's value.

Issue: Where the Government condemns lands whose value is augmented by their proximity to Government lands, must the Government pay compensation for the added value attributable to the location?

Rule: (Rehnquist, J.) The Government as condemnor is not required to compensate a condemnee for elements of value that the Government has created, or that it might have destroyed under the exercise of governmental authority other than the power of eminent domain.

Dissent: (Powell, J.) The Government must pay the market value of the land, including any value attributable to the land's proximity to the government lands.

United States v. 564.54 Acres of Land (S.Ct. 1979)

Facts: 564.54 Acres Corp. operated three nonprofit summer camps used as a public recreational project. In 1970 the United States condemned these properties.

Issue: When the Government condemns property owned by a private nonprofit organization and operated for a public purpose, is the condemnee entitled to replacement costs or merely fair market value?

Rule: (Marshall, J.) The just compensation requirement of the Fifth Amendment does not require compensating condemnees for the nontransferable value arising from the owner's unique need for the property. Therefore, fair market value, not replacement costs, is the measure of compensation due.

Loretto v. Teleprompter Manhattan CATV Corp. (S.Ct. 1982)

Facts: A New York statute mandated that landlords must allow a cable television company to install its cable facilities on their property. Loretto purchased an apartment building, and then discovered that the cable installation occupied portions of her roof and the side of her building. Loretto challenged the statute.

Issue: Does a minor but permanent physical occupation of an owner's property authorized by the government constitute a "taking" of property for which just compensation is due under the Fifth and Fourteenth Amendments of the Constitution?

Rule: (Marshall, J.) A permanent physical occupation authorized by government is a taking without regard to the public interests that it may serve.

Dissent: (Blackmun, J.) A takings rule based on technical distinctions is inherently suspect and inappropriate for modern social problems. Instead, the court should consider the interests of all private parties and the benefit to the public.

Lucas v. South Carolina Coastal Comm'n (S.Ct. 1992)

Facts: Lucas purchased land for residential development purposes. Before he was able to erect any permanent structures on the land, the state passed an act barring their development. He filed suit, claiming that the act constituted a taking because it extinguished his property's value.

Issue: Is a taking established where a regulation causes a landowner to lose the economically viable use of his land?

Rule: (Scalia, J.) If a regulatory action deprives an owner of all economically viable use of his land, a taking exists, and the state must compensate the landowner, unless the prohibited use of the land constitutes a nuisance under the state common law.

Dissent: (Blackmun, J.) The Court has created a new taking doctrine for which there is no justification. Furthermore, a landowner does not lose all economically viable use of his land where, as here, numerous sticks in his bundle of rights are still available, such as, his right to use the land and the right to exclude others.

Dissent: (Stevens, J.) The chance that property might be rendered valueless is a risk inherent in investment. If this is the result of a generally applicable Act motivated by a compelling purpose, such an Act does not constitute a taking.

PA Northwestern Distribs., Inc. v. Zoning Hearing Board (1991)

Facts: PA Northwestern appealed the passage of an amendment of the zoning ordinance to regulate "adult commercial enterprises." The amendment, which passed not long after plaintiff had opened an adult book store, would have forced plaintiff to close his business.

Issue: Is a zoning ordinance which requires the amortization and discontinuation of a lawful pre-existing nonconforming use confiscatory and violative as a taking of property without just compensation?

Rule: The amortization and discontinuance of a lawful preexisting nonconforming use is per se confiscatory and violative as a taking of property without just compensation.

Commons v. Westwood Zoning Board of Adjustment (1980)

Facts: Commons (plaintiff) applied for a variance to build a house which did not conform with the city's zoning plan. The zoning ordinance permitted the issuance of variances if certain criteria were met. Without clearly specifying its reasons, the Zoning Board (defendant) rejected the plaintiff's variance application.

Issue: Must a zoning board specify its reasons for granting or rejecting a variance application?

Rule: A zoning board must expressly address all relevant factors in determining whether the statutory criteria for a variance were satisfied.

Cope v. Inhabitants of the Town of Brunswick (1983)

Facts: The plaintiff's application for an exception to a zoning ordinance was rejected by the defendant board because "granting it," said the board, "would adversely affect the health, safety, or general welfare of the public and alter the essential characteristics of the surrounding property."

Issue: Is a zoning ordinance unconstitutional when it grants the zoning board authority to grant or deny exceptions based upon its own determination of whether the proposed use would "adversely affect the health, safety or general welfare of the public?"

Rule: Whether a use of property will generally comply with the health, safety and welfare of the public and the character of the area is a legislative question. The determination of this issue cannot be delegated to a local zoning board without specific guidelines as to what unique or distinctive characteristics of a particular use will render it detrimental to the neighborhood.

Arnel Development Co. v. City of Costa Mesa (1980)

Facts: Arnel Development Co.'s (plaintiff) housing proposal for its fifty acres was thwarted by an initiative circulated by a neighborhood association and approved by voters.

Issue: Is the rezoning of specific, relatively small parcels of land essentially adjudicatory in nature and thus incapable of being enacted by initiative?

Rule: Zoning ordinances are legislative acts and may be enacted by initiative.

Metromedia, Inc. v. City of San Diego (S.Ct. 1981)

Facts: A San Diego ordinance restricted the use of certain kinds of outdoor signs, including all noncommercial advertising and offsite commercial advertising. Metromedia claimed that the ordinance was unconstitutional.

Issue: Do the First and Fourteenth Amendments prohibit an ordinance which bans noncommercial advertising and some types of commercial advertising?

Rule: (White, J.) An ordinance which permits some kinds of commercial speech cannot ban all noncommercial advertising.

Concurrence: (Brennan, J.) A ban is constitutional only if it is shown to directly promote a government interest that cannot be advanced by a more narrowly drawn ordinance.

Dissent: (Burger, C.J.) A city may make a distinction between different types of commercial advertising whereas it may not do so for noncommercial advertising. Therefore, the ordinance is valid.

Elliott v. City of Athens (1992)

Facts: Elliott sought a rezoning of his property located in a single-family residential district so that he could sell it to a group for use as a center for alcohol and drug rehabilitation.

Issue: Is a zoning ordinance which holds that there is a maximum occupancy limitation for unrelated persons exempt from the Fair Housing Act?

Rule: Where a zoning restriction is reasonable, i.e., it represents a city's strong and legitimate interests in controlling density, traffic and noise, it is exempt from the Fair Housing Act.

CHAPTER 9 THE SALE OF LAND

I. THE STATUTE OF FRAUDS
A contract for the sale or purchase of an interest in land must be in writing to be enforceable. When one says a contract "falls within" the statute, it will only be enforced if it is in writing. A contract that "falls outside the statute" will be enforced even if it is not in writing.

A. Contracts for an interest in land that require a writing

Mnemonic:
When parties convey land, They Must Leave Evidence.

1. Timber
Contracts for the sale of timber, minerals and oil must be written if the buyer will remove the same after title to the land passes to him.

2. Mortgages
A promise to give a mortgage as security for a loan must be in writing. Assigning rights to a mortgage may be oral.

3. Leases
Some states allow oral leases of less than one year.

4. Easements

B. A contract which by its terms is incapable of being performed within one year is unenforceable if not in writing.

1. The one year period begins to run from the signing of the contract, not from the beginning of performance.

2. The fact that performance within a year is very unlikely will not place a contract within the statute as long as the agreement may theoretically be performed within a year.

C. Requirement of a Writing
A contract or memorandum will satisfy the statute of frauds if the writing contains the following elements.

Mnemonic: <u>T</u>he <u>S</u>tatute <u>I</u>s <u>R</u>eally <u>S</u>trict

1. <u>T</u>erms and conditions (essential terms) of the agreement are specified.

2. <u>S</u>ubject matter identified.

3. <u>I</u>dentity of the parties to the contract.

4. <u>R</u>ecital of consideration.

5. <u>S</u>ignature of the party to be charged.

Note: Under UCC § 2-201 the requirements of a writing are satisfied if a memorandum is "sufficient to indicate that a contract for sale has been made between the parties, and it is signed by the party against whom enforcement is sought."

D. A party that has performed a contract that was later invalidated by the Statute of Frauds may be entitled to recover on the theories of unjust enrichment and promissory estoppel.

II. MARKETABLE TITLE
Unless otherwise specified, a contract for the sale of real property implies that the seller will deliver marketable title at the closing. Marketable title is "free from reasonable doubt" as to its validity as that which a prudent and experienced businessman would be willing to accept.

There are a number of common defects that may make a title unmarketable:

A. Defects in the Chain of Title

1. Wrong names

2. Improper description

3. Defective recording

4. Incompetent conveyor

5. Inability to establish a record

       6. Adverse possessor

B.   Encumbrances

       1. Mortgage

       2. Lien

       3. Covenant

       4. Easement

       5. Encroachment

III.   TIME
Time is not usually "of the essence" in contracts for the sale of real property. A party may enforce a contract even though he is not unreasonably late (usually a few weeks will be considered not unreasonably late) in tendering performance. Although time is not of the essence, a party that is late in tendering performance may be liable for damages.

A.   Suits for damages (action in law) will assume that time was "of the essence."

B.   Suits for specific performance (action in equity) will *not* assume that time was "of the essence."

C.   Time may become "of the essence" if the parties expressly agree to that effect, or one party gives notice that time will be important, or circumstances show that time was important.

IV.   RISK OF LOSS: EQUITABLE CONVERSION

A.   Majority Rule
The buyer bears the risk of loss between the time the contract was signed and the closing.

    1. **Note:** This rule relies on the doctrine of equitable conversion that establishes equitable ownership in land at the time a contract is signed. Legal title remains with the seller who has a lien for the sale price. The reasoning of this rule is that a buyer has a

right to specifically enforce the contract after the signing. "Equity regards as done, that which ought to be done."

2. Exceptions
In the following two situations, risk of loss will not pass to the buyer even though the majority rule is followed.

   a.   Title was not marketable at the time the contract was signed.

   b.   The loss was caused by the seller's negligence.

B.   Minority Rule
The risk of loss remains with the seller until legal title is conveyed regardless of who retains possession between signing and closing.

C.   Uniform Vendor and Purchaser Risk Act (another minority view)
Seller bears the risk of loss until the possession or title shifts to the buyer.

V.   INSTALLMENT CONTRACTS
Most sales of real property involve a small down payment by the purchaser, who borrows the balance of the purchase price from a lender, who will receive the property if the purchaser defaults. Under an installment contract the purchaser does not receive a deed to the property until he makes the final payment.

A.   Default by Buyer
Judicial proceedings are not necessary, the seller retains the deed and all payments previously made by the buyer.

B.   Some states have enacted statutes to soften the legal effects of a default by the buyer.
Examples:

   1. Foreclosure safeguard
   When a buyer has paid a substantial portion of the loan he has the rights of a mortgagor (see below).

   2. Redemption
   Buyer may pay off the loan balance and keep the land despite his default.

   3. Reinstatement

Buyer pays the amount of his default and continues the contract as if the breach never occurred.

4. Restitution
Buyer recovers payments in excess of damages incurred by the lender as a result of the default.

VI.   MORTGAGES

A.   Definitions

1. Mortgagor
Borrower who gives the mortgage.

2. Mortgagee
Lender who receives the mortgage.

3. Mortgage
A document giving a lender the right to claim real property if a borrower defaults on a loan.

B.   The Mortgage
When a buyer finances a purchase of property by using a mortgage he receives a deed to the property. (Contrast with an installment sale.) The buyer gives a mortgage to a lender in exchange for a loan. The mortgage gives the lender the right to foreclose on the property in case the borrower defaults. The lender returns the mortgage to the borrower after all the payments have been made.

VII. DEEDS

A.   Definition of a Deed
A deed is a written document that effectuates a transfer of real property.

B.   A deed will be effective if:

1. It is delivered by the grantor.

2. It is accepted by the grantee.

3. It is valid.

C.   Delivery of a Deed

1. A deed need not be physically delivered to satisfy this requirement. Conduct or words of a grantor that indicate his present intent to make the deed operative will satisfy the requirement of delivery. Intent is the key.

2. Manual Delivery

a.   If the deed was physically transferred to the grantee, a presumption in favor of delivery will be created.

b.   If the grantor retains physical possession, a presumption against delivery will exist.

3. A grantor's attempts to revoke a delivery previously effectuated will be futile because title passes at the moment a deed is delivered.

4. Delivery of the deed to the county recorder's office will be a valid delivery.

5. Delivery will be effective even if the deed contained a condition. **Example:** A deed specifies that the grantee must live until age 21. Delivery will be effective if the grantee is 18 years old and he will have a contingent estate.

6. Fine Line Distinction: Revocation of Deed vs. Revocation of Estate.
If a grantor delivers a deed that by its terms reserves a right of revocation in the grantor, the grantor retains a right to revoke the estate and he may do so, but he may not revoke the delivery after it was accomplished.

7. Escrow
A delivery in escrow is a delivery to an impartial third party who holds the deed until certain conditions are met. The delivery will be effective if the grantor relinquished all control. (Title will pass when the conditions of escrow are fulfilled, not when the deed physically passes from the third party to the grantee.)

D.   Acceptance by the Grantee

The grantee must accept the deed. Such acceptance is presumed.

E. Validity of a Deed
    Information Required on the Face of the Deed

    Mnemonic: **O**ld **D**eeds **N**ever **S**urvive

    1. **O**perative words of conveyance

    2. **D**escription of the property
       Methods of Description:

       a. by metes and bounds: "calls and distances" in relation to a "monument" (a landmark).

       b. by government survey.

       c. by a particular map.

    3. **N**ames of grantee and grantor

    4. **S**ignature of the grantor (seals have not been required for a long time).
       Notes:

       a. some states require attestation (a disinterested witness) or acknowledgment (notarizing).

       b. consideration is not required.

VIII. COVENANTS FOR TITLE
      There are two classes of deeds.

A. Quitclaim Deed
    Grantor conveys whatever title he owns without warranty as to his title.

B. Warranty Deed
    Grantor makes representations concerning titles. There are six general classes of covenants.

    Mnemonic:
    Even **F**ilthy **S**coundrels **R**eject **Q**uestionable **W**arranties.

1. <u>E</u>ncumbrances
   Grantor warrants that his conveyance is free of encumbrances: liens, mortgages, easements, etc.

2. <u>F</u>urther assurance
   Grantor warrants that he will make any conveyance within his power in order to perfect grantee's title. This covenant is rarely used today.

3. <u>S</u>eisin
   Same as the right to convey.

4. <u>R</u>ight to convey
   A personal covenant that the grantor has the right to convey.

5. <u>Q</u>uiet enjoyment
   Historical differences between this covenant and the covenant of "warranty" have been abolished so that they are identical.

6. <u>W</u>arranty
   Grantor covenants that grantee's use or enjoyment of the property will not be disturbed by a third party.

   a.   This covenant is "real" and will run with the property.

   b.   This is the broadest covenant.

   c.   Damages for breach are limited to the value of the property.

IX.   APPLICABILITY OF COVENANTS TO FUTURE GRANTEES
      Covenants that "run with the land" may be enforced by a future grantee. Whether a covenant will run with the land depends on whether it is a "Present" or "Future" covenant.

A.   Present Covenants
      Covenants that are breached at the moment the conveyance is made. They generally do not run with the land.

      1. Covenant of seisin.

      2. Covenant of right to convey.

      3. Covenant against encumbrances.

B.   Future Covenants
Covenants that are only breached when a party is later evicted. Future covenants always run with the land.

1. Covenant of quiet enjoyment.

2. Covenant of warranty.

3. Covenant of further assurance.

CASE CLIPS

Shaughnessy v. Eidsmo (1946)

Facts: The Shaugnessys (plaintiffs) leased land by oral agreement from Eidsmo (defendant). Eidsmo also gave the plaintiffs an option to buy the demised premises. Before expiration of the lease, the Shaugnessys performed their part of the option, and exercised the option, but no contract was ever written. Eidsmo refused to complete the sale.

Issue: Does possession and part performance of an oral option to purchase leased premises constitute a defense to the Statute of Frauds?

Rule: The taking of possession, coupled with the making of part payment, in reliance upon and with unequivocal reference to the vendor-vendee relationship constitutes a defense to the Statute of Frauds.

Burns v. McCormick (1922)

Facts: J.A. Halsey (decedent) orally promised the plaintiffs that in return for their services he would give them his house. After his death, neither deed nor will existed to evidence the agreement.

Issue: Must a vendee's conduct be unequivocally referable to a contract for sale of land when the vendee seeks specific performance of an oral agreement to sell the same?

Rule: For equity to decree specific performance, acts of part performance must be solely and unequivocally referable to a contract for sale of land.

Hickey v. Green (1982)

Facts: Green (defendant) orally agreed to sell a lot to the Hickeys (plaintiffs). Green accepted a deposit from the Hickeys who, in reliance on the contract, contracted to sell their home. Green, although aware of the plaintiffs' sale of their home repudiated the contract.

Issue: Does a vendee's reasonable reliance upon an oral contract to sell land constitute a defense to the Statute of Frauds?

Rule: A contract for the transfer of an interest in land may be specifically enforced notwithstanding failure to comply with the Statute of Frauds if it is established that the party seeking enforcement, in reasonable reliance on the contract and on the continuing assent of the party against whom enforcement is sought, has so changed his position that injustice can be avoided only by specific enforcement.

Pearson v. Gardner (1918)

Facts: Pearson (plaintiff) orally agreed to sell land to the Gardners (defendants). The Gardners refused to complete the contract after taking possession, making partial payment and so altering the premise's character as to diminish its value.

Issue: May a vendor seeking specific performance rely on the vendee's part performance as grounds to avoid the Statute of Frauds?

Rule: A vendor may seek specific performance of a contract which has been part performed on the grounds of mutuality.

Ward v. Mattuschek (1958)

Facts: The Mattuschek brothers (defendants) executed a contract with a real estate broker granting the broker an exclusive right to sell land. The contract, signed by the defendants, contained the essential terms of the defendants' offer to sell. The broker found Ward, a buyer, who unconditionally accepted. The Mattuscheks subsequently refused to convey the property. Ward sued for specific performance.

Issue: Is a contract between a seller and real estate broker granting the broker the right to sell the land and stating therein the essential terms of seller's offer invalid under the Statute of Frauds?

Rule: A contract between a vendor and broker that states the essential elements of the seller's offer is sufficient to take a contract of sale between vendor and vendee out of the Statute of Frauds.

King v. Wenger (1976)

Facts: King (plaintiff) and Wenger (defendant) executed an informal memorandum in which they agreed to a transfer of real estate. The parties, however, contemplated negotiating, drafting, and executing a formal contract in the future.

Issue: Are parties bound to an informal agreement when they were negotiating with an understanding that the terms of the contract were not fully agreed upon and a written formal agreement was contemplated?

Rule: Parties to an informal agreement are not bound thereby when the intent of the parties was that the terms of the contract were not fully agreed upon and a written formal agreement was contemplated.

Niernberg v. Feld (1955)

Facts: The Felds (plaintiff) and the Niernbergs entered a sales agreement to transfer land. Before the agreement was performed, the parties orally rescinded the contract.

Issue: Must a rescission of a written executory sales contract of real estate be in writing?

Rule: An executory contract involving title to, or an interest in, lands may be rescinded by a mutual parol agreement.

Kasten Construction Co. v. Maple Ridge Construction Co. (1967)

Facts: Maple Ridge Constr. Co. (plaintiff) contracted to purchase land from Kasten Constr. Co. The contract specified that settlement was to be made in sixty days but did not stipulate that time was of the essence. Maple Ridge performed most of its contractual duties before the closing date. Five days after the contract's expiration, Maple Ridge notified the defendant of its intention to complete the contract, but that an additional three weeks would be required to complete a title examination. The defendant, in response, repudiated the contract. Maple Ridge sued for specific performance.

Issue: When a contract for the sale and purchase of realty fails to expressly state that time is of the essence and circumstances surrounding the transaction do not imply such an intent, what will be the effect of a deadline?

Rule: In a case involving specific performance, time is not of the essence of the contract of sale and purchase of land unless a contrary purpose is disclosed by its terms or is indicated by the circumstances and object of its execution and the conduct of the parties.

Doctorman v. Schroeder (1921)

Facts: A land sale contract executed by Schroeder (defendant) and Doctorman (plaintiff) provided that time was of the essence, and further, if the plaintiff failed to complete payment by a certain hour, Doctorman would forfeit the down payment and terminate the contract. The plaintiff was unable to raise the amount required, and sued to recover the down payment.

Issue: May equity relieve a defaulting party of the consequences flowing from a land sale contract when the agreement distinctly provides that time is of the essence, and that the purchaser's rights shall cease unless payment is made at the time stipulated?

Rule: When parties to a land sale contract expressly provide that time is of the essence, equity will not, when a purchaser defaults, prevent a forfeiture.

Gerruth Realty Co. v. Pire (1962)

Facts: A land sale contract contained a "subject to financing" clause. Pire (defendant) could not get financing and refused to complete the contract.

Issue: May a land sale contract be held void for indefiniteness when there are insufficient facts surrounding the transaction for a court to construe with reasonable certainty a "subject to financing" clause?

Rule: When a land sale contract contains a "subject to financing" clause, and a court cannot infer the terms of the clause either from the evidence or by means of current practices in the community, the contract is void for indefiniteness.

Skendzel v. Marshall (1973)

Facts: The Marshalls contracted to purchase land from Burkowski. The sales contract provided for periodic payments, and the vendee's forfeiture of all previous payments and possession if the contract was breached. Before breaching, the Marshalls (defendants) paid $21,000 of the $36,000 purchase price.

Issue: When a liquidated damages clause results in damages being disproportionate to the loss actually suffered, may equity find the clause void as a penalty and require the injured party to seek redress through foreclosure?

Rule: When a liquidated damages clause results in damages disproportionate to the actual loss suffered, equity will hold the clause void as a penalty and compel the injured party to seek foreclosure.

Union Bond & Trust Co. v. Blue Creek Redwood Co. (1955)

Facts: The vendee (plaintiff) willfully defaulted on an installment land sale contract that provided for forfeiture in the event of a breach.

Issue: Does a willfully defaulting buyer have a right to remedy his breach and continue the contract in force?

Rule: A purchaser who willfully defaults on an installment sale may, where there has been substantial part performance or substantial improvements on the property, complete the contract within a specified time by paying the entire purchase price together with the seller's damages resulting from the delay in performance.

Wallach v. Riverside Bank (1912)

Facts: Wallach desired to purchase certain property from Riverside Bank. In order to carry out the transaction Wallach (plaintiff) agreed to accept from Riverside Bank a quitclaim deed to certain property, then refused to complete the transaction because the defendant's title was clouded.

Issue: Must a vendor provide marketable title to a vendee who signed a land sales contract to accept a quitclaim deed?

Rule: A vendor always covenants by implication to give a good title, unless such a covenant is expressly excluded by the terms of the contract.

Bartos v. Czerwinski (1948)

Facts: Bartos (plaintiff) agreed to purchase realty if the defendant would provide marketable title. Bartos then refused to accept the conveyance unless the defendant took certain actions to clear the title. When the defendant refused, Bartos sued for specific performance.

Issue 1: If a possible outstanding interest in a property in one other than the vendor exists, is the vendor's title marketable?

Rule 1: A title is unmarketable if a reasonably careful and prudent person, familiar with the facts, would refuse to accept the title in the ordinary course of business because of a doubt or uncertainty that could reasonably form the basis of litigation.

Issue 2: Where a vendor who contracts to convey land by quitclaim deed fails to convey marketable title, is the vendee entitled to specific performance?

Rule 2: The equitable remedy of specific performance is not one of right, but rests in the discretion of the court. Where a vendor who contracts to convey land by quitclaim deed fails to convey marketable title, and clearing title would require substantial action, the court may deny specific performance.

Luette v. Bank of Italy Nat. Trust & Savings Ass'n. (1930)

Facts: The plaintiff agreed to buy land from the defendant provided the defendant would supply marketable title. The installment contract provided that the land would be conveyed only when paid in full. The plaintiff sought rescission prior to closing, claiming that the defendant was not then in possession of a marketable title.

Issue: May a vendee, prior to the date when the vendor will be required to convey title under an installment contract, seek to rescind on account of an uncertainty as to the state of the vendor's title?

Rule: There can be no rescission by a vendee of an executory contract of sale merely because of lack of title in the vendor prior to the date when performance was due.

Cohen v. Kranz (1963)

Facts: Cohen (plaintiff) contracted to purchase Kranz's house. Prior to the closing date, Cohen (vendee) notified Kranz (vendor) that the title was unmarketable and demanded return of his down payment. Neither party tendered, nor demanded performance. Cohen sued to recover the deposit.

Issue: May a vendee, who does not tender his performance recover his deposit when the vendor's title is curably defective?

Rule: A vendee is barred from recovering his deposit from a vendor whose title defects were curable in a reasonable time and whose performance was never demanded.

Handzel v. Bassi (1951)

Facts: The vendee (plaintiff) entered an installment land sales contract with the defendant, under which the plaintiff could not assign the contract without the defendant's consent. When the plaintiff violated this provision, the defendant proclaimed the contract void and the plaintiff's prior payments forfeited. Despite the plaintiff's tender of full performance, the defendant refused to complete the contract.

Issue: Is a provision prohibiting assignment of an installment land sales contract enforceable when, after the vendee assigns the contract, vendee offers and is able to complete the performance of the contract?

Rule: Since the primary purpose of a provision prohibiting a vendee from assigning an installment land sales contract is to ensure vendee's performance, the vendor cannot forfeit the contract on the grounds that the vendee assigned his interest if the vendee has tendered performance.

Kramer v. Mobley (1949)

Facts: Mobley (plaintiff) contracted to purchase land from Kramer. Mobley notified Kramer of a cloud on Kramer's title. Kramer offered to institute a quiet title action and reimburse Mobley in the amount of the disputed lien on the property if Mobley would complete the transaction. Before he would complete the contract, Mobley insisted Kramer pay the purported lienholder and obtain a release. When Kramer refused, Mobley sued for the benefit of his bargain.

Issue: When a vendor's title is defective, may a vendee recover the difference between the contract price and the market value of the property, either at the time of breach or at the time fixed for delivery, when the vendor acted in good faith and was guilty of no positive or active fraud?

Rule: A vendee of real estate is not entitled to damages for the loss of his bargain upon the inability of the vendor to obtain a good title if the vendor acted in good faith and was guilty of no active nor positive fraud in the transaction.

Smith v. Warr (1977)

Facts: Warr (defendant) contracted to sell land to Smith. The defendant was unable to convey the land because a third party successfully asserted an adverse possession claim. The plaintiff sued for benefit-of-the-bargain damages.

Issue: Is the correct measure of damages for a breach of contract for the sale of real property out-of-pocket loss, or benefit-of-the-bargain damages?

Rule: The measure of damages where the vendor has breached a land sale contract is the benefit-of-the-bargain damages, i.e., market value of the property at the time of the breach, less the contract price to the vendee.

Clay v. Landreth (1948)

Facts: Landreth (defendant) contracted to purchase land from Clay, Rezoned between the time of making the contract and the time for delivery of the deed, the land became unusable for its intended purpose. Clay sued for specific performance.

Issue: Will a contract for the sale of land be specifically enforced when the agreed purpose for which it was bought and sold was defeated?

Rule: Equity will not compel specific performance if hardship and injustice would be forced upon one of the parties through a change in circumstances not contemplated by the parties when the contract was made.

Shay v. Penrose (1962)

Facts: Carol Shay entered into separate contracts to sell four parcels of land. Each contract specified that the buyer would pay in installments, Carol Shay died before all the payments were made. She was survived by her husband Arthur Shay (plaintiff), and her sister and heir, Grace Penrose (defendant). Arthur contended the unpaid balance on an installment land sale contract was personalty, Penrose, the decedent's heir, contended the installment was realty.

Issue: When a valid installment land sale contract is executed, does the seller hold a real property interest in the land?

Rule: When one enters into a valid and enforceable contract for the sale of his land, he continues to hold the legal title in trust for the buyer, and the buyer becomes the equitable owner and holds the purchase money in trust for the seller. Therefore, in this case, the plaintiff is entitled to the unpaid balance of the purchase prices.

Clapp v. Tower (1903)

Facts: Charlemange Tower (decedent) sold land by executory contract which was foreclosed subsequent to his death. The executors, claiming Charlemange's interest in the land converted to personalty, sold it to Clapp (plaintiff). The Towers (defendants and Charlemange Tower's heirs) contended that the decedent retained a real property interest and it therefore devolved to his heirs.

Issue: Does realty sold under an executory contract convert the seller's interest in the land to personalty?

Rule: When a vendor sells land under an executory contract, his property, as viewed by equity, is no longer real estate in the land, but personal estate in the price. If he dies before payment, it goes to his administrators, and not to his heirs.

Eddington v. Turner (1944)

Facts: The decedent devised a life estate in certain land to Turner (defendant). He subsequently gave Eddington (plaintiff) an option to buy the same land. Eddington properly exercised the option after the decedent's demise.

Issue: When an option to purchase realty is granted after the execution of a will, will exercise of the option after the death of the optionor operate as an equitable conversion of the property relating back to the date of the option so that the proceeds of sale would pass to the personal representatives rather than to the specific devisee of the land?

Rule: Equitable conversion cannot occur prior to the exercise of an option, for until then no duty rested on anyone in connection with the land. Consequently, when there has been no conversion of land during a testator's life, the testator did not have a claim for the purchase price transmissible to his personal representatives.

Bleckley v. Langston (1965)

Facts: Prior to vendee taking possession, an ice storm substantially destroyed improvements on the land conveyed, decreasing its value. The parties had a valid executory contract and the vendor was able to convey good title.

Issue: If an enforceable contract exists between two parties and the vendor is able to convey good title, which party bears the risk of loss?

Rule: Regardless of which party maintains possession, risk of loss rests with a vendee after the contract is executed, if the vendor is able to convey good title.

Sanford v. Breidenbach (1960)

Facts: Sanford (plaintiff) contracted to sell to Breidenbach certain lands which included a house and outbuildings. Prior to having met the conditions of the contract of sale, the house was destroyed by fire. Breidenbach (defendant) repudiated the agreement. Sanford sued for specific performance.

Issue: When real property is destroyed before the vendor is able to meet the conditions of the contract for its sale, is the risk of loss borne by the vendee?

Rule: Prior to fulfilling the conditions of a contract calling for conveyance of good title, a vendor cannot maintain an action for specific performance. Equitable conversion does not occur until a vendor can convey good title and is entitled to specific performance; therefore, the risk of loss remains with the vendor.

Raplee v. Piper (1957)

Facts: The subject matter of a contract was destroyed before the performance date. As required by the contract, the vendee (plaintiff) purchased insurance on the property in the vendor's name.

Issue: Where, pursuant to a contract, a vendee buys fire insurance covering the subject property in the vendor's name and the property is destroyed by fire prior to the performance date of the contract, is the vendee entitled to have the insurance proceeds applied against the unpaid balance of the purchase price?

Rule: When a contract to purchase land requires the vendee to keep the property insured against fire, insurance recovered by the vendor for a fire that occurred before performance of the contract was completed is to be applied to any remaining balance of the purchase price.

State ex rel. Indiana State Bar Ass'n v. Indiana Real Estate Ass'n, Inc. (1963)

Facts: Indiana's Bar Association sought to enjoin real estate brokers from selecting and completing standardized legal forms.

Issue: Does the selection and use of forms of legal instruments prepared by attorneys and the insertion of words within the printed forms in connection with the real estate transactions in which they are involved, constitute the unauthorized practice of law by real estate brokers who are not attorneys?

Rule: The use and filing of certain forms by real estate brokers incidental to their real estate transactions does not constitute the practice of law, if they require only the use of common knowledge regarding the information to be inserted in the blanks and general knowledge regarding the legal consequences involved.

Tristram's Landing, Inc., et al. v. Wait (1975)

Facts: Tristram (plaintiff), acting as Wait's (defendant) broker, located a buyer for Wait's realty. Wait and the vendee entered a purchase and sale agreement, but the transaction was never consummated.

Issue: Is a real estate broker producing a buyer who is ready, willing and able to purchase a vendor's property, and who is in fact accepted by the vendor, entitled to a full commission if the transaction is never consummated?

Rule: When a seller engages a real estate broker, the broker earns his commission when he produces a purchaser ready, willing and able to buy on the terms fixed by the owner, the buyer enters into a binding contract with the owner to do so, and the buyer completes the transaction by closing the title in accordance with the provisions of the contract.

French v. French (1825)

Facts: The plaintiff leased land of which he was seized to his father by bargain and sale deed. A statute required deeds to be attested to by two witnesses. Because only one person witnessed this deed, the plaintiff challenged its validity.

Issue: Is every deed not conforming to a statute invalid?

Rule: In passing the statute, the legislature intended to abolish livery of seisin only, not conveyances such as bargain and sale deeds, which need no attestation.

First Nat'l Bank of Oregon v. Townsend (1976)

Facts: Both grantor and grantee were deceased. The plaintiff, the grantee's representative, found a deed among the grantee's effects. The deed was ambiguous regarding the extent of the interest the grantor intended to convey and extrinsic evidence did not resolve the doubt.

Issues: When neither the deed nor extrinsic evidence reveals the extent of the interest a grantor intended to convey, will the grantee be deemed to take the larger interest?

Rule: When there is doubt as to whether the parties intended that a deed transfer a fee simple or a lesser interest in land, that doubt should be resolved in favor of the grantee and the greater estate should pass.

Grayson v. Holloway (1958)

Facts: Holloway and wife (grantors) executed a deed in which the granting clause conflicted with the habendum clause.

Issue: When a granting clause and habendum clause of a deed conflict, does the granting clause control?

Rule: When seeking to determine what estate was conveyed by a deed, the intention of the grantor shall be ascertained if possible by giving to every word of the deed its appropriate meaning, and by enforcing that intention regardless of the formal divisions of the instrument.

Womack v. Stegner (1956)

Facts: Leaving blank the space for the grantee's name, W.B. Womack executed a deed, delivered it to D.R. Womack, and authorized him to fill in his or any name in the blank as grantee.

Issue: When a grantor leaves the grantee's name blank in a deed, but authorizes the grantee to fill in his or any name, does title pass?

Rule: When a deed with the name of the grantee in blank is delivered by the grantor with the intention that title shall vest in the person to whom the deed is delivered, and that person is expressly authorized at the time of delivery to insert his or any other name as grantee, title passes with the delivery.

Clevenger v. Moore (1927)

Facts: Clevenger (plaintiff) placed a deed in escrow to be delivered upon the occurrence of certain conditions. Although the conditions were not met, the depository delivered the deed to the grantee who conveyed the land to Moore (defendant).

Issue: Is a deed absolutely void when it is placed in escrow and delivered to a grantee without performance of the conditions for delivery and thus ineffective to convey title to either the grantee or the grantee's bona fide purchaser for value?

Rule: A deed placed in escrow to be delivered to a grantee upon the performance of certain conditions will not be valid for any purpose until the condition upon which it is to be delivered to the grantee is met, even though a claimant thereunder was an innocent purchaser for value.

Bybee v. Hageman (1873)

Facts: Hageman (defendant) held a mortgage on real property. The description of the land in this mortgage was ambiguous as to the land's boundaries. When Hageman sought to foreclose on the mortgage, Bybee (plaintiff), who held a second mortgage on the same land, contended that Hageman's mortgage was not valid due to indefiniteness.

Issue: May a mortgage's latent ambiguities be explained by parol evidence?

Rule: Extrinsic evidence is admissible to explain latent ambiguities in mortgages.

Walters v. Tucker (1955)

Facts: Despite the clear description of the lot conveyed by the plaintiff's deed, the trial court allowed the defendant to present extrinsic evidence in an attempt to show that the grantor intended to convey less land than the deed described.

Issue: When a description in a deed is clear, definite and unambiguous, both on its face and when applied to the land, may extrinsic evidence be admitted to show that the grantor intended to convey a different sized lot?

Rule: When there is no inconsistency on the face of a deed and, on application of the description to the ground, no inconsistency appears, parol evidence is not admissible to show that the parties intended to convey either less, more or different ground from that described.

Pritchard v. Rebori (1916)

Facts: Rebori (defendant) covenanted to convey unencumbered land. When the grantee (plaintiff) built on the land, he discovered he had infringed on a railroad's easement. The boundary of the easement was unmarked. Both parties believed a retaining wall located inside the easement's outer boundary represented the extent of the easement. In describing the lot conveyed, however, the deed referred to both the wall and the easement.

Issue: When determining the boundaries of conveyed land, is there an absolute hierarchy among natural objects, artificial markers, boundary lines of adjacent owners, and courses and distances?

Rule: The rule that resort is to be had in determining boundaries first to natural objects or landmarks, next to artificial monuments or marks, then to boundary lines of adjacent owners, and finally to courses and distances, is not inflexible or absolute.

Parr v. Worley (1979)

Facts: Parr conveyed to Worley land adjacent to a highway described as "lying to the East of the highway. Parr later purported to convey to a third party the mineral interests under both sides of the highway described as "lying west of the east right-of-way line of" the highway. Worley argued that he owned the eastern half of the highway. Parr (plaintiff) contended that Worley's land's boundary was the eastern edge of the highway.

Issue: When monuments are used as boundary lines, must the presumption that the line runs through the center of the monument be expressly rebutted by language in the deed?

Rule: Absent an expressed contrary intent in a deed, a conveyance of land abutting a road, highway, alley, or other way (i.e., monument), is presumed to take the fee to the center line of the way or monument.

Hocks v. Jeremiah (1988)

Facts: Hocks gave his sister (defendant) four bonds in person in return for her love and her service to their mother. The goods were placed in a joint deposit box and each held a key. The defendant never opened the box while Hocks was alive, but Hocks left notes saying the contents of the box were the defendant's. Hocks added more bonds and a diamond to the box. The representative of Hocks' estate (plaintiff) claimed the goods.

Issue: Does the placing of property in a jointly leased safety deposit box constitute delivery of the property to a cotenant and, thereby, a present gift?

Rule: The joint letting of a safety deposit box is not delivery of property, absent clear and convincing evidence that the cotenant parted with control and possession of the property therein.

Newman v. Bost (1898)

Facts: Prior to death, the decedent intestate handed keys to the plaintiff Newman telling her that everything in the house was here upon his death. A life insurance policy was found in decedent's bureau.

Issue: May a gift made in anticipation of death (causa mortis) be constructively delivered when actual delivery is possible?

Rule: When an item was present and could have been manually delivered, constructive delivery is insufficient to constitute a gift causa mortis.

McCarton v. Estate of Watson (1984)

Facts: McCarton (plaintiff) cared for Mrs. Watson while she was dying, and she had him write out her will as she dictated it. In it, she left many goods to McCarton. Mrs. Watson's estate contested the will, as another was already in existence.

Issue: Will delivery by the donor and possession by the donee that is as complete as the nature of the property and the circumstances permit establish a valid gift causa mortis?

Rule: Where the other requisite elements are present, a valid gift causa mortis is established where delivery by the donor, and possession by the donee, are as complete as the nature of the property and the circumstances permit.

In Re Nols' Estate (1947)

Facts: Prior to and in contemplation of his impending death, the decedent gave Vander Zanden (plaintiff) a parcel and stated, "if I don't come back, you can have it."

Issue: Is a gift causa mortis a testamentary disposition and therefore invalid unless there is compliance with the Statute of Frauds?

Rule: The doctrine of gifts causa mortis is an exception to the rule against testamentary disposition except by will. Thus, a gift conditioned upon the donor's death is valid.

In Re Estate of Thompson (1981)

Facts: R.L. Thompson deposited funds in two joint and survivorship savings accounts. His wife was the other party to the accounts. Thompson withdrew all the funds prior to his wife's death.

Issue: Do joint account holders share equally in the ownership of funds on deposit?

Rule: During their lives, a joint account belongs to the parties in proportion to the net contributions made by each, unless there is clear and convincing evidence of a different intent.

Hoban v. Cable (1984)

Facts: Cable (defendant), who claimed title by adverse possession, contended that he lacked notice of the plaintiff's predecessor in interest. The deed's technical description of the lot was in error because it did not define an enclosed lot.

Issue: Is a deed valid when the land conveyed therein is insufficiently defined but nevertheless identifiable?

Rule: When the lot a grantor intended to convey is identifiable from the deed's description, the deed is valid even though the land's description was technically insufficient.

Campbell v. Noel (1986)

Facts: Campbell (plaintiff) and defendant were adjacent landowners but were uncertain of the proper boundary between their parcels. The defendant had the area surveyed and erected a fence along the boundary. Five years later, when the plaintiff had the property surveyed, he discovered that the fence was erected 60 feet into his property.

Issue: Where dispute existed as to where a boundary should be, but one landowner allows a fence between the lots to stand before he discovers a defect, is that landowner equitably estopped from reclaiming his land?

Rule: Under the doctrine of equitable estoppel, a boundary by agreement arises where (1) there exists uncertainty as to the true boundary; (2) the parties agree that a certain line will be treated as the true line; and (3) the parties subsequently occupy their lands in accord with the agreement for a period of time sufficient to show a settled recognition of the line as the permanent boundary.

McMahon v. Dorsey (1958)

Facts: Dorsey (defendant) lived and worked on McMahon's farm for many years. After McMahon's death, a deed conveying the farm was found in a safe deposit of which McMahon and the defendant were joint lessees. The decedent's sole heirs sued to have the deed put aside on the grounds that no delivery was made.

Issue: Must manual delivery of a deed be shown for the deed to be a valid conveyance?

Rule: Delivery of a deed is strictly a matter of the intention of the grantor as manifested and evidenced by the words, acts, and circumstances surrounding the transaction. Manual delivery is but one factor evidencing delivery.

Martinez v. Martinez

Facts: The grantor sold land to the grantee, who agreed to assume mortgage payments on it. The grantors gave to the grantees a deed to the land, and orally gave instructions that the grantee take the deed to the bank, where it was to be held in escrow until the mortgage was paid in full. Before delivering the deed into escrow, the grantee recorded the deed. None of the documents mentioned an escrow agreement. Later, the grantee defaulted on the mortgage payments, but claimed title to the land.

Issue: Is parol evidence admissible to determine the intent of the grantor as to when a deed was to take effect?

Rule: Parol evidence is admissible to determine the intent of the grantor as to when a deed was to take effect. There is no legal delivery, even where a deed has been physically transferred, when the evidence shows that there was no present intent on the part of the grantor to divest himself of title to the land.

Thomas v. Williams (1908)

Facts: Before his death, Lewis conveyed land to Williams (defendant) by deed, contingent on the grantee surviving the grantor. The plaintiff claimed the deed was testamentary in character and therefore void.

Issue: Is a deed unenforceable as a testamentary instrument when the grantor, though grantee's enjoyment is postponed, intends to pass an interest presently vesting?

Rule: If by the terms of the instrument a right or interest passes at once, subject to a contingency over which the grantor has no control, it is a deed and irrevocable even though the enjoyment of the thing granted is postponed until grantor's death.

Smith v. Fay (1940)

Facts: White deeded land to G.E. White, contingent on the grantee surviving the grantor. The grantor left the deed with a third party together with instructions to deliver it to the grantee after the grantor's death.

Issue: Does a grantor's act of leaving a deed with a third party with instructions to deliver it to the grantee after the grantor's death effectuate an absolute delivery?

Rule: Delivery of a deed to a third party, with instructions to deliver it to the grantee upon the grantor's death and no reservation of a right to recall the deed, constitutes good delivery with title passing immediately to the grantee subject to the grantor's reserved life estate.

Raim v. Stancel (1983)

Facts: William L. Raim conditionally delivered a deed to Stancel.

Issue: Is an inter vivos gift valid when a conditional delivery is tendered?

Rule: Unless donor has a clear intention to pass all right, title, and dominion over the gift to the donee, an inter vivos gift is invalid. When a deed is delivered to the grantee with intention that it become operative only on the death of the grantor, it will not pass title.

Merry v. County Board of Education of Jefferson County (1956)

Facts: Snedecor negotiated the sale of land with the County Board of Education (defendant) shortly before her death. She left with her lawyer an executed deed with instructions to deliver it when a deal was struck. The proposal was not accepted, nor the deed delivered before her death. The plaintiffs, the executors of the estate, sought cancellation on the grounds that the deed was never delivered.

Issue: Is an escrow revocable if not supported by a contract?

Rule: An escrow is revocable at any time before it is accepted by the grantee, and if not done in the lifetime of the grantor, it is ipso facto revoked on her death.

Irons v. Smallpiece (1819)

Facts: A gift of an interest in horses was verbally promised to the plaintiff but never delivered.

Issue: Is a gift valid when delivery of the property is absent?

Rule: In order to transfer property by gift there must either be a deed or instrument of gift, or there must be actual delivery of the gift to the donee.

Newell v. National Bank (1925)

Facts: When Reynolds was seemingly terminally ill, he gave Newell (plaintiff) a ring. Reynolds recovered, and lived for years after he gave the gift.

Issue: May a donor under apprehension of death make an inter vivos gift?

Rule: A donor under apprehension of death may make an inter vivos gift if he intends to have the gift take effect in the present, irrevocably and unconditionally, whether he lives or dies.

Grymes v. Hone (1872)

Facts: In apprehension of death, the donor, who was advanced in years, assigned stock to Grymes (plaintiff). He gave the instrument conveying the assignment to his wife to hold as his agent until his death, whereupon she was to give the instrument to the plaintiff. The donor lived for five months after giving the instrument to his wife.

Issue 1: Where a donor wishes to assign stock to a donee after his death, does the delivery of the assignment instrument to an agent constitute delivery to the donee?

Rule 1: Because the donor parts with all of his interest in the stock assigned to the donee, and the donee becomes the equitable owner against every person but a bona fide purchaser without notice, an assignment coupled with delivery of the assignment instrument to a third party until the donor dies constitutes delivery to the donee.

Issue 2: Must a donor be in extremis for a gift causa mortis to be valid?

Rule 2: A gift causa mortis will only be valid if the donor did not recover from the illness prompting the gift. The donor does not have to be in extremis at the time he made the gift.

Meyers v. Meyers (1926)

Facts: Meyers (the donor) while ill and just prior to an operation following which he died, signed and left a deed of assignment with his lawyer. The donor instructed the lawyer to put the deed on record if anything happened to him.

Issue: Is a delivery effectuated when a donor retains the object of a deed of assignment but instructs a third party to deliver the deed upon the donor's death?

Rule: A gift made by delivering a deed with donative intent is a valid symbolic delivery even though the subject does not accompany the deed.

Innes v. Potter

Facts: Warren Potter took a certificate of 1,000 shares of stock, endorsed upon it an absolute assignment to the H. Marcia Potter. The certificate he enclosed in an envelope and gave to Casey with directions to deliver it to Marcia Potter in case of Warren Potter's death.

Issue: Is it competent for a person to make a gift of personal property by delivery of the subject of the gift to a trustee where delivery by the trustee to the donee and beneficial enjoyment by the donee are postponed until the death of the donor?

Rule: Where a grantor executes a deed and deposits it with a third person, to be delivered by him to the grantee after the death of the grantor, and reserves to himself no right to control or recall the instrument, the transaction is a valid one and full and complete title is vested in the grantee after death of the grantor.

Tygard v. McComb (1893)

Facts: Wilson transferred the entire balance of his bank account to the credit of his minor daughters. He frequently made withdrawals from the funds and told friends he only transferred the funds for his own convenience.

Issue: Does a valid inter vivos gift result when a donor retains dominion over the purported gift?

Rule: A valid inter vivos gift will only result when the donor had an absolute and unequivocal intention to presently pass title and possession to a donee.

In Re Totten (1904)

Facts: F.A. Lattam deposited money in passbook savings accounts in her name as trustee for E.R. Lattam, her nephew. The nephew was unaware of the account and the aunt retained complete control over the funds.

Issue: When a savings account depositor who retained complete control over the funds puts the account in his name in trust for another, is an irrevocable trust established?

Rule: A deposit by a person of his own money as trustee for another establishes a tentative trust, revocable at will until the depositor dies or completes the gift in his lifetime by some unequivocal act or declaration. If the depositor dies before the beneficiary without revocation or some decisive act or declaration of disaffirmance, the presumption arises that an absolute trust was created as to the balance on hand at the death of the depositor.

Malone v. Walsh (1944)

Facts: Wishing to keep her estate from certain relatives, decedent deposited money in bank accounts naming her brother as a joint tenant. Decedent retained complete dominion over the funds.

Issue: When a depositor places her own funds in a joint deposit over which she retains complete control, is a present interest vested in the other tenant?

Rule: When the depositor of one's own funds to a joint account intends joint ownership but retains complete control over the funds during life, an inter vivos present interest is created in the other as joint tenant(s), which ripens into complete ownership and enjoyment on the death of the depositor before the other tenant's death.

Smith's Estate (1891)

Facts: The decedent (T. Smith) bought bonds for the benefit of his nephew, Kelly. The decedent Smith informed Kelly's father that he bought the bonds for Kelly and listed them as Kelly's property in his private records.

Issue: Must a settlor make a declaration of trust to someone beside himself?

Rule: If it appears that a deceased settlor wrote and preserved for the inspection of others a declaration of trust, it is sufficient to establish the settlor's intent to create a trust. Others need not be informed of the settlor's actions during his life.

Elyacher v. Gerel Corp. (1984)

Facts: The plaintiffs brought an action against their 85-year-old father to compel him to surrender certain stock certificates. They claimed that their father had made them a gift of the interests represented by these certificates despite the fact that he retained physical possession of the certificates themselves.

Issue 1: What are the requirements for a valid inter vivos gift of stock?

Rule 1: In order to establish a valid gift transfer of an ownership interest a plaintiff must show that the donor *intended* to make a gift of a *present* ownership interest, the donor *delivered* the property in such a manner as to permanently divest himself of the ownership interest, and the donee *accepted* the gift.

Issue 2: May a donor retain control of the corporate interests despite having transferred his ownership interest?

Rule 2: A donor may retain control of the corporate interests through the creation of an inter vivos trust or through a retained life interest in the property. In the latter instance the donee holds a remainder interest in the property.

Hessen v. Iowa Automobile Mutual Insurance Co. (1922)

Facts: Hessen (plaintiff) purchased an automobile from someone whom he believed had clear title. He then purchased from the defendant company an insurance policy on the car. The policy contained a condition that the owner's title be "unconditional." When Hessen tried to recover on the policy, it was discovered that the car had been stolen.

Issue: Will an insurance policy for an automobile which includes a condition that the owner's title be clear and unconditional be voided if it turns out that the policy's owner was a bona fide purchaser of a stolen automobile?

Rule: The requirement that the insurance policy holder have clear and unconditional title to the insured property is a valid provision. It is the duty of the insured to establish that he has the interest which is defined in the policy.

Morgan v. Hodges (1891)

Facts: The plaintiff rented two horses, a harness and a buggy to Seaman. Seaman then sold the horses and equipment to Hodges (defendant). When plaintiff discovered where the objects were, he said to Hodges, "if you return to me the equipment, then I will let you keep the horse." Hodges agreed, and gave the harness and buggy to the plaintiff. The plaintiff then brought this suit to recover the value of the horse, arguing that the agreement was void for lack of consideration, since Hodges never had title to the harness and buggy.

Issue: If property is stolen from its true owner and then sold to a bona fide purchaser, what is the effect of the true owner's request to that purchaser to have the property returned?

Rule: If property is stolen from its owner and then sold to a bona fide purchaser, and the true owner later asks that purchaser to return the property, then if the purchaser does not acknowledge the true owner's claim to the property, then the bona fide purchaser can use the property as valid consideration in a contract with the true owner. If he does not acknowledge that the true owner has superior title, then the bona fide purchaser loses any claim to the property, and cannot use the property as valid consideration in a contract with the true owner.

Donald v. Suckling (1866)

Facts: The plaintiff deposited debentures with Simpson, as security for the payment at maturity of a bill of exchange, dated August 25, 1864, and payable six months after. Before that date, Simpson deposited the debentures with the defendant as security for a loan to Simpson. The plaintiff, without having satisfied his debt, sued to recover the debentures.

Issue: If a debtor deposits debentures with a creditor as security for the repayment of a loan, can the creditor convey the debentures before the day on which the loan is due?

Rule: A deposit of debentures with a creditor to secure repayment of a loan to him on a given day, with the power to sell in case of default on that day, creates an interest and a right of property in the debentures which is more than a mere lien. The transfer of the debentures by the creditor before the specified day does not annihilate the contract between the parties, nor the interest of the creditor in the debentures under that contract.

Sherer-Gillett Co. v. Long (1925)

Facts: Sherer-Gillett Co. contracted to sell to Taylor a display counter for a grocery store, for which Taylor agreed to pay monthly payments until the full purchase price was paid. The title was to remain in Sherer-Gillett until full payment had been made. Two days later Taylor sold the counter to Long, who had no knowledge of the sales agreement between Taylor and Sherer-Gillett. Sherer-Gillett brought an action for replevin.

Issue: Is a reservation of title by the seller good against a bona fide purchaser from a buyer in possession under a contract of conditional sale?

Rule: Where goods are sold by a person who is not the owner thereof, and who does not sell them under the authority or with the consent of the owner, the buyer acquires no better title to the goods than the seller had, unless the owner of the goods is by his conduct precluded from denying the seller's authority to sell.

O'Connor, Administratrix v. Clark (1895)

Facts: O'Connor, who was in the business of renting out wagons, employed Tracy, a well-known piano mover, O'Connor hired Tracy, and painted the words, "George Tracy, Piano Mover" on a wagon, with the intention of retaining the goodwill Tracy had established with the community. Later, Tracy sold the wagon to the Clark (defendant), who was persuaded by the words that the wagon was Tracy's. O'Connor's administratrix sued to recover the wagon.

Issue: Is an owner of property estopped from asserting title to the property if he takes actions designed to convince another that the property belongs to a third person, and that third person conveys the property?

Rule: An owner is prevented from asserting title to and is deprived of his property by the act of a third person if (1) the owner clothed the person with apparent title or authority to dispose of it, and (2) the person alleging the estoppel acted and parted with value upon the faith of such apparent ownership, so that he would be the loser if the appearances which he trusted were not real.

Phelps v. McQuade (1917)

Facts: Walter J. Gwynne falsely represented to the Phelps (plaintiffs) that he was Baldwin J. Gwynne, a man of financial responsibility. Relying upon this statement, the plaintiffs delivered to him upon credit a quantity of jewelry. Gwynne in turn sold it to the defendant, who bought it without knowledge of any defect in title. After discovering the deception, the plaintiffs sued to recover the jewelry.

Issue: Where an owner of personal property intends to sell his goods to the person with whom he deals, but is deceived of the person's identity, does title pass?

Rule: Where an owner of personal property intends to sell his goods to the person with whom he deals, then title passes, even if he were deceived of the person's identity. If the owner intends to sell to another, whom the buyer is impersonating, then title does not pass. It is purely a question of the vendor's intention.

Hurd v. Bickford (1892)

Facts: Gross was indebted to Bickford (defendant). Gross fraudulently purchased a horse and sleigh from Hurd. Bickford purchased the horse and, in payment therefor, discharged Gross' debt, Bickford was not aware of Gross' fraudulent purchase of the horse. Hurd (plaintiff) sued to recover the horse, contending that Bickford was not an innocent purchaser.

Issue: Where a debtor fraudulently purchases chattel and conveys it to the creditor in satisfaction of the debt, is the creditor an innocent purchaser?

Rule: Where a debtor fraudulently purchases chattel and conveys it to the creditor in satisfaction of the debt, the creditor is not an innocent purchaser. This rule arises because if the title to the chattel turns out to be false, then such conveyance did not constitute valid consideration for the discharge of the debt, and the creditor can yet demand payment of the debt. Since the creditor never gave up unconditionally his claim to the debt, he gave no consideration for the chattel.

Higgins v. Lodge (1888)

Facts: Levy made a fraudulent purchase of goods from Lodge (plaintiffs). Levy then sent them to Higgins (defendant) for public sale. Higgins made advance payments for the goods.

Issue: Is a purchaser of goods which were obtained by the vendor through fraud a bona fide purchaser?

Rule: If in any purchase, there be circumstances which would put a reasonable person acting as vendee upon inquiry, then the vendee will be presumed to have made that inquiry, and will be charged with notice of every fact which that inquiry would have revealed.

Wooden-Ware Co. v. United States (1882)

Facts: Indians from the Oneida tribe cut and removed timber from public lands. They transported the timber to the town of Depere and sold it to the Wooden-Ware Co. (defendant). The defendant had no knowledge of the vendors' wrongdoing. The United States sued to recover from Wooden-Ware the value of the timber.

Issue: If a party wrongfully removes timber from another's land, and sells it to a bona fide purchaser, is the bona fide purchaser protected from recovery against the original owner?

Rule: Where a party wrongfully removes timber from another's lands and sells it to a bona fide purchaser, the original owner of the timber can recover from the bona fide purchaser the market value of the timber at the time and place of the purchase.

Richtmyer v. Mutual Live Stock Commission Co. (1932)

Facts: Richtmyer owned pure bred cattle which were valued in Cherry County at $3500. The cattle were stolen from Richtmyer's ranch, and sold in Omaha by the thief to the Mutual Live Stock Commission Co. (defendant). The defendant, which had no knowledge of the theft, subsequently sold the cattle on the market as beef cattle for $1000. Richtmyer (plaintiff) sued to recover from the defendant the value of the cattle. The parties disputed the measure of damages.

Issue: Where property is stolen from its owner and then removed to another market where the property's price differs from its value in the owner's market, and sold to an innocent purchaser, what measure of damages can the owner recover from the bona fide purchaser?

Rule: The general rule for the measure of damages for conversion is the value of the property at the time and place of conversion. Where the property was transported by the wrongdoer between markets in which the property fetches different prices, the "time and place of conversion" which controls on the question of value is that fixed by the acts of the innocent purchaser in its dealing with the property, rather than the original taking in which it had no part.

Sechrest v. Safiol (1981)

Facts: Safiol contracted to purchase land from Sechrest. A provision of the sale agreement allowed Safiol to terminate the contract if he was unable to secure approval from the public authorities for the construction he planned. Safiol never submitted building plans to the authorities, nor did he seek any other necessary town approval. Subsequently, Safiol was unable to find a builder and attempted to terminate the contract. Sechrest sought to retain the deposit on the purchase agreement.

Issue: Does a provision in a purchase agreement allowing a buyer to terminate the contract if conditions are not fulfilled obligate the buyer to take action reasonably calculated to satisfy those conditions?

Rule: When a purchase and sale agreement permits a buyer to terminate the contract on the buyer's failure to meet certain conditions, the buyer is obligated to undertake activity reasonably calculated to meet those conditions.

Moses Brothers v. Johnson (1890)

Facts: Johnson (defendant) purchased forested land from Moses Brothers under an installment contract. By the contract's terms, the land was security for Johnson's payment obligations. When Johnson began cutting trees down, Moses Brothers sought an injunction to prevent waste.

Issue: Can a vendor holding legal title to land sold as security for the purchase money obtain an injunction against a buyer committing waste?

Rule: In an installment sale contract, a vendee committing waste that impairs the security or renders it insufficient can be enjoined from committing further waste.

Layman v. Binns (1988)

Facts: Layman(buyer) had an unhindered opportunity to examine the basement of the premises. Layman saw the bulging, obviously defective basement wall.

Issue: Can a buyer of defective real estate recover when the defect was obvious and there was ample opportunity to discover the defect?

Rule: The doctrine of caveat emptor precludes recovery in an action by the purchaser of real estate where the condition complained of is open to observation or discoverable upon reasonable inspection, the purchaser has ample opportunity to examine the premises, and there is no evidence of fraud on the part of the vendor.

Sweeney, Administratrix v. Sweeney (1940)

Facts: The decedent Maurice Sweeney had two deeds drawn at the same time. The first deed, which was recorded, conveyed a farm to the defendant. The second deed was not recorded because Maurice was afraid he would predecease the defendant. The second deed conveyed the farm back to the decedent. Maurice took home both deeds, which were attested. The plaintiff contended that the farm was part of Maurice's probate estate.

Issue: May a deed delivered to a grantee be held conditional?

Rule: Because conditional delivery must be made to a third party, conditional delivery to a grantee vests the grantee with absolute title.

Johnson v. Johnson (1903)

Facts: The grantor left a deed with a third party and instructed the third party to deliver the deed to the grantor's daughter if the grantor should die. The grantor continued to exercise dominion over the property during her life. Upon her death, the third party delivered the deed to the daughter.

Issue: To effect a valid delivery of a deed, must a grantor divest himself of any right of future control over the deed?

Rule: In order to constitute a delivery, the grantor must absolutely part with the possession and control of the deed.

Stone v. Duvall (1875)

Facts: Duvall (plaintiff) deposited a deed in escrow which was to be delivered upon his death to his daughter, Mary Stone. When she died, Duvall sought to abrogate the deed, thereby preventing Mary's husband from inheriting the land.

Issue: Is a deed in escrow abrogated when the grantee dies before the performance of the condition of delivery?

Rule: The death of a grantee prior to the performance of a condition of a deed held in escrow does not abrogate the deed.

Mays v. Shields (1903)

Facts: Shields (plaintiff) deposited a deed in escrow. The deed was subsequently improperly delivered and recorded. Shields did not act to have the record expunged. Mays (defendant), an innocent purchaser for value, had no notice that there had been an escrow or that the deed had been recorded.

Issue: May a grantor who deposited a deed in escrow and knew that it was improperly delivered and recorded be estopped from denying the title of an innocent purchaser when the grantor did not act to prevent the improper recording?

Rule: To avoid being estopped from denying the title of an innocent purchaser buying on the faith of the record, a grantor of an escrow deed who has knowledge of the deed's improper recording must take steps to expunge the record.

Smith v. Hadad (1974)

Facts: Smith and Hadad were owners of adjacent portions of property, both of which were previously owned by Nichols. The deeds from Nichols were ambiguous as to whether Nichols intended to measure their respective lots from the edge or center of an abutting road.

Issue: In the absence of expressed intent by the parties to a transaction, will a measurement given in a deed as commencing on a public way be presumed to begin at the center or at the side line of that way?

Rule: In the absence of a clear showing of contrary intent, a measurement given from a stream or public or private way shall be presumed to begin at the side line of that stream or way.

Bernard v. Nantucket Boys' Club, Inc. (1984)

Facts: Potter owned a lot located directly north of the northernmost of Adams' three adjacent lots. Adams conveyed to the defendant land described in the deed as both bounded to the north by other land of grantor and as being entirely enclosed by fences. At the time of the conveyance, there was a single fence around all of Adams' lots but no fence separating the separate lots. Additional evidence failed to clarify whether the parties intended to include Adams' northernmost lot in the conveyance.

Issue: If a deed contains conflicting descriptions of real property conveyed, which description will govern?

Rule: When a deed contains inconsistent descriptions of the land conveyed, and the parties' intent is unclear, and neither description is more specific, then the grantee is entitled to that interpretation which will be most beneficial to him.

Hilliker v. Rueger (1920)

Facts: Rueger (defendant) covenanted that he was "seised of the said premises in fee simple and had good right to convey the same," and conveyed the property to Hilliker. When he tried to sell the same, Hilliker discovered that Rueger did not in fact have title to part of the premises. Hilliker contends that damages should be only nominal since the plaintiff had not actually been evicted.

Issue: May a grantee recover damages for breach of a covenant of seisin if he was not evicted?

Rule: If a covenant of seisin be broken at all, it is at the time of the delivery of the conveyance. If the covenant be broken by the failure of title then an action can be maintained to recover the damages which result directly from the breach. It is not essential in an action to recover damages for the breach of such a covenant that the grantee should be evicted.

Schofield v. Iowa Homestead Co. (1871)

Facts: The plaintiff sold a portion of land which he had bought from the defendant. The defendant's deed contained a covenant of seisin. The plaintiff subsequently sold the land to another. Later, the plaintiff discovered that the covenant of seisin had been breached, but did not suffer any damages.

Issue: Does a covenant of seisin run with the land?

Rule: A covenant of seisin runs with the land. The first grantee who purchases land under a covenant of seisin and then conveys the land to another is thereafter not entitled to recover for a breach of that covenant. The remote grantee who suffers the injury can maintain an action upon the covenant.

Solberg v. Robinson (1914)

Facts: Robinson (defendant) conveyed land to the Smiths, who in turn conveyed the same to Solberg (plaintiff). Robinson's deed contained covenants of seisin and quiet enjoyment. Neither Robinson nor Smith was ever in possession of the premises. The parties later realized that Robinson was not the true owner.

Issue 1: Does a covenant of seisin run with the land?

Rule 1: A covenant of seisin does not run with the land. Therefore, remote grantees cannot recover from the original grantor upon this covenant.

Issue 2: Is actual possession necessary for the covenant of a grantor without title to inure to the benefit of his remote grantees?

Rule 2: Constructive possession of a grantee is sufficient to carry a covenant of quiet enjoyment (future covenant) forward. Thus, a grantor without title is estopped by deed from claiming he had no estate in the land attempted to be conveyed, and is therefore liable to remote grantees who are evicted.

State v. Buyers Service Company (1987)

Facts: The State alleged that Buyers Service, a commercial title company which also assists homeowners in purchasing residential real estate, engaged in the unauthorized practice of law. Some of its practices included: preparing documents affecting title to real property, handling real estate closings, and recording legal documents at the courthouse.

Issue: Do the preparation of deeds, notes, and other instruments related to mortgage loans and transfers of real property, the preparation of title abstracts for persons other than attorneys, the performance of real estate closings, and the practice of mailing or hand-carrying legal instruments to the courthouse for recordings constitute activities that entail the practice of law?

Rule: The practice of law is not confined to litigation. It extends to activities in other fields, including: the preparation of documents which entail specialized knowledge and ability, the conducting of title examination, and the preparation of title abstracts. Moreover, real estate and mortgage closings should be conducted only under the supervision of attorneys, and the delivering to and mailing of documents to a courthouse for the purpose of effecting a real estate transfer falls within the definition of legal practice.

Lohmeyer v. Bower (1951)

Facts: The buyer (Lohmeyer) sued to rescind a contract for the sale of land on the grounds that the land contained violations of both private and public restrictions. The contract provided that the defendant would convey merchantable title.

Issue: Is a title to real property marketable when the property is in such a condition that it does not comply with public and/or private restrictions?

Rule: Title to real property is unmarketable when the violation of a land-use restriction imposed by covenant is of substantial character and may expose the party holding title to the risk of litigation.

Conklin v. Davi (1978)

Facts: Conklin's title to a portion of real estate that the Davi (defendant) was to purchase was claimed by adverse possession. The contract of sale required the vendor to convey a "marketable and insurable" title.

Issue: Is a title procured by adverse possession unmarketable?

Rule: A marketable or insurable title is a less stringent requirement than a title valid of record. Hence, a title resting in adverse possession, if clearly established, is marketable.

Stambovsky v. Ackley (1991)

Facts: The Stambovskys, after contracting to purchase a house, discovered that it was widely reputed to be possessed by poltergeists.

Issue: Does the doctrine of caveat emptor apply in situations where it would be unlikely for the buyer to discover any undisclosed details concerning the home he has contracted to purchase?

Rule: Where a condition which has been created by the seller materially impairs the value of the contract and is undiscoverable by or unlikely to be within the scope of knowledge of a purchaswer exercising due care, nondisclosure constitutes a basis for rescission as a matter of equity.

Johnson v. Davis (1985)

Facts: The Davises contracted to buy a house from Johnson. When Davis asked about damage to a window and the ceiling, Johnson stated that the problem was corrected and that the roof and ceiling had never been a problem. Davis then gave Johnson an additional deposit. Davis later observed water entering the house from various parts of the ceiling and elsewhere.

Issue: Does the seller of a home have a duty to disclose latent material defects to a buyer?

Rule: When the seller of a home knows of facts materially affecting the value of the property that are not readily observable and are not known to the buyer, the seller is under a duty to disclose the defects to the buyer.

Lempke v. Dagenais (1988)

Facts: The Lempkes purchased a garage from the original owners. Shortly afterward, they noticed structural problems which were undiscoverable at the time of purchase.

Issue: May a subsequent purchaser of real property sue the builder or contractor on the theory of implied warranty of workmanlike quality for latent defects?

Rule: A subsequent purchaser may sue a builder or contractor under an implied warranty of workmanlike conduct for latent defects which manifest themselves within a reasonable time after purchase and which cause economic harm.

Frimberger v. Anzellotti (1991)

Facts: A wetlands area was filled without a permit and in violation of state statute. Unaware of the violations, Frimberger conveyed the property to Anzellotti by warranty deed, free of all encumbrances, but subject to all building and zoning restrictions as well as easements and restrictions of record.

Issue: Does a latent violation of a restrictive land use statute or ordinance, existing at the time a fee is conveyed, constitute a breach of the warranty deed covenant against encumbrances?

Rule: Encumbrances cannot be expanded to include latent conditions on property that are in violation of statutes or government regulations.

Rockafellor v. Gray (1922)

Facts: Connelly purchased Rockafellor's land at a foreclosure sale. He sold the land by warranty deed to Dixon, who sold it by warranty deed to Hansen and Gregory. Subsequently, the court invalidated the foreclosure sale. Hansen & Gregorson, the remote grantees, sued the remote grantor, Connelly, for breach of the warranty of seisin.

Issue: Does a covenant of seisin run with the land even though the original grantor never had actual possession of the land conveyed?

Rule: A remote grantee can maintain an action on a covenant of seisin given by the grantor in the original deed, regardless of whether the original grantor ever had actual possession of the land.

St. Louis County National Bank v. Fielder (1953)

Facts: Kessler deeded his residence to the defendant Fielder, but reserved a life estate in himself and the power of revocation upon his death. Kessler's will left all of his estate, real and personal, to the plaintiff.

Issue: When a grantor retains the power to revoke a deed, is the deed void as an invalid testamentary disposition?

Rule: A grantor has the right to reserve the power of revocation and such a reservation in itself does not make a deed testamentary.

Murphy v. Financial Development Corp. (1985)

Facts: Financial (mortgagee) foreclosed on Murphy's (mortgagor's) property. Financial acted in good faith to arrange a foreclosure sale. A poor showing at that sale resulted in a sales price far below the property's market value.

Issue: Must a mortgagee foreclosing on property exercise due diligence to obtain a fair price for the property, thereby securing the mortgagor's equity?

Rule: A mortgagee must exercise due diligence to obtain a fair price for foreclosed property.

Bean v. Walker (1983)

Facts: Bean contracted to sell Walker a single-family home. The sellers retained legal title to the property, until payment was completed, at which time title was to go to the purchasers. When approximately one-half of the contract was paid off, the Walkers defaulted and the Beans sued for repossession.

Issue: What are the relative rights between a vendor and a defaulting vendee under a land purchase contract?

Rule: A vendee acquires equitable title and a vendor merely holds the legal title in trust for the vendee until such time that the purchase price is paid in accordance with the terms of the contract. Therefore, before a vendor may file an action for repossession, he must first attempt to foreclose the equitable title or bring an action at law for the purchase price.

CHAPTER 10 RECORDING AND TITLE ASSURANCE

I.   COMMON LAW

A.   First in Time Rule
When two parties have conflicting valid claims to the same parcel of land, the first in time will prevail.

Example: A conveys his home to B. The next day A conveys the same home to C. B will prevail over C.

B.   Exceptions

1. Conflicting claims are equitable and the first party is estopped from benefiting under the rule because of his actions.

2. Conflicting claims are equitable and the second purchaser later acquired "legal title" in good faith and for valuable consideration.

3. A holder of a legal interest will always prevail over one who holds an equitable interest if the legal interest was acquired first. The holder of the legal interest will prevail over the holder of the equitable interest even if the legal interest was acquired later in time if the legal holder acquired the title in good faith and for value.

4. A party who conveys land to another before obtaining title, and then obtains title and records first in an attempt to claim superior title, may be estopped from arguing that he did not hold title at the time of the conveyance.

II.   RECORDING STATUTES

A.   In General
Recording statutes were enacted to provide a buyer with more title assurance than the common law allowed. Recording acts establish how title to property is determined.

B.   Effect of a Recording Act
A recording act will determine who obtains title to real property. The act will not affect a contractual or other relationship.

Example: A pays B $100,000 for title to land. A later discovers that he cannot receive title to the land because another purchaser has already recorded his interest. A may sue B for breach of contract.

C.   Types of Recording Acts

1. Pure Notice Acts
A bona fide purchaser will prevail over an earlier purchaser regardless of who was the first to record.

2. Pure Race Acts
A subsequent purchaser, whether bona fide or not, will prevail against an earlier purchaser if he (the second purchaser) recorded first. The second purchaser may prevail even if he had notice of the first purchaser. (The winner of the "race" to record will receive title). This rule is only followed in two states.

3. Race-Notice Acts
A subsequent bona fide purchaser will prevail against a previous purchaser if the subsequent purchaser recorded first without notice of the earlier conveyance.

III.   MECHANICS OF RECORDING

A.   Deposit with County Recorder
The grantee brings the deed to the county recorder who stamps, copies and files the deed.

B.   Indices
The deeds are indexed by grantor and grantee. Some jurisdictions require indexing by tract, the most accurate method to follow a title.

IV.   INTERESTS TO BE RECORDED

A.   Interests That Must Be Recorded

1. Instruments that affect title to real property such as deeds, mortgages, powers of attorney, covenants, tax liens, etc.

2. Instruments that modify title to real property or any interest in the examples above.

B. Interests That Need Not Be Recorded

   1. Adverse possession

      a. An adverse possessor will prevail over a grantee if the adverse possessor's claim ripened before the grant. This rule is consistent with the rule that the earlier of two legal claims will prevail.

      b. Abandonment of the property by the adverse possessor after his title ripens will not extinguish his priority over a subsequent grantee, because an adverse possessor's title is not extinguished by physical abandonment of his premises.

   2. Short-term leases.

   3. Executory contract of sale.

   4. Easements by implication and necessity.

C. The Bona Fide Purchaser
    A bona fide purchaser will be entitled to certain rights. The general requirements are:

   1. Purchaser for value
      Does not have to be fair market value but nominal consideration will not suffice.

   2. Antecedent debt

      a. Cancellation of a debt in return for a conveyance of property will constitute valid consideration.

      b. Courts are split if a mortgagee maintains the same rights of collection.

   3. Persons not considered purchasers for value:

      a. Those who promise to pay at a future date given in exchange for the conveyance.

    b. Donees, heirs, devisees.

    c. Lien creditors (some states will consider lien creditors purchasers for value).

    d. Unsecured creditors.

V.   NOTICE

The purchaser must show he did not have notice. There are three kinds of notice: actual, record, and inquiry (good faith) notice.

A.   Actual Notice

B.   Record Notice

If a deed was recorded and appeared in the chain of title, the purchaser will be charged with notice. The mere fact that a deed was recorded will not confer notice if the recording was outside the chain of title.

1. Problems in the Chain of Title

A deed that is outside the chain of title is one that would not be discovered by due diligence and therefore would not provide "notice" to a purchaser. A deed may fall outside the chain of title for a number of reasons:

    a. Link was not recorded.

    b. "Wild" deed

A deed given by a grantor whose claim to title came from a source which was not recorded.

    c. Error by county indexer

A deed misindexed by the recorders office will *not* remove the deed from the chain of title (majority rule).

    d. Deed recorded late

Courts are split when a subsequent purchaser records before a previous purchaser of whom he had no notice.

    e. Deed recorded early

A deed recorded before the title actually passed will not be in the chain of title and will not serve as notice. (**Minority**

Rule: the recording in such cases becomes effective when the title actually passes).

    f. Easements and servitudes on land that is eventually subdivided
Courts are split whether the purchaser of a subdivision is on notice of the easements and servitudes.

2. Defective Document
Will not serve as notice—Most states have passed "curative acts" allowing a defective writing to be valid notice if a technical defect is not challenged within a certain amount of time.

3. Requirements of a Proper Search:

    a. Check grantor, grantee and other applicable indices maintained by the county.

    b. Trace title for the statutorily required period (e.g., 60 years).

    c. Trace mortgages, probate proceedings and other encumbrances discovered.

C. Inquiry (Good Faith) Notice
Notice imputed to a purchaser who had neither record notice nor actual notice, but had information that would cause a "reasonable person" to make further inquiries about the title. A purchaser's obligations include:

1. Investigate an unrecorded transaction referred to in a recorded document.

2. Physically examine the premises.

3. Quitclaim deed
In a majority of states a quitclaim deed in the chain of title will not place the purchaser on notice.

VI. THE TORRENS SYSTEM
A title registration is merely evidence of title to real property. Under the Torrens System, the act of registration provides the title. This system is followed only in a minority of jurisdictions and is only optional in these jurisdictions.

VII. TITLE ASSURANCE

A. Generally

A purchase of real property is usually accompanied by a covenant of title (see Chapter 9). Very often a buyer may not be able to recover for breach of a covenant because the seller is insolvent, dead, or hiding in Paraguay. To protect himself, a buyer's lawyer will seek assurance of the validity of the title to be conveyed. Since tracing a title is cumbersome and time-consuming, lawyers usually purchase an abstract or title insurance from companies that specialize in these services.

B. Abstract

1. Definition

A summary of the conveyance history of real property.

2. Practical use

A lawyer will examine an abstract and then render an opinion as to the validity of title.

3. Liability

a. Lawyers are liable for results of their negligence but not for the negligence of the abstract company.

b. Abstract companies are liable for their negligence to the purchaser of the real property even though they never had actual dealings.

c. Third parties relying on an abstract may recover from a negligent abstract company.

C. Title Insurance

1. Definition

Insurance against any loss incurred by a buyer due to an imperfect title.

2. The insurance usually encompasses any covenant extended to a future buyer by the insured.

3. Coverage

May be limited by the policy but usually extends to all risks that would be disclosed by a competent examination of the public records.

4. Defects that an insurer will *not* be liable for if not discovered:

   a. Public records relied upon that were incorrect.

   b. Encroachment of the insured onto adjacent property and encroachment of adjacent property owners onto the insured's property.

   c. Violation of setback rules.

   d. Adverse possession claims.

   e. Taxes, assessments and other charges that do not appear as liens.

5. Negligence
   The insurer will be held liable for a negligent search even though the purchaser's loss would have been excluded from the policy.

CASE CLIPS

Mountain States Telephone & Telegraph Co. v. Kelton (1955)

Facts: Kelton, a contractor, damaged the telephone company's underground cable buried in a certain location under a perpetual easement. The easement was recorded. The telephone company sued the contractor and the property owner to recover damages.

Issue: Must a contractor with no interest in the title to the land where he is working search the record to locate easements?

Rule: A contractor without an interest in the title of the land on which he is working has no duty to search the record and is not therefore on constructive notice as to an easement's location.

Stone v. French (1887)

Facts: Although recorded, French's deed was void for lack of delivery. Stone, who was unaware that the deed was void, bought the land from French.

Issue: Does the recording of a void deed validate a transfer of an interest in land represented by the void deed?

Rule: A void deed, though recorded, is still void and a purchaser of realty from a person holding under a void recorded deed, though in fact a bona fide purchaser, cannot obtain a good or valid title.

Earle v. Fiske (1870)

Facts: In 1864, Fiske conveyed her interest in land by deed which was not recorded until 1867. In 1865, she died and her sole heir by a valid and recorded deed conveyed the same real property to Earle, who lacked actual notice of the prior conveyance.

Issue: Does an unrecorded deed void a subsequent transaction involving the same land when the purchaser lacks actual knowledge of the prior conveyance?

Rule: Although an unrecorded deed is binding upon the grantor, his heirs and devisees, and all persons having actual notice of it, it is not valid and effectual as against any other persons.

Mugaas v. Smith (1949)

Facts: Mugaas (plaintiff) gained title to land by adverse possession but did not record his title. Smith (defendant), without actual notice of the Mugaas's claim, purchased property by legal description and with record title that included Mugaas's land.

Issues: Under a recording statute, does a conveyance of the record title to a bona fide purchaser extinguish a title acquired by adverse possession?

Rule: Since recording statutes relate exclusively to written titles, a conveyance of the record title to a bona fide purchaser will not extinguish a title acquired by adverse possession.

Mortensen v. Lingo (1951)

Facts: In 1941 McCain conveyed realty to Anglin. The deed was recorded but not indexed. In 1947, McCain conveyed the same land to Lingo (defendant), who conveyed by warranty deed to Mortensen (plaintiff). Mortensen brought suit against Lingo, contending that Anglin threatened to evict him.

Issue: Is a deed properly recorded in the office of the district where the land lies, but not indexed, constructive notice against subsequent innocent purchasers for value?

Rule: The recording of a deed without indexing is insufficient to give constructive notice to a bona fide purchaser for value.

Patterson v. Bryant (1939)

Facts: Bryant (defendant) sold the same timber rights twice, first to the plaintiff who failed to promptly record title, and secondly to another who promptly recorded and thereby defeated title pursuant to the recording statute.

Issue: Is a grantee's failure to promptly record title a defense in a restitutionary action against a grantor?

Rule: Recording statutes only protect subsequent purchasers. Hence, a grantee's failure to promptly record his title is not a defense in a restitutionary action against a grantor who subsequently sells the same property again.

Simmons v. Stum (1882)

Facts: To secure a debt, in 1874 Stum (plaintiff) took a mortgage from McHenry. McHenry conveyed the property to Cochran and Strong, both of whom had actual notice of the mortgage. Stum recorded his mortgage on March 15, 1879. Two days earlier, Cochran and Strong conveyed to the defendant, who did not claim actual notice of the mortgage.

Issue: Under a race-notice statute, must a bona fide purchaser for value without notice prove in a title conflict that she recorded her deed prior to the recordation of an outstanding mortgage in order to defeat the mortgagee's interest in the land?

Rule: Under a notice-race statute, a bona fide purchaser for value without notice must prove that in a title conflict her deed was recorded prior to an outstanding mortgage in order to defeat the mortgagee's interest in the land.

Eastwood v. Shedd (1968)

Facts: On December 2, 1958, a donor deeded land to Eastwood (defendant) who recorded on October 16, 1964. On October 15, 1963, the donor conveyed the same land to the plaintiff who recorded on October 23, 1963, Shedd (plaintiff) had no actual notice of the prior conveyance. Both conveyances were gifts, Shedd brought suit to quiet title.

Issue: In a jurisdiction with a race-notice statute, must a subsequent grantee purchase the conveyed property to be protected by the recording statute?

Rule: Since the legislature deleted the language "purchaser" from the statute, the statute grants priority to a second grantee only if he takes the instrument without notice of the prior conveyance and has his instrument recorded ahead of the prior instrument. (This case represents a minority view).

Strong v. Whybark (1907)

Facts: A common grantor, S.D. Heyden, conveyed land to Moore by warranty deed through which Strong's (plaintiff) title derived. Subsequently, S.D. Heyden conveyed by quitclaim deed and for nominal consideration the same land to J. Heyden, through which Whybark's (defendant) title derived. The quitclaim deed was recorded prior to the warranty deed.

Issue 1: When a grantee has a quitclaim deed in his chain of title, is he a bona fide purchaser for value without notice of the title of the true owner?

Rule 1: A purchaser for value by quitclaim deed is as much within the protection of the registry act as one who becomes a purchaser by a warranty deed; thus a quitclaim deed, without more, does not put the purchaser on notice.

Issue 2: Is one who purchased a deed that recited nominal consideration considered a bona fide purchaser for value?

Rule 2: Under a recorded deed, it is not necessary (absent fraud) that the consideration be adequate in point of value.

Note: Rule 2 represents a minority view.

Gabel v. Drewrys Limited, U.S.A., Inc. (1953)

Facts: Drewrys Limited, Inc. (plaintiff) received from a debtor a note secured by a mortgage. Concurrently, the parties agreed that Drewrys would forbear collection, but no definite time extension was mentioned. The debtor previously mortgaged the property to secure a debt owed to Gabel (defendant) who recorded his mortgage after Drewrys who, without notice of Gabel's mortgage, recorded theirs.

Issue: When a mortgage is given to secure a preexisting debt, is a mortgagee a purchaser for value and thus protected by the recording statute?

Rule: If a mortgage is taken to secure a preexisting debt and no new contemporaneous consideration passes (either of benefit to the mortgagor or detriment to the mortgagee), then the mortgagee does not thereby become a purchaser.

Osin v. Johnson (1957)

Facts: Osin (plaintiff) sold land to Johnson (defendant), who promised but fraudulently failed to properly record a trust on the land. The defendant then executed deeds of trust to others on the land which were recorded. Still other creditors obtained judgment liens on the land. Osin brought suit for equitable relief.

Issue: Does a constructive trust which is incapable of being recorded have a superior claim to subsequent lienholders who rely on the record title when deciding to extend credit?

Rule: A constructive trust only has priority over lienholders who did not rely on the record title when deciding to extend credit.

Wineberg v. Moore (1961)

Facts: Barker sold land to Wineberg (plaintiff), who took possession of the land but failed to record his deed. Subsequently, Barker sold the land to the defendant by a deed which was recorded. Wineberg brought suit to quiet title.

Issue: When land is patently in the possession of one who is not the record owner, are subsequent grantees who fail to inquire bona fide purchasers in good faith?

Rule: The law imputes to a purchaser all information which would be conveyed to him by an actual view of the premises, and if such inspection reveals possession by another, the purchaser has notice of the possessor's interest in the property. In the absence of such inspection, purchasers are on constructive notice as to all facts which such inspection would have revealed, as well as to facts discoverable by inquiry suggested by such inspection.

Kindred v. Crosby (1959)

Facts: In 1938, Kindred (plaintiff) received a quitclaim deed from Crosby. This deed was not recorded until 1957. In 1953, Crosby executed and recorded a joint tenancy deed of the same interest to himself and his wife. Crosby died soon thereafter. Crosby's wife (defendant) now claims to own an undivided half-interest in the property.

Issue: Does a subsequent purchaser have the burden of proving that he was a subsequent purchaser for valuable consideration without notice?

Rule: One claiming to be a bona fide purchaser as against the holder of a prior unrecorded conveyance or encumbrance has the burden of showing by evidence apart from the deed that he paid a valuable consideration for the conveyance.

Sabo v. Horvath (1976)

Facts: Before title passed to him, Lowery conveyed real estate to Horvath by deed recorded in January 1970. In August 1973 Lowery received title to the land and in October 1973, he deeded the land to Sabo by a deed recorded in December 1973. After Lowery obtained title, Horvath did not rerecord his deed. Horvath brought suit to quiet title.

Issue: Where a grantor-grantee index is used, does a wild deed (i.e., a deed recorded outside the chain of title) give constructive notice to subsequent innocent purchasers for value?

Rule: Only instruments which are recorded after the grantor obtains title, and therefore are within the chain of title, serve as constructive notice to a subsequent purchaser who duly records.

Petersen v. Hubschman Construction Co., Inc. (1979)

Facts: Petersen (plaintiff) contracted with Hubschman Construction Co. (defendant) for construction of a new house. Petersen refused to complete the contract because although the house was habitable, it contained substantial defects. Petersen sued to recover all money already paid to the construction company.

Issue: Does a contract for the sale of a house contain an implied warranty of habitability that the house is free of latent defects that would make it unfit for use as a residence?

Rule: Implied in a contract of sale from the builder-vendor to the vendees is a warranty that when completed and conveyed to the vendees the house is free from latent defects so that it is reasonably suited for its intended use.

G-W-L, Inc. v. Robichaux (1982)

Facts: The Robichaux (plaintiffs) contracted with a builder-vendor, G-W-L, Inc. (defendant) for the construction of a new house. The language of the contract stated that "no ... warranties, express or implied, in addition to said written instruments" existed between the parties. The contract did not include a warranty of the house's habitability.

Issue: Must language waiving the implied warrant of habitability be clear and free from doubt in a sales contract between a builder-vendor and a purchaser of a new house?

Rule: In a sales contract between a builder-vendor and a purchaser of a new house, language waiving the implied warranty of habitability must be clear and free from doubt. In this case, the language was clear and the waiver was valid.

Connor v. Great Western Savings and Loan Ass'n (1968)

Facts: Great Western Savings and Loan Association financed the construction of a subdivision. Connor purchased a home in this subdivision. Thereafter the home suffered serious damage due to negligent construction. The plaintiff sought rescission or damages.

Issue: Does a lender of a construction enterprise owe an independent duty of care to home buyers who are not in privity with the lender?

Rule: When a lender voluntarily assumes a relationship with a builder wherein its financing took on ramifications beyond the domain of the usual money lender, it actively participates in and has the right to extensively control the construction enterprise. The lender owes an independent duty of care to the home buyers if the following factors are present: (1) the transaction was intended to affect the home buyers; (2) the lender could reasonably foresee the risk to the home buyers; (3) it is certain the homeowners suffered injury; (4) the injury suffered is proximately caused by the lender's conduct; (5) substantial moral blame attaches to the lender's conduct; and (6) imposing liability advances public policy.

Sunnen Products Co. v. Chemtech Indus., Inc. (1987)

Facts: Sunnen Products Co. purchased property from Chemtech Industries, who had used the site as a chemical factory. The plaintiff alleged that the property was environmentally contaminated, and brought suit for damages under the Comprehensive Environmental Response, Compensation and Liability Act.

Issue: Where the owners of contaminated property prove that a previous owner contaminated the property, may the previous owner be held liable for the clean-up costs under CERCLA?

Rule: The owner who contaminated the property is strictly liable for the necessary costs of response incurred by its successor in interest.

Brown v. Lober (1979)

Facts: An owner of land reserved a two-thirds interest in the mineral rights of land he conveyed to the Bosts. The Bosts conveyed the land to the Browns (plaintiffs) by general warranty deed with no exceptions. The Browns discovered they owned only a one-third interest in the sub-surface estate when they conveyed the land. The statute of limitations barred a suit on the present covenants. Therefore the Browns sued the Bosts estate on the covenant of quiet enjoyment.

Issue: If a covenantee fails in his effort to sell an interest in land because he discovers that he does not own what his warranty deed purported to convey, has he suffered a constructive eviction entitling him to bring an action against his grantor for breach of the covenant of quiet enjoyment?

Rule: The mere existence of a paramount title does not constitute a constructive eviction. Hence, an action for breach of a covenant of quiet enjoyment will not lie.

Leach v. Gunnarson (1980)

Facts: A property owner gave Leach (defendant) an irrevocable license to construct a well on a piece of land. The well was an obvious physical structure. The owner subsequently conveyed with a covenant against encumbrances to Gunnarson (plaintiff) who was, at the time of the conveyance, cognizant of the well. The original owner told Gunnarson that the defendant had no enforceable right to use the well. Leach filed suit seeking a decree that they owned an easement for drawing water from the well.

Issue: Is an irrevocable license to use a spring on a grantee's land a breach of the grantor's covenant against encumbrances if the license is an open, notorious, and visible physical encumbrance?

Rule: Absent an express exclusion in a deed, a grantor's covenant against encumbrances in a warranty deed protects the grantee against all encumbrances existing at the time of delivery of the deed even if the grantee knew about the encumbrance.

Davis v. Smith (1848)

Facts: Before his death, N.H. Harris conveyed to Laney a deed containing a covenant of warranty. Laney's heirs sued the estate of

Harris claiming breach of the covenant of warranty. The parties disputed the measure of damages.

Issue: How are a grantee's damages measured when, due to a grantor's defective title, he is evicted from premises to which he was given a covenant of warranty?

Rule: If a grantor breaches a covenant of warranty, the grantee is entitled to the purchase price of the land plus interest from the date of the purchase.

Madrid v. Spears (1957)

Facts: The Madrids (defendants) obtained land under a deed on which Spears' name was forged. During four years, the Madrids occupied the land, made valuable improvements thereon, and realized profits from the land. Spears brought suit to cancel the deed and quiet title.

Issue 1: May one who in good faith improved land owned by another before he was ejected recover the enhanced value of the land?

Rule 1: One who is permitted to recover for improvements to real property is entitled to the reasonable value of his labor and materials, or to the amount which his improvements have added to the market value of the land, whichever is smaller.

Issue 2: Is a rightful owner of land entitled to a credit for the rents and profits received by a good faith improver of land that accrue after the owner serves his complaint?

Rule 2: An owner successfully prosecuting an ejectment action against a good faith improver of the land is entitled to the rental value of the land in its raw state without its improvements. In the absence of any such proof, he is not entitled to recover any of the rents and profits.

Robben v. Obering (1960)

Facts: Meirink executed an oil and gas lease to Obering (defendant). Obering's lease included a covenant of warranty. Meirink, who at the time of the lease had thought he owned the land, later discovered he only owned a 25 percent interest. He then acquired another 25 percent which he later reconveyed to his brother. This brother sold the 25 percent interest to Robben (plaintiff). Robben brought suit for a declaratory judgment.

Issue: When a lessor's lease includes a covenant of warranty to property in which he has only a partial interest, does an interest acquired after the conveyance pass to the lessee?

Rule: The doctrine of after-acquired title or estoppel by deed is applicable to a lease which contains an express warranty of title. The doctrine holds that where one who has no interest, or but a part thereof, in land he undertakes to convey, and afterwards acquires title, the interest he acquires passes to the grantee.

First American Title Insurance Co., Inc. v. First Title Service Co. of the Florida Keys, Inc. (1984)

Facts: First Title Service Company (defendant) prepared abstracts for the sellers of two lots. First American Title Insurance Company (plaintiff), relying on the abstracts, issued owners' and mortgagees' title insurance policies to the buyers of the two lots and their lender. The abstracts failed to note the existence of a recorded judgment against a former owner of the lots, and that the holder of the judgment had made demand on the new owners for payment of the judgment. The plaintiff brought suit as a third-party beneficiary of the contract of employment of the abstractor.

Issues: Can an abstracting company be held liable to a landowner's title insurance company for abstracts that were negligently prepared for the landowner?

Rule: If the abstractor knew or reasonably should have known that his customer requested an abstract for purposes of inducing third parties to rely on it as evidence of title, the abstractor is liable to those third parties for damages caused by the negligent production of the abstract.

United States v. Ryan (1954)

Facts: The United States (plaintiff) had a tax lien against property in Minnesota, a Torrens System state. Pursuant to state law, all lienholders had to obtain a court decree directing the registrar to issue a new certificate of title noting the lien on the property. The plaintiff, who did not comply with the state law, contended that Ryan (defendant) purchased the land subject to the lien.

Issue: In a state using the Torrens System, may the U.S. perfect a lien against real estate even though it does not comply with state registration law?

Rule: The U.S. government is not exempt from state laws affecting title to property. Failure to have a certificate of title altered to reflect a tax lien as required by state law will mean that a tax lien is not perfected.

White v. Western Title Insurance Co. (1985)

Facts: The Whites (plaintiffs) purchased title reports and insurance from the defendant. The defendant failed to mention a water easement on the property either in the reports or the insurance policy. The easement was a matter of public record. The contract between the plaintiffs and the defendant excluded coverage for claims or title to water rights. When the Whites discovered the existence of the easement, they sued for damages.

Issues: Where a title insurance policy excepts from coverage certain easements, is the insurer nonetheless liable in negligence for failure to advise an insured of recorded easements in the subject land?

Rule: A title insurer has a duty to list all matters of public record regarding the subject property, and failure to so do is prima facie negligence from which the insurer cannot, by contract, exculpate itself.

Transamerica Title Insurance Co. v. Johnson (1985)

Facts: Transamerica Title Insurance Co. (plaintiff) issued title insurance to Johnson's vendees. Johnson (defendant) paid the premiums. Johnson contractually agreed to convey unencumbered land. When it was discovered that the land was encumbered, the plaintiff paid the assessments and sued Johnson under its policy subrogation rights. Johnson argued that the plaintiff, who negligently failed to disclose the encumbrances, was liable to the defendant for its failure to disclose, Johnson knew of the encumbrances long before the plaintiff became involved in the transaction.

Issue: Is a title insurance company liable to noninsured vendors who pay title insurance premiums for failure to reveal encumbrances on the land?

Rule: A title insurance company is liable to noninsureds for failure to disclose encumbrances only when the noninsured shows foreseeable reliance on the title search.

Beaullieu v. Atlanta Title & Trust Co. (1939)

Facts: Beaullieu purchased a piece of property and obtained a title guaranty policy from Atlanta Title & Trust Co. (defendant). The plaintiff subsequently discovered that a third party owned an easement over the property. Beaullieu sued for breach of contract. The parties disputed the measure of damages.

Issue: What is the measure of damages owed an insured by an insurer for breach of its contract of title insurance?

Rule: The measure of damages for a breach by an insurer under a policy insuring title against encumbrances or encroachments is the difference between the value of the property when purchased with the encumbrance or encroachment thereon, and the value of the property as it would have been if there had been no such encumbrance or encroachment.

Howard v. Kunto (1970)

Facts: Due to an inaccurate survey of a lot the Kuntos (defendants) occupied and used seasonally, the Kuntos' deed description did not coincide with the land they and their predecessor in title actually occupied. When the holder of the true deed to the property sued to quiet title, the Kuntos claimed title by adverse possession.

Issue 1: May a claim of adverse possession be defeated because the physical use of the premises was restricted to summer occupancy?

Rule 1: Because the requisite possession required to successfully claim by adverse possession is possession and dominion as ordinarily marks the conduct of owners of property of like nature and condition, seasonal occupancy will not defeat a claim of adverse possession.

Issue 2: May a person who received record title to tract A under the mistaken belief that he had title to tract B (immediately contiguous to tract A) and who subsequently occupies tract B for the purpose of establishing title to tract B by adverse possession, use the periods of possession of tract B by his immediate predecessors who also had record title to tract A?

Rule 2: When several successive purchasers received record title to tract A under the mistaken belief that they were acquiring tract B immediately contiguous thereto, and when possession of tract B was transferred and occupied in a continuous manner for more than 10 years by successive occupants, sufficient privity of estate is present to permit tacking and thus establish adverse possession as a matter of law.

Failoni v. Chicago & North Western Railway Co. (1964)

Facts: Failoni (plaintiff) owned the surface estate above a severed mineral estate. That severed mineral estate had been purchased by the Chicago & North Western Railway Co. (defendant). The defendant railway company had never removed any of the minerals, nor did it pay taxes on the separate mineral estate. Failoni claimed title by adverse possession.

Issue: Is a claim of adverse possession of a mineral estate successfully made solely by ownership of the severed surface estate?

Rule: To possess a mineral estate by adverse possession, one must undertake the actual removal thereof from the ground or do such other act as will apprise the community that such interest is in exclusive use and enjoyment of the claiming party.

Mercer v. Wayman (1956)

Facts: The Mercers (plaintiffs) and the Waymans (defendants) were cotenants of realty. The Mercers occupied the land for thirty-four years, paid taxes and executed mortgages on the property. The Mercers never asserted to the defendants or their predecessors in title any claim of possession adverse to them. The Mercers filed suit to have themselves declared sole owners of the property.

Issue: Can a cotenant in possession sustain a claim of adverse possession against his fellow cotenant(s) if he never asserted, orally or by conduct, any claim of possession adverse to the cotenant(s) not in possession? (i.e., sufficient to start the statute of limitations running?)

Rule: In order to start the statute of limitations running against a cotenant, it must be shown either that the tenant in possession gave actual notice to the tenant out of possession that he was claiming adversely, or that the tenant out of possession had received notice of such claim of the tenant in possession by some act which would amount to an ouster or disseisin.

Short v. Texaco, Inc. (1980)

Facts: The Mineral Lapse Act stated that when a mineral estate remained unused for twenty years, it automatically transferred to the surface estate owner. By its terms, there was a two-year grace period from the Act's effective date wherein owners could preserve their interests. When Short filed suit to obtain title over an unused mineral estate, Texaco (defendant) argued that such transferral was unconstitutional.

Issue: Does Due Process require notice to those affected by a statute that automatically divests them of their property interests?

Rule: Due Process has not been violated if a self-executing statute that is rationally related to promoting a paramount public interest provides reasonable time for those adversely affected by the law's provisions to preserve their interests.

Presbytery of Southeast Iowa v. Harris (1975)

Facts: The Marketable Title Act required holders of future interests in land to file notice of their interest in the land within one year of its enactment. If notice was not filed, their interest was to expire twenty-one years after the Act's creation. In 1898, Elizabeth Cline conveyed land to the Presbytery of Southeast Iowa (plaintiff) by a deed which required that a church building be built on the land within two years of the conveyance, or the premises would revert to the grantor. When the plaintiff brought suit to quiet title, the heirs of Mrs. Cline challenged the statute.

Issue: Does a statute requiring future interest holders to record their interest before they may enforce their rights violate substantive Due Process?

Rule: When an act does not abolish or alter any vested right but simply modifies the procedure for effectuation of the remedy by conditionally limiting the time for enforcement of the right, it does not bar a claimant's remedy before he has had an opportunity to assert it, and is therefore not violative of substantive Due Process.

Messersmith v. Smith (1953)

Facts: Messersmith (plaintiff) acquired title to real estate by quitclaim deed, but did not immediately record the deed. In the interim, the same vendor deeded mineral rights in the property to defendant Smith. Smith in turn deeded his interest to defendant Seale. This deed was recorded before plaintiff's deed, but the act of recording was not in conformity with statutory law. A second statute voided unrecorded deeds if an innocent purchaser for value recorded his deed first. Messersmith brought suit to quiet title.

Issues: Must a deed be acknowledged in conformity with the applicable statute to be validly recorded?

Rule: To be validly recorded, an instrument conveying title of real estate must conform to the statutory requirements of the recording laws.

Stegall v. Robinson (1986)

Facts: The defendants purchased lots in a subdivision that was laid out in a plat by their predecessor in title. No general restrictions were filed with the plat, but the predecessors included in their first recorded conveyance out of lots in the subdivision a page of restrictions. The plaintiffs sued to enforce the restrictions.

Issue: Where restrictive covenants governing a subdivision were not recorded as part of the subdivision plat but were recorded with the first conveyance out of lots in the subdivisions, does a purchaser have record notice of the covenants?

Rule: A title examiner must read prior conveyances to determine that they do not contain restrictions applicable to the use of the subject property; accordingly, a purchaser has notice of all duly recorded documents.

Mayers v. Van Schaick (1935)

Facts: On May 22, 1933, a title insurer (defendants) issued a certificate to the plaintiff stating that as of that date, title to certain land was free of liens or encumbrances. The plaintiff bought the land, relying on the certificate. The certificate made no mention that in 1928, the village had levied on each lot in town a special assessment to pay for a park. The plaintiff brought suit against the company to recover the sum due under the special tax.

Issue: Does title insurance protect against special assessments or taxes that, at the time the policy is issued, are not yet liens on the property?

Rule: Title insurance operates to protect a purchaser or a mortgagee against defects in or encumbrances on a title existing at the date of such insurance. An assessment for local improvements is not a lien or encumbrance. Therefore, a title insurance policy which contracts to insure against liens and encumbrances does not undertake to protect against assessments for improvements.

Shada v. Title & Trust Co. of Florida (1984)

Facts: Shada (plaintiff), in purchasing property, relied upon the defendant title insurers' commitments instead of obtaining an attorney's opinion of title. When the plaintiff later discovered that the title was clouded, the defendant refused to indemnify the plaintiff.

Issue: Does failure to cure or schedule title defects constitute a breach of contract or actionable negligence?

Rule: A title insurer has a duty to exercise reasonable care when it issues a title binder or commitment and its failure to do so may subject it to liability in either contract or tort.

Minnich v. Guernsey Savings & Loan Co. (1987)

Facts: Ohio's Marketable Title Act stipulates that any person having an unbroken chain of title of record to any interest in land for forty years or more, has a marketable record title to such interest. The plaintiffs showed a chain of title dating from a conveyance by Isaac McIlwee in 1890. However, in 1883, Isaac McIlwee had conveyed the full subsurface rights to the Akron & Cambridge Coal Co. The defendants could demonstrate a chain of title to the subsurface rights originating with a deed of 1892. There was no link between the 1883 deed and the 1892 deed, however.

Issue 1: Can a stray or "wild" recorded deed be the basis for marketable record title?

Rule 1: Under the Marketable Title Act, a stray recorded deed can be the basis for marketable record title if the other requirements are satisfied.

Issue 2: If title to a severed mineral estate is lost, can the owner of the current valid deed to the land claim title to that mineral estate?

Rule 2: An owner of land with valid title cannot claim title to a severed mineral estate where a rival deed to that mineral estate, derived from a wild deed, exists, as Jong as that deed has been rendered valid by statute.

Hebb v. Severson (1948)

Facts: The plaintiffs, a title insurance company, contracted to sell to Severson (defendant), a piece of property, and to insure the title by warranty deed. Severson subsequently discovered the seller's title to be encumbered and unmarketable. The title insurance company sued for specific performance.

Issue: Must a purchaser accept the unmarketable title of a seller when an insurer will nevertheless insure the title?

Rule: A purchaser is not compelled to accept an unmarketable title when an insurance company is willing to insure the title.

Regent International v. Lear (1981)

Facts: Lear (plaintiff) agreed to sell property to Regent International (defendant) by a title that created certain undefined easements. The defendant failed to tender the purchase price, alleging that the undefined nature of the easements resulted in an inability to transfer marketable title and excused it from tendering the purchase price. The deed excepted easements both of record and not of record from any warranties. Lear sued for specific performance.

Issue: Do easements that are stated in a purchase agreement to be of an undefined nature and to be determined in a later document make the title unmarketable?

Rule: As a matter of law, undefined easements are an encumbrance on title that do not come within an easement exemption contained in a deed.

Bryant v. Willison Real Estate Co. (1986)

Facts: Bryant contracted to purchase a building from the defendants. Before the deed was delivered, a water line broke. The contract of sale allocated the risk of loss to seller. Bryant asked the defendants to correct the water damage or to rescind the contract. The defendants refused the request. Bryant then refused to pay the purchase price, and the defendants, believing Bryant to have breached the contract, sold the property to a third party. Bryant sued for rescission of the contract and return of the deposit.

Issue: Under an executory contract, what remedy is available to purchaser where risk of loss is on the vendor and damage has been done to the property?

Rule: Where a contract places risk of loss on the vendor and damage to the property occurs without the fault of either party, the purchaser may recover his down payment where the vendor refuses to repair the damage or give an abatement in the purchase price.

Note: Had the contract not allocated the risk of loss, the doctrine of equitable conversion would have placed the risk of loss on buyer.

Berlier v. George (1980)

Facts: In 1976, the Berliers (plaintiffs) agreed to buy property from George (defendant) on the condition that George obtain fire insurance coverage of $15,000 for the house for the first year. George bought a policy with $30,000 coverage that extended beyond the one year period of his obligation. In 1978, the house was destroyed by fire.

Issue: Where a seller insures property for more than a contract requires, must the extra insurance proceeds received be credited to the contract price?

Rule: The party who bears the risk of loss (here, the buyer) is entitled to any and all insurance proceeds, less an offset for the amount required to reimburse the payor of the premiums, regardless of who contracts for the coverage.

In Re Walker (1986)

Facts: Debtor filed for bankruptcy in 1985. Mortgagor sold the property to Purchaser in February 1986. Purchaser failed to record the trustee's deed until March 24, 1986. Debtor recorded a notice of the filing of the bankruptcy on March 13, 1986.

Issue: Does a debtor's recording of a bankruptcy filing defeat the rights of a third-party bona fide purchaser with a prior unrecorded deed?

Rule: Under a "race-notice" recording statute, a debtor who recorded notice of the bankruptcy before the purchaser's recordation of the trustee's deed may void the prior purchase.

Ayer v. Philadelphia & Boston Face Brick Co. (1893)

Facts: Waterman gave two mortgages on his property. Subsequent to both mortgages, the first mortgagee foreclosed and sold the land to Barstow, who later sold it back to Waterman, who conveyed it to Philadelphia & Boston Face Brick Co. (defendant). The second mortgage contained a covenant of warranty and mentioned the first. The second mortgage came into the hands of Ayer (plaintiff), who foreclosed on the defendant. Ayer claimed that when Waterman reacquired title, the doctrine of estoppel by deed applied, and Waterman's new title inured to the second mortgagee.

Issue: In a deed with a covenant of warranty, does a title subsequently acquired by a grantor inure by way of estoppel to a grantee?

Rule: Under a deed with covenants of warranty, a title afterwards acquired by the grantor inures by way of estoppel to the grantee, not only as against the grantor, but also as against one holding by descent or grant from him after acquiring the new title.

Morse v. Curtis (1885)

Facts: In 1872, Hall mortgaged the land to Morse. In 1875, Hall mortgaged the land to Clark, who had notice of the earlier mortgage. The mortgage to Clark was recorded in January 1876. The mortgage to the plaintiff was recorded in September 1876. In October 1881, Clark assigned his mortgage to the tenant, who had no actual notice of the mortgage to the plaintiff. The plaintiff claimed superior title.

Issue: Must a purchaser who finds in the registry a record of a conveyance to his grantor giving the grantor perfect record title, further search to determine if there has been any prior unrecorded deed of the original owner?

Rule: If a purchaser examines the registry and finds a conveyance from the owner of the land to his grantor which gives him a perfect record title, he is entitled to rely upon such record title and is not obliged to search the records further in order to see if there has been any prior unrecorded deed of the original owner.

Buffalo Academy of the Sacred Heart v. Boehm Brothers (1935)

Facts: The plaintiff agreed to discharge an indebtedness to the defendant by conveying to it marketable title to certain realty. Boehm (defendant) rejected as unmarketable the plaintiff's title to lots that the plaintiff attempted to deed to Boehm because the plaintiff had previously conveyed the subdivision lots with restrictions on their use. Although not mentioned in his deed or chain of title, Boehm contended the restrictions were binding on him.

Issue: Do restrictions placed on lots in a subdivision bind a purchaser of different lots in the subdivision when no mention of such restrictions is made in the deed or chain of title, thereby making the grantor's title unmarketable?

Rule: In the absence of actual notice either before or at the time of purchase or of other exceptional circumstances, an owner of land is only bound by restrictions if they appear in some deed of record in the conveyance to himself or his direct predecessors in title.

Note: A purchaser of a lot which formed part of a larger tract is not charged with notice of restrictive covenants contained in a prior deed from the same grantor to any other lot or parcel of the same general tract although the deed is recorded and by its terms applies to all other lots.

Guillette v. Daly Dry Wall, Inc. (1975)

Facts: A vendor of land sold a lot to plaintiffs by a deed which contained restrictions intended explicitly to bind all the lots in the subdivision. The defendant subsequently purchased a lot from the grantor under a deed which did not contain the restriction, and without knowledge thereof.

Issues: Is a purchaser of land bound by a restriction contained in a deed to its neighbor from a common grantor, when he took without knowledge of the restriction and under a deed which did not mention them?

Rule: Where the owner of several lots conveys one of the lots by a deed containing a restrictive covenant which explicitly binds all of the remaining lots, then a subsequent purchaser from the vendor acquires title subject to the restrictions in the earlier deed.

Galley v. Ward (1880)

Facts: Jane Smith conveyed land to Galley. The deed was erroneously executed such that Smith only released dower and homestead. Galley took the land and remained in notorious and open possession. Ward, a creditor of Jane Smith who was unaware of Galley's possession, checked the registry and found that J. Smith apparently retained legal title. He obtained a lien on the land. Galley (plaintiff) claimed superior title.

Issue: Is a creditor who is unaware of the notorious occupation of land by one who holds title charged with constructive notice of an unrecorded deed or equitable claim to the land by the title holder in possession?

Rule: Where a party is in open and notorious possession of land, both purchasers and creditors are charged with constructive notice of an unrecorded deed or equitable claim to title by the party in possession, whether they know of such possession or not.

Toupin v. Peabody (1895)

Facts: Toupin's (plaintiffs) lessor executed a written unrecorded five year lease with a renewal option for five additional years. By statute, unrecorded leases for more than seven years are invalid against those who have no actual notice other than the lessor and his heirs. Peabody (defendant) bought the premises from Toupin's lessor, who represented that the lease was oral.

Issues: Is an unrecorded five-year, renewable lease within a statute invalidating the effect of unrecorded leases of terms exceeding seven years against purchasers of the demised premises who lack actual notice of the lease?

Rule: An unrecorded five-year, renewable lease is within a statute invalidating the effect of unrecorded leases of terms exceeding seven years against purchasers of the demised premises who lack actual notice of the lease?

Brinkman v. Jones (1878)

Facts: In 1870, Jones conveyed by deed land to Shove, who by unrecorded contract, agreed to reconvey to Jones if he paid a debt to Shove. Jones and his son (plaintiff) continuously occupied the land until

1876 when Shove deeded the land to Brinkman. Brinkman (plaintiff) brought an ejectment proceeding.

Issue: Is a purchaser charged with actual notice if he has actual knowledge of such facts "as would put a prudent person upon inquiry that would lead to actual notice of the right or title in conflict with that which he is about to purchase?"

Rule: When a subsequent purchaser has knowledge of such facts as would put a prudent person upon inquiry which would lead to actual notice of the right or title in conflict with that which he is about to purchase, it becomes his duty to make inquiry, and he is guilty of bad faith if he neglects to do so. Consequently, he will be charged with the actual notice he would have received if he had made the inquiry.

Toland v. Corey (1890)

Facts: After Corey (plaintiff), a life tenant, purchased the remainder, her son mortgaged the premises without her knowledge. Corey, who was in open and notorious possession, recorded her deed after the mortgages were recorded.

Issue: Does exclusive and notorious possession of land constitute actual notice to subsequent purchasers and creditors of the occupier's title?

Rule: An occupant's possession is actual notice of his title and all persons with notice of such possession have a duty of inquiry, regardless of what the record shows.

Durst v. Dougherty (1891)

Facts: Daugherty (plaintiff) purchased land as a bona fide purchaser, without knowledge that the defendants had a claim to the land. Daugherty argued that he should receive the entire tract of land, and the seller should recover the unpaid contract price.

Issues: What measure of protection should be given to an innocent purchaser of land whose title is challenged by another, valid title?

Rule: In determining what measure of protection should be accorded to a bona fide purchaser of land, it is necessary to ascertain and consider fully the equities of the parties. These include the price paid by the innocent purchaser with respect to the market price, whether or not he made improvements on the land, whether the land is in a condition to be partitioned, and whether either party is more at fault

McDonald & Co. v. Johns (1911)

Facts: Johns executed two mortgages on his land as security for preexisting debts. Both mortgages were given to secure the payment of a preexisting debt, and no new or additional consideration or extension of time of payment was given as an inducement to the extension of either mortgage. McDonald & Co.'s (plaintiff) mortgage, although executed last, was recorded prior to the first mortgage, McDonald claimed to be a bona fide purchaser.

Issue: Is a creditor a bona fide purchaser for value if he takes a mortgage to secure the payment of a preexisting indebtedness when no new or additional consideration or extension of time of payment was given as an inducement to the execution of the mortgage?

Rule: A creditor is not a bona fide purchaser for value if he takes a mortgage on realty merely as security for the payment of a debt already due him without giving any new consideration or being induced to change his condition in any manner.

Eliason v. Wilborn (1930)

Facts: Eliason (plaintiff) entrusted his certificate of title to Napletone who fraudulently obtained a new certificate in his name. He then conveyed the land to the defendant. (Illinois follows the Torrens System.)

Issue: Where one knows that the transfer of land is governed by the Torrens System and entrusts his certificate to another, who fraudulently obtains title, is the registrar obligated to rescind the fraudulent title?

Rule: An owner of land governed by the Torrens Act who entrusts another with his certificate of title bears the risk that the trustee will convey the land to a third party.

Abrahamson v. Sundman (1928)

Facts: The holder of a good title duly registered under the Torrens Act conveyed the land by warranty deed to S.J. Johnson who conveyed to Abrahamson (plaintiff). Neither Johnson's nor Abrahamson's deed was noted on the certificate of title. Abrahamson took possession. Glass-Melone Lumber Co., Johnson's lienholder, subsequently foreclosed on the land, obtained a new certificate by court decree, and conveyed the land to the defendant. Abrahamson was not made a party to the lien foreclosure proceeding. Abrahamson claimed superior title.

Issue: Under the Torrens System, can the lienholder who forecloses terminate all rights and interests to the property by limiting the parties to the suit to those whose names appear on the certificate or some memorial or notation thereon?

Rule: Under the Torrens Act, one who takes possession without any notation or memorial of his right upon the registration certificate is charged with knowledge that his possession is not notice of any interest in him, and that such possession will never ripen into a right adverse to the registered owner.

Killam v. March (1944)

Facts: Killam (plaintiff) purchased land registered under the Torrens System. Prior to the purchase, the plaintiff had actual notice that the defendant had a valid, though unregistered, twenty-five year lease granting the defendant use of the plaintiff's driveway from the plaintiff's predecessor in interest.

Issue: Does one purchasing registered land take the land subject to an unregistered lease if he has actual notice of the lease?

Rule: A subsequent purchaser of registered land does not have an indefeasible title as against interests of which he had actual notice.

State Street Bank & Trust Co. v. Beale (1967)

Facts: Beale (defendant) defrauded the plaintiff out of title to registered land. A statute required a defrauded owner to "petition for review" a fraudulently obtained registration decree within one year of the decree's entry. Two years after the decree's entry, the plaintiff sought a constructive trust.

Issue: May an action to impose a constructive trust on registered land be properly treated as a "petition for review" of the registration decree, and thus pursuant to statutory law, only be brought within one year of that decree?

Rule: Since the remedy of restitution only operates against the person who has committed fraud, not against the registration decree itself, an action seeking a constructive trust is not barred by the registration statute's time limitations.

Bothin v. California Title Insurance & Trust Co. (1908)

Facts: Excepting from coverage the "tenure of the present occupants . . . [and] instruments . . . not shown by any public record," the defendant insured the plaintiff's record title from defects. A neighbor who adversely claimed a portion of the plaintiff's land recorded a deed of trust evincing his conveyance of a part of the plaintiff's lot.

Issue: When an insurance policy expressly excepts the "tenure of present occupants," does the adverse possession of the insured's land or the adverse claimant's recorded deed of trust constitute a breach of the policy?

Rule: Since a policy excepting the tenure of present occupants and non-public instruments insures the record title only, neither adverse possession nor the adverse possessor's deed of trust constitutes a defect in the record title in breach of the insurance policy.

Metropolitan Life Insurance Co. v. Union Trust Co. (1940)

Facts: Union Trust (defendant) excepted encumbrances, liens and charges existing at or prior to the policy date from its title insurance policy issued to the plaintiff. Before the policy date, local public improvements were completed and paid for by bond. The bond assessment did not take effect until after the policy date.

Issue: Is a title insurer liable for the cost of the assessments to the insured when assessment for local public improvements is levied after a title insurance policy is executed, but improvements are completed prior to the policy date?

Rule: Title insurance is not prospective in its operation and has no relation to an assessment that is not an actual, fully matured lien at the time the policy is executed.

Glyn v. Title Guarantee Trust Co. (1909)

Facts: Title Guarantee Trust Co. acted both as conveyancer and as insurer for Glyn when she purchased property. The defendant failed to articulate precisely the encumbrances upon the property it conveyed to Glyn, but stated that these encumbrances did not affect the title's marketability. Relying on the defendant's assertions, the plaintiff bought the land and later discovered that the encroachments interfered with the free use of her property. Glyn brought suit for negligence and for breach of policy.

Issue 1: Does a title insurer acting as a conveyancer, who examines the title and undertakes to advise a prospective purchaser on the issue of its marketability, owe a duty of due care to a prospective purchaser?

Rule 1: An insurer in the role of a conveyancer assumes all the obligations of an attorney to his client and must advise the prospective purchaser of the exact character and nature of encroachments.

Issue 2: Do encroachments on an insured's property not rendering the title unmarketable violate a policy insuring against encumbrances?

Rule 2: An encroachment that might interfere with or prevent the free use and improvement of property that the owner could not remove at will, and that was not specifically exempted by a policy constitutes an encumbrance diminishing the title's marketability.

Luthi v. Evans (1978)

Facts: Owens assigned to the defendant "all interest of whatsoever nature in . . . all Oil and Gas leases in Coffey County, Kansas." Owens later assigned to Burris, a third party, a lease known as the Kufahl lease, which was in Coffey County. Defendant claimed superior title.

Issue: Does the recording of a deed which intends to convey real property and which describes that property as "all the grantor's property in a certain county" constitute constructive notice to subsequent purchasers?

Rule: The recording of a deed which purports to convey real property and which describes that property as "all the grantor's property in a certain county" is not effective as to subsequent purchasers unless they have actual notice of the transfer.

Orr v. Byers (1988)

Facts: Orr received a judgment from Elliott, whose name was misspelled by Orr's attorney and thus, was recorded erroneously. When Elliott later obtained title to property, it became subject to Orr's judgment lien. Elliott then sold the property to Byers, who conducted a title search which failed to disclose the abstract of judgment. This action sought to obtain judicial foreclosure of Orr's judgment lien.

Issue: Does the doctrine of *idem sonans,* that though a person's name has been written inaccurately, the identity of such person will be presumed from the similarity of the sounds between the correct pronunciation and the pronunciation as written, apply to title records as based upon constructive notice?

Rule: In undertaking a title search, where a name is misspelled, an individual does not have constructive notice the error in an abstract of judgment under the doctrine of *idem sonans,* as it would place an undue burden on the transfer of property.

Board of Education of Minneapolis v. Hughes (1912)

Facts: In 1906, Hughes (defendant) received a deed on which the name of the grantee was not inserted. He filled in the name shortly before he recorded the deed on December 16, 1910. In April 1909, the same owner gave a quitclaim deed to a broker, who did not record the deed until December 21, 1910. In November 1909 the broker had delivered a deed for the lot to the plaintiff, who recorded it in January 1910. The plaintiff claimed superior title.

Issue 1: Is the delivery of a deed by the grantor with the name of the grantee omitted a valid conveyance?

Rule 1: A deed that does not name a grantee is inoperative as a conveyance until the name of the grantee is inserted with either the express or implied authority of the grantor.

Issue 2: Does a record of a deed conveyed from an unrecorded owner constitute notice to a subsequent purchaser?

Rule 2: If a grantee's deed shows no conveyance from an owner of record, it is not sufficient to provide subsequent purchasers with notice.

Woods v. Garnett (1894)

Facts: In 1891, Riley executed a defective deed which was recorded. In May 1892, Riley executed a second deed to the same property to another party, Oliver. Before accepting the second deed, the grantee searched the record, observed the defective deed and, believing it ineffective, recorded his deed. In October 1892 the first deed was corrected and rerecorded. On November 19, 1892, the plaintiff Woods, under the 1891 deed, and Garnett, under Oliver's 1892 deed and without notice of Woods' purchase, bought the same lot on the same day. Woods claimed superior title.

Issue 1: Is a subsequent purchaser who discovered an improperly recorded deed a bona fide purchaser?

Rule 1: One who sees an instrument improperly recorded upon the record and fails to make further inquiry is not a bona fide purchaser.

Issue 2: Does the corrected rerecording of an initially defectively recorded deed render the deed effective against subsequent purchasers?

Rule 2: A defectively recorded conveyance becomes effective upon the date of its corrected recording, and trumps the claim of a second, bona fide buyer who buys the land after the corrected recording. In this case, therefore, Woods had superior title.

Alexander v. Andrews (1951)

Facts: Alexander sought to obtain quiet title of land conveyed to him and sought to remove a deed, for the same property, held by Andrews.

Issue: When two individuals hold title to the same deed, what are the rights of a subsequent holder of the deed?

Rule: Where there are two holders of a deed, and the subsequent holder of the deed is without notice of the former deed and pays a valuable consideration for its conveyance, relief may be granted only if the transaction is complete upon actual or constructive notice, i.e., if full consideration is paid before the former deed is recorded.

Harper v. Paradise (1974)

Facts: In 1922, Susan Harper deeded a farm to Maude Harper as life tenant with remainder to her children. The deed was subsequently lost, and later discovered and recorded in 1957. In 1928, Susan's heirs conveyed to Maude by quitclaim their interest in the land with an instrument that referred to the lost deed. In 1933 Maude conveyed the farm to Thornton. The plaintiff Paradise, who had an unbroken chain of title from Thornton, recorded a deed for the property in 1955. Maude Harper's children claim title under the first (lost) deed as remaindermen.

Issue: Does a purchaser have a duty to ascertain the contents of an earlier deed referred to in his chain of title and the interests conveyed therein?

Rule: A deed in the chain of title which is discovered and which contains references to other deeds constitutes constructive notice of those other deeds. Any investigator who discovers such deed is obligated to inquire into those deeds to which it refers.

Waldorff Ins. and Bonding, Inc. v. Eglin Nat'l Bank (1984)

Facts: The defendant Waldorff purchased a condominium in a building owned by Choctaw. Waldorff installed furniture and began to occupy the unit. Despite Waldorffs prior purchase, Choctaw represented to Eglin National Bank that it owned the unit, and obtained a mortgage on the unit. Subsequently, Eglin foreclosed, claiming title to the condominium unit. Waldorff claimed superior title.

Issue: Does actual possession of a condominium unit constitute notice of the occupier's interest in the property to those subsequently acquiring any title or lien on the property?

Rule: Actual possession is constructive notice to anyone having knowledge of the possession of whatever right the occupants have in the property.

Heifner v. Bradford (1983)

Facts: Heifner and her sisters sought quiet title to and partition of their share of the oil and gas rights in land, which were reserved for them when their grandparents conveyed the property's surface rights.

Issue: Is a marketable record title subject to a title transaction, even if the title transaction is part of an independent chain of title recorded after the required statutory period?

Rule: A marketable record title is subject to an interest arising out of a title transaction, even if the title transaction is part of an independent chain of title.

Marshall v. Hollywood, Inc. (1970)

Facts: Hollywood's chain of title originated from a forged deed. Forty-two years after the forged deed was recorded, the plaintiff Marshall discovered the fraud and sued to establish his interest in the property. Hollywood, whose title descended from the forged deed, contended that Florida statutory law validated any recorded chain of title more than 30 years old.

Issue: Does the Marketable Record Titles to Real Property Act confer marketability to a chain of title arising out of a forged or wild deed; so long as the strict requirements of the Act are met?

Rule: The act declares a marketable title on recorded chains of title which are older than the statutorily stipulated age, subject to certain exceptions. All competing interests which are older than the root of the recorded chain of title are nullified.

Walker Rogge, Inc. v. Chelsea Title and Guaranty Co. (1989)

Facts: Walker Rogge purchased real estate without conducting a land survey. It instituted this action upon discovering that it had only acquired 12.5 acres of land, 5.5 acres less than the 18 acres it paid for and thought it had purchased.

Issue: Is a shortage of acreage an insurable loss under a policy?

Rule: In the absence of a recital of acreage, a title company does not insure the quantity of land. To obtain coverage, an insured should provide the title company with an acceptable survey that recites the quantity of land described or obtain an express guarantee that the quantity of land purchased is insured in the policy.

Lick Mill Creek Apartments v. Chicago Title Ins. Co. (1991)

Facts: Plaintiffs took out three policies from Chicago Title Insurance for three parcels of land. At the time that the policies were issued, however, various agencies had records disclosing the presence of hazardous substances on the lots. Plaintiffs incurred costs for removal and cleanup of the hazardous substances and then sought indemnity from the defendants.

Issue: Where a clause in an insurance policy protects against unmarketability of title, can an insured claim coverage for a property's physical condition?

Rule: Where a clause insures against the unmarketability of title, and the market value of land is not encompassed by the definition of marketable title, a plaintiff cannot claim coverage for the physical condition of his land.

Radovanov v. Land Title Co. of America (1989)

Facts: The Radovanovs brought suit to recover damages incurred by the failure of defendant to disclose the existence of a pending lawsuit concerning building code violations that were supposed to have been resolved by the time of closing, or to obtain the provision of coverage for financial loss that resulted from the lawsuit.

Issue: Does an exclusion clause protect an insurance title company from covering claims that affect the marketability of land when the litigation causing the damages was pending before the title commitment and policy were issued?

Rule: Where a title insurance company contracts to provide coverage for damages resulting from unmarketability of title, an obligation is created to provide coverage for damages rendering a title unmarketable even if they were caused by pending lawsuits which predate the issuance of title commitment and policy.

TABLE OF CASES